Crowood Travel Guides are the essential starting point for a holiday to remember – and they'll be the signpost to enjoyment every step of the way. Easy-to-follow, practical advice, combined with a warmth and enthusiasm for the peoples and cultures of the world, mean that they'll be turned to again and again for direction and inspiration.

Jamaica and
the Greater Antilles

First published in 1991 by
The Crowood Press Ltd
Gipsy Lane, Swindon
Wiltshire SN2 6DQ
© The Crowood Press Ltd. 1991

British Library Cataloguing in Publication Data
Booth, Elizabeth
  Jamaica and the Greater Antilles. – (Crowood travel guides)
  I. Title
  917.290452

  ISBN 1–85223–462–8

Photographs by the author except:
Cayman Tourist Office, pages 18, 26-27, 30, 32, 35, 38, 40-41, 45, 53, 56
Jamaica Tourist Board, pages 6-7, 125, 150, 154, 158, 161, 172, 174, 175, 177, 178, 180, 182, 184, 185, 186, 195, 198, 202, 204, 211, 219, 226, 237, 238-39, 240, 247, 355
Puerto Rican Tourism Company, pages 250-51, 253, 254, 253, 273, 274, 276-77, 279, 288-89, 299, 318, 320, 326
Les Mitchell, pages 58-59, 104

The hotel and restaurant prices quoted in this book were correct at the time of writing but are subject to change and should only be taken as a guide. All prices change in mid-December when they go up for the high season and then drop back in mid-April.

Maps by Taurus Graphics
Typesetting and page layouts by Visual Image
Printed and bound by Times Publishing Group, Singapore

Jamaica and
the Greater Antilles

Crowood Travel Guide

Elizabeth Booth

The Crowood Press

Jamaica and the Greater Antilles

Contents

Montego Bay

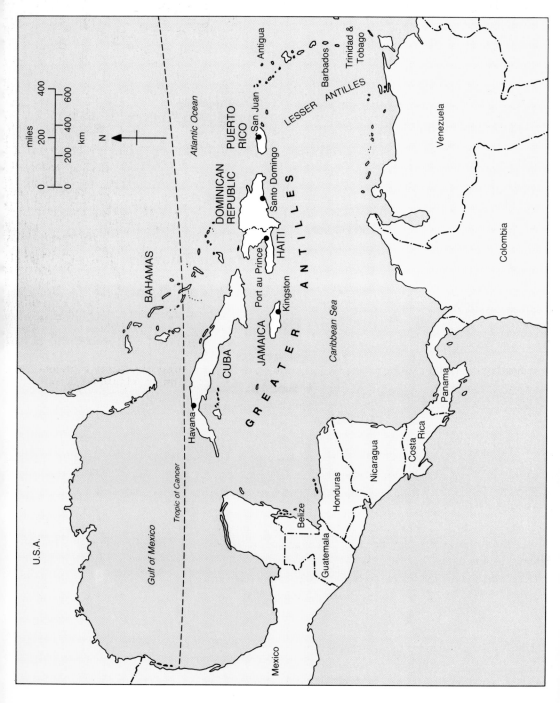

Introduction With well over fifty islands in the Caribbean, it is difficult to sum up the region in one line. Sun, sea and sand are the images that the word Caribbean conjures up in most people's minds but the islands are far more than that.

Seven Mile Beach on Grand Cayman, fringed by palms

The region is tremendously varied. Four languages are spoken with countless local dialects. The economies are also widely different and the islands compete against each other for world markets. Even the geology is quite different, with some islands made of volcanic rock and others, just a few kilometres away, made up from coral. And the people themselves have come from all over the world to make up the races, creeds and colours of the different islands.

One thing that all the islands do have in common is the warm welcome that they offer visitors. Language barriers are soon broken down and they all work hard to give visitors the holiday of a lifetime.

The islands can be split into three geographical regions. The Greater Antilles are the most westerly islands and include the largest such as Hispaniola, Jamaica and Puerto Rico. To the east

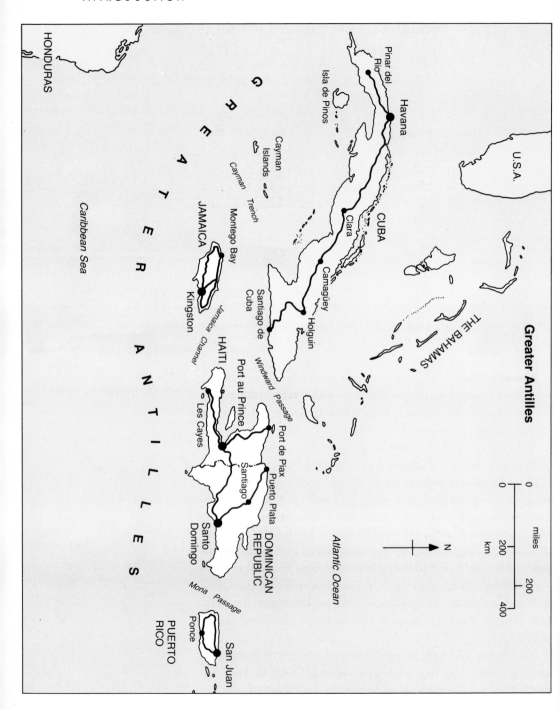

Greater Antilles

are the mass of small islands that make up the US and British Virgin Islands, Antigua, St Kitts and Nevis down to Guadeloupe which are collectively known as the Leeward Islands. To the south are the Windward Islands and names like Barbados, St Lucia, Grenada, Trinidad and Tobago.

Each island, or small cluster of islands, has its own government, some have their own airlines and all are fiercely independent. The different languages are the result of the various European powers colonizing the region in the 1500s. Many of the islands were hard fought over because of their wealth. Later sugar became King and those with rich, fertile volcanic soils amassed great fortunes for the plantation owners. The plantations needed workers and so slaves were imported, adding the African heritage to the existing culture.

Many people are amazed by the region's rich history. Discovered in 1492 by Christopher Columbus on his way to discovering North America, there are still relics of that bygone age. The year 1992 will be very important for the islands when most will take part in the 500th anniversary celebrations. Whole towns are being renovated and much of the history rediscovered in readiness. And, one thing is for certain, the islanders know how to throw a good party.

The book concentrates on the Greater Antilles' islands of the Dominican Republic, Haiti, Jamaica and Puerto Rico. The Cayman Islands are included although they are not, strictly speaking, part of the Greater Antilles.

History The Dominican Republic was among the first Caribbean islands to be landed on by Christopher Columbus and his men, and became home to the majority of his family. Arguments rage across the islands as to exactly where the Spanish first landed and discovered the Americas. The Bahamas usually claims the honour but now the Turks and Caicos Islands are also claiming they have proof he went there first. The opportunity to make such a claim will probably have enormous financial rewards for whichever island wins the battle and can celebrate as the first landing place during the 1992 Columbus celebrations. But even later voyages throw up some questions for the islanders. Many know that Columbus was the first European to land on their shores but the historical evidence varies as to where he actually first set foot on their soil. Museums abound in the region, filled with artifacts, anchors and documents from those first trips.

What is definitely known is that Columbus first thought he had arrived in the Far East and in India, hence the naming of the local people Indians. It is also certain that he travelled to the Bahamas, Turks and Caicos and to the island of Hispaniola on his first voyage, but it was on Hispaniola that he left his brother Bartlomé to found a colony. Since that first voyage, the European settlers started to arrive *en masse* in the islands, and the history of the region is well documented. Much of the furniture and books of those early settlers are still on the islands and, even more surprisingly, some of the very first houses are still in use today.

It was from the Dominican Republic that many famous Spanish explorers set out to find fame and fortune. Expeditions to colonize Puerto Rico, Jamaica and even Mexico set out from the capital port of Santo Domingo.

Once the Spanish had established a firm foothold in the area, the English, French and Dutch were eager to steal some for themselves. Wars raged for hundreds of years, with some islands having new rulers every couple of years. The Dominican Republic celebrates Re-Independence Day as well as the original Independence Day in honour of the fact that the islanders only managed independence for two years before the Spanish and French regained control. They then had to wait many years before getting a second chance at ruling for themselves.

The Caribbean was an important staging post for the Spanish galleons carrying gold home to Europe from South America. With so much wealth in the large ships and with so many islands to hide on or behind, it was a natural home for pirates – and the English navy. Jamaica's Port Royal was the home to pirates in the days of Blackbeard, and their success made them so wealthy and respectable while doing such damage to the Spanish fleets that they were rewarded by the British Government with large plantations and posts in the island's government.

The Cayman Islands were controlled by Jamaica for many years and are now one the few remaining British colonies left. The Cayman Islands also had a chequered past, becoming a tax haven as a reward for saving a fleet of British ships but also being home to pirates who are rumoured to have hidden their treasure in the many caves of Cayman Brac.

Puerto Rico managed to stay firmly in Spanish control despite numerous attempts by the British to win this important staging post. But in the end it was the Americans who conquered the Spanish here and turned the island into a colony. Puerto Rico is still part of the USA and Puerto Ricans hold American passports, although the island does have some autonomy and its people do not have the right to vote in the USA.

Economy For a couple of hundred years the islands were important economically to their European masters but, in many cases, once the slaves had staged rebellions and won their freedom, the agricultural wealth disappeared. The sugar price has now sunk so low that it actually costs some farmers to produce it, and most of the island's agriculture is for home consumption rather than export.

The only remaining signs of those wealthy times are the old plantation houses, many renovated and turned into palatial hotels or museums, a few sugar-cane mills, again used by the entrpeneurial as hotels or museums, and a few working sugar-cane plantations. Many of these take advantage of the tourist industry to keep afloat financially. Some will do tours, showing visitors the different farming methods through the years and teaching them about the local foods.

The sugar is still used locally to supply the home market as well as the rum industry. Over 80 per cent of the world's white rum comes from Puerto Rico, while Jamaica is famous for its dark rum.

Many of the successful crops were actually imported, such as; bread-fruit. Captain Bligh was bringing bread-fruit to the region on his ill-fated voyage on the *Bounty*. Although that attempt failed, bread-fruit was brought to the islands and transplanted so well that it appears as frequently as the indigenous fruits.

There was mineral wealth on some of the islands, although tales of gold cost the original Indian inhabitants dear. The tribes who first lived here came from South America; there were three main tribes: the Taino, Caribs and Arawaks. The Taino was the oldest culture, while some theories are that the Arawak and Carib Indians were actually two factions of the same tribe. But they were totally different in nature.

The Arawaks were friendly farmers while the Caribs were extremely warlike, constantly killing. They would turn on each other if there was no one else around to kill. They were also cannibals as they would eat any available meat, human or animal. One theory is that the Caribs killed many Arawak men and used their women as concubines. These women are thought to have incited the Caribs to even more violence, hoping they would destroy each other in revenge for destroying the Arawak families.

When the Spanish first arrived on Puerto Rico, the friendly Taino Indians told the crew of the gold that could just be picked out of the rivers. These tales inspired Juan Ponce de Leon to set off from the Dominican Republic to find all this wealth. When he got there, he found a small amount of gold in the rivers but nothing more. This caused great friction between the Spanish and Indians, who were soon put to work for the Europeans. Within a few years they had disappeared, unable to cope with the physical labour and the enslavement by the Europeans.

It was the same story on many of the other islands but, although the Indians died out quickly, they did leave their culture behind, and many of their burial or ceremonial sites have been rediscovered in recent years. Archaeologists have discovered much about the Indian way of life despite the fact that the first settlers kept few records of the Indian cultures.

Soon after the Caribbean gold had run out, the Europeans discovered gold in South America and, instead of neglecting the islands, realized their importance as a staging post between the old and new worlds. They also looked for other minerals and these have been mined on the islands more recently. Jamaica was once one of the world's most important bauxite producers. The bauxite used to be exported in huge quantities for use in aluminium smelting but this market collapsed a few years ago. Some bauxite is still mined and exported but it does not create the wealth it once did.

With the decline in both agriculture and in mining, the islands have had to look in new directions to support their economies. Some have had help from their colonial bosses. After the Second World War, the USA introduced Operation Bootstrap to bolster the Puerto Rican economy, giving American corporations huge tax incentives to set up manufacturing bases on the island.

But, for the majority of the islands, tourism has taken over – it both employs a high number of local people and brings in the much needed foreign currency. In some ways, you could sympathise with local people for jealousy towards the visitors. In the Dominican Republic the government is quite open about its policy of supplying electricity and water to the hotels first and the general population second. In Jamaica Hurricane Gilbert brought much destruction and, again, it was the hotels who had help first. The government's theory was that to get the foreign money coming in and to keep employing many local people they would be able to afford the necessary repairs to the rest of the island.

This attitude has caused jealousy and the belief that all tourists are rich, resulting in some violence and theft. Some islands, particularly Jamaica and Puerto Rico, are worse than others. The governments have worked hard to stamp out this problem and are winning the battle, although it is still a good idea to travel by taxi at night in both Kingston and San Juan. In Jamaica the government has introduced tourism into the school curriculum from primary stage upwards to teach future generations that thieving and violence will stop tourists from visiting the country and create real problems for everyone.

Some of the governments have tried nationalizing the industry but have since discovered that allowing the private sector to own the properties helps improve investment by foreigners with hard currency. Most of the islands are keen to get as much hard currency as they can and have strict rules about the import and export of money.

Politics Politically, most of the islands are stable although there are a few notable exceptions. In the Greater Antilles, Haiti appears the most turbulent. The extreme poverty there probably contributes to the country's problems, which in the past have spilled over to neighbouring Dominican Republic. People from both sides of Hispaniola set sail for Puerto Rico on a regular basis. If they can sneak past the vigilant coastguards and become resident in Puerto Rico, they hope to become eligible for an American passport.

Tourism in the Dominican Republic is increasing fast, and conditions are improving. Standards of living are also improving and more people have a chance of earning a reasonable wage. They are eager to work, and those who make it into the international hotels are very proud of their work. The Dominican Republic has only recently emerged from the shadow of a harsh

15

dictator, and the people still get very excited and agitated at election time. Likewise, Haiti has overthrown numerous rulers in the past few years and the people are desperate for general elections and democracy, but many experts believe it will be some time before the problems can be ironed out.

Although many of the islanders are excitable and politics appears to be the cause of most trouble on the islands, the people generally are affable and laid-back. Even the political upheaval tends to be tempered with a bit of 'island time'. Nothing is done in a hurry on the islands and one of the joys of a holiday here is the relaxed, laid-back atomosphere – more than a little frustrating for those who are trying to work.

Travel Travelling to the islands is easy from either Europe, Canada or America. The only problem there can be is in booking a seat far enough ahead. There is a huge demand for direct flights from Europe, particularly around Christmas time when seats can be booked up to a year in advance.

Most of the major airlines travel to one or another of the islands and many American companies travel to the majority of them. Inter-island travel is also relatively easy, either by an international airline or by the island's own airlines. There are also ferry services between the closer islands.

Travelling around the islands themselves can be a slow process. You can hire cars relatively easily, although in the majority of cases it is expensive because every car has to be imported and waiting lists for cars are months long. Spare parts are also hard to find and the roads are not that good so spares are always in demand.

When you are driving around, allow much more time than you would normally take. Also, expect to get lost because the maps are not always up to date. If you are on an island where they speak a foreign language, make sure you take your dictionary, and it is worth having some loose change for tolls on the highways. In some places you might get stopped by police or army road-blocks. They usually wave tourists straight through but lots of smiling does the trick if you get stopped. The locals will probably have to pay to get through.

Tourism The islands have been learning through experience with tourism. While the Caribbean has always been seen by the

British as a destination for the rich and famous, it has long been a weekend getaway place for the Americans. The mass American market, however, appears to be on the decline and instead the islands are cultivating the European markets. But rather than going purely for numbers they have, in many cases, deliberately set out to woo the exclusive tourist. They are creating luxurious resort hotels as well as improving the network of plantation houses or places where a house-party atmosphere prevails. These tend to be expensive but you pay for the isolation, private beaches and good hospitality.

Most of the hotels use 110 volt electricity so it is a good idea to take an adaptor. A few hotels have 240 volts so it is always worth checking before you plug anything in. Most hotels have spare adaptors if you need them.

In areas such as the Dominican Republic, the hotel industry is labour intensive and everyone is keen to do a good job. You may well find your hotel room is cleaned several times a day and the hoteliers are always quick to provide you with information about what is happening in the resort.

Communications are good. Some of the islands may have some of the poorest people in the world living there, but the majority are used to western ways and particularly to the Americans. Most major hotels will have direct international dialling. But watch out for the costs. In some places, such as a few Jamaican hotels, you will have to pay for the calls first or leave a credit card print-out as a deposit. On most islands, local calls are free but the hotels will charge you a commission for using the telephone – usually about US$1 per call. International calls, however, are marked up much higher and if you intend making long calls it might be worth finding a local Post Office or telecommunications centre. Most of the hotels also have fax and telex facilities. Be warned: during a storm the telephone lines are often the first things to come down.

Conservation Preserving the best of what they have got has not been exclusive to the hoteliers using plantation houses. The islands have long kept their rich history and there are plenty of worthwhile museums to visit. Most of the major hotels and tour operators will have set up tours of all the local sights. Some of these might be too packaged for some people but the sights are

17

An enormous coral attracts two scuba divers

generally worth visiting. River rafting or climbing the Dunn's River Falls in Jamaica; a visit to a rum factory in the Dominican Republic; or climbing the famous Citadelle of Haiti are just a tiny sample of what the islands have to offer other than their beautiful beaches and warm, sunny climate.

The islanders are also keen conservationists. Many of the coral reefs are protected and the forests are nature reserves. The Puerto Ricans have spent millions of US dollars in breeding programmes to try to save rare species, while their rain forest is always open to the public to enjoy in an attempt to show people it is worth saving. And, although tourism is new and the world-wide move towards saving the environment even newer, it is a surprise to discover that many of the national parks on the islands have been around for many years. Some started life as fashionable therapeutic mineral spas but others were preserved almost a hundred years ago by forward-thinking people who realized that certain areas were totally unique, such as Hell on the Cayman Islands, or that they were in danger of disappearing forever, such as the El Yungue rain forest of Puerto Rico.

Many of the islands have underwater reserves. Providing stunning sites for scuba divers and snorkellers, the large coral reefs are alive and anyone picking the live coral will be destroying that natural habitat. Hawkers will sell large seashells to sunbathers on the beach but it is always worth asking where they got them from. Many go out fishing for the live shells and kill the shellfish just to provide a pretty shell for tourists. But there are still shells, pieces of coral and unusually shaped driftwood to be found, particularly after storms.

All the islands have a wealth of bird life as well as rare and often unique plants and trees. Orchids and exotic flowers abound and, in some areas, you will find up to 300 orchids growing within an area of just a few miles. Jamaica, in particular, has many botanical gardens. Some of them were established hundreds of years ago and have been carefully preserved.

Climate However well preserved the gardens might be, they have a few of Nature's worst conditions to cope with. Hurricanes are an annual event in this part of the world. It comes as a shock to open the telephone directory and find the emergency procedures for hurricanes. The good thing is that the islands are well prepared and the hotels are designed to withstand even the fiercest storms. In the unlikely event that you get caught in a bad hurricane – the bad ones apparently only happen every sixty years and it seems that different areas of the Caribbean get hit each time – there are plenty of shelters all across the islands, and the weather forecasters are getting good at giving everyone at least a day to prepare.

With the good communications world-wide, television pictures of the devastation left in the wake of the hurricane are now commonplace in European homes. These work two ways for the islands. The shock of the damage helps the islands in their appeal for international aid to put right the mess, but it also frightens away many tourists who think that the islands will never recover.

In fact, most of the islands can get back to normal within a few days and all but the worst hit have the usual facilities for tourists. Sometimes the worst part of the hurricane for hoteliers is that it washes away the beach, but this can also happen in reverse and some owners have hurricanes to thank for providing them with their best assets. The hurricanes mostly happen in the quieter summer season when there are relatively few visitors, and the islanders work hard to ensure they are ready for the hectic winter months.

Hurricanes apart, the Caribbean is known for its constantly good weather. The hottest time is in the summer months of April through to September. It is also the wettest time and can become humid, so most people prefer to travel in the slightly cooler but drier months of December to April. These have become the most expensive months and hotel accommodation can double in price. The resort towns can become crowded and the most popular beaches hives of activity.

The British have traditionally travelled in the summer when they can have peace and quiet. The islanders have more time to stop and chat, the tourist attractions are less crowded, and bars and restaurants have fewer bookings. Do not be put off by the thought of rain; it is usually in the form of short summer showers and is often quite refreshing. The only slight disadvantage of travelling in the summer is that this is the time of year when there are more mosquitoes and other insects around. It is worth taking insect repellent with you and applying it liberally in the evenings. And be careful walking on the sand late in the afternoons or at night. Many of the beaches are crawling with sandflies which can give you a nasty nip.

Health The Caribbean is generally a healthy place to visit, with a few exceptions. AIDS is reported to be rife in Haiti, and most of the other islands issue health warnings against the disease. Casual sex without protection is a bad idea, and added to the advice against taking drugs is the warning about used syringes. Many people travel with small first-aid packs which include clean syringes and plasma. You will not always get these through customs and, if you do, you will probably have to spend some time explaining yourself first. Hospital care on the islands is good, in most cases, and there should be no need for such a kit.

Drinking water varies from island to island. Jamaica has hundreds of fresh, fast-flowing rivers and the islanders are proud of their clean, healthy water. But on the Dominican Republic or in Haiti you are advised to stick to drinking bottled water which is available in most hotel and resort areas.

The Dominican Republic is notorious among its visitors for giving everyone a bout of stomach trouble. There are three main causes to watch out for. One is the water, so used bottled water for cleaning teeth as well as drinking. The second is the food: the cooking standards are not always up to European quality, and less than hygienic kitchens combined with unusual foods can cause problems. The third is the sun. Most people forget just how hot the midday sun can be. On the north coast, a regular afternoon breeze always picks up, cooling the beaches. But don't be deceived, the sun is still burning and many people advise leaving the beach by 11 a.m. for the shade of the palm trees. One of the main symptoms of heat-stroke or severe sunburn can be an upset stomach.

Most people are well aware of the dangers of too much sun but it is worth remembering to pack sunhats, particularly for young children, and to use plenty of suncream, and re-apply it after swimming.

It is also worth checking with your GP before you go, to see if he recommends any particular vaccinations. Most will suggest taking malaria pills before visiting Hispaniola and also having up-to-date typhoid, tetanus and polio protection.

Money Most of the islands have their own currency, but most will also accept the US dollar in their shops, restaurants and hotels. Sterling is not so widely accepted, although most banks will change it.

Puerto Rico uses the US dollar, while the Cayman Islands have a fixed rate for the Cayman Island dollar against the US and both can be used anywhere on the islands. The Jamaican dollar and the Dominican Republic peso both offer you favourable exchange rates with the US dollar rather than with sterling. All the island accept most major credit cards, and the majority of visitors will take little cash with them in favour of credit cards.

With foreign currency so crucial to their economies, there are strict rules about the import and export of money. Most will not allow you to export their own currency.

The Caribbean is an expensive region and visitors should expect to spend heavily while there. Some of the islands, such as the Dominican Republic, are still cheap but the cost of food and drinks in the resort areas will still be at least three times what it is in local towns. Other places, such as the Cayman Islands, are very expensive for everybody and, although it is a tax haven, many local people have two jobs to support themselves and their families.

Jamaica has several all-inclusive hotels springing up across the island in response to demand. Everything is paid for in advance and there are no hidden extras. Some people feel they have seen little of the island by the time they leave, while others are glad of the security of the hotel complex and knowing that they can not spend over budget.

Shopping In an effort to attract tourists, particularly the cruise-ship trade, the islands have invested heavily in duty-free shopping areas. A few years ago the majority of these centres were filled with china, glass and jewellery but now many have had to switch to cater for a different type of traveller – those on cheap packages – and the shops are filled with cheap souvenirs and T-shirts. There are some exceptions. The Cayman Islands still have some high-quality centres and on all the islands there are still some nice shops to be found. Much of the crystal and china has been brought over from Europe and is only really cheap for the American visitors rather than for the Europeans.

Away from the formal shopping centre, nearly every Caribbean town and village has its own market. Most are used by locals every day, while others such as the Straw Market in Montego Bay, Jamaica, have become tourist attractions in their own right. They contain the locally grown fruit and vegetables, as well as freshly caught fish in the seaside towns.

Culture The mixes of cultures that have resulted in the cosmopolitan islanders have also resulted in the interesting mix of arts and crafts. Places like Puerto Rico are dominated by their Spanish heritage mixed with an American efficiency. Their culture, however, is also influenced by Africa combined with a style, developed uniquely within the country.

Theatre and music play an important part in all island life, together with religion which forms the basis of many of the islands' celebrations. The Dominican Republic is dominated by its *merengue* music which turns the whole of the capital into an open-air party for most of July, while Jamaica is world famous as the original home of reggae music. Bob Marley was born and raised on the island and his home is now a museum dedicated to reggae music.

Dreadlocks and Rastafarians abound in the islands and many of these people contribute to the crafts, making a living by selling to tourists. Each island has its own distinctive art. Haitian paintings are known for their bright colours and scenes of village life, while paintings from the Dominican Republic can be much the same but always with a bright-red flame tree somewhere in the picture.

Wooden carvings are also found everywhere in the region, many influenced by the African heritage of the former slaves. Others are influenced by religion, such as the *santos* in Puerto Rico, where each family has its own style of *santos*, or wooden carving depicting saints, passed down from generation to generation.

Clothing Informality is the keyword on most of the islands and a selection of light cottons is most suitable. But to visit some of the religious centres of the islands, you will need to wear skirts below the knee for women or long trousers for men.

Some of the hotels like guests to dress for dinner and ask guests not to wear swimwear while walking through the foyer or main public areas. On some islands, such as Puerto Rico and Dominion Republic, it is advisable to cover up if you leave the beaches to avoid comment from the locals. Some islands allow topless or nude sunbathing but it is usually only in certain well-marked areas and it is discouraged anywhere else.

Sports With the islands' warm climate and the calm Caribbean Sea, the area has become a haven for sports-lovers. Every island has a wide range of water sports facilities, from water-skiing and jet-skiing to deep-sea fishing or scuba diving. Some islands, such as the Cayman Islands, are world famous for their scuba-diving sites, some just a few metres off-shore, and Sting Ray City off Grand Cayman is a name most divers recognize as being the only place in the world where sting ray will come to divers and eat out of their hands. The Cayman Islands also operate two submarines in which tourists can travel along the edge of the 1,220metre(4,000ft.) wall to marvel at the marine life. There are over twenty dive operators willing to teach beginners and to offer experienced divers night dives, daytime dives or photographic trips.

Day trips on catamarans or sailing boats are also common on the islands and offer guests the chance to enjoy the islands from the sea. Jamaica has some well-known fishing tournaments – the October Marlin contest at Port Antonio is one of the oldest competitions in the Caribbean – while on Grand Cayman they go for grand prices, fishing in competition for a million dollars in June's Million Dollar Month. River and lake fishing are popular in the mountain areas of Puerto Rico

Apart from the watersports, one of the fast-growing sports in the region is golf. Many of the islands have golf-courses designed by Robert Trent Jones, and the course at the Hyatt Hotel on Grand Cayman is the only one in the world to use the Cayman Ball, designed by Jack Nicklaus. It floats on the water – an essential requirement on a course where many of the holes are punctuated by inlets from the sea.

The islands attract major international tournaments annually for tennis and polo and for the more adventurous there is the hot-air balloon contest held annually in Montego Bay, Jamaica. Jamaica and Puerto Rico both have annual marathon contests, and in Puerto Rico there are many cycling races every weekend. Some sports are seasonal, such as baseball or basketball which follow the North American seasons, while others are peculiar to the islands, such as cock fighting.

Windsurfers travel from far and wide to try out the excellent surfing conditions at Caberete, Dominican Republic

New sports centres are opening up all the time, both in resort areas and for local people. San Juan in Puerto Rico has an Olympic Centre, while in Kingston, Jamaica, there are also excellent facilities.

In the Dominican Republic there is the Casa de Campo resort on the south coast with its excellent sports and arts facilities.

The islanders are keen sports fans and if you have the misfortune to travel during a cricket test series between England and the West Indies, and England just happen to be losing, you can rest assured everyone will let you know the latest score and every taxi driver in Kingston will manage to take you past the cricket ground to point out that is where your cricketers are busy losing the match.

As well as the competitive marathons, there are also numerous trails. Jamaica's Blue Mountain is really only accessible on foot and is a climb for the fit and healthy. In Puerto Rico, there are numerous trails through the El Yungue rain forest as well as mountain trails in the western hills. Many of these areas are rarely visited by tourists and give visitors a real opportunity of getting to know the islands and their people.

For the even less competitive, there are plenty of swimming-pools complete with swim-up bars. Glass-bottom boats take the effort out of underwater sightseeing or try a day at the dog or horse races for another spectator sport.

Children are well catered for with many hotels offering baby-sitting services and arranging a full day of beach activities to give parents a day off.

Eating out in the region is varied, leaving visitors to choose between exotic local foods, international cuisine or good home cooking. Trying the different restaurants and bars gives you an opportunity to meet local people and learn how the islands work.

Set in the Caribbean Sea, the islands of the Greater Antilles are some of the largest in the region. They are also large in history and colour. They may not be among the wealthiest nations in the world but they still have a lot to offer visitors, making them feel they have come to a very special place. But size does not matter: the large islands have their secluded bays and beaches while the small islands still have a mass of sights for visitors to enjoy as well as the beaches.

But one of the biggest pleasures of the region is that if you prefer a quiet, get-away-from-it-all holiday to yourselves, people will be happy to oblige. They let you choose the pace and direction of any trip and are just there to help make it happen.

Part One: **The Cayman Islands**

**The sea bar where some
couples get married at the
Divi Tiara Hotel, Cayman Brac**

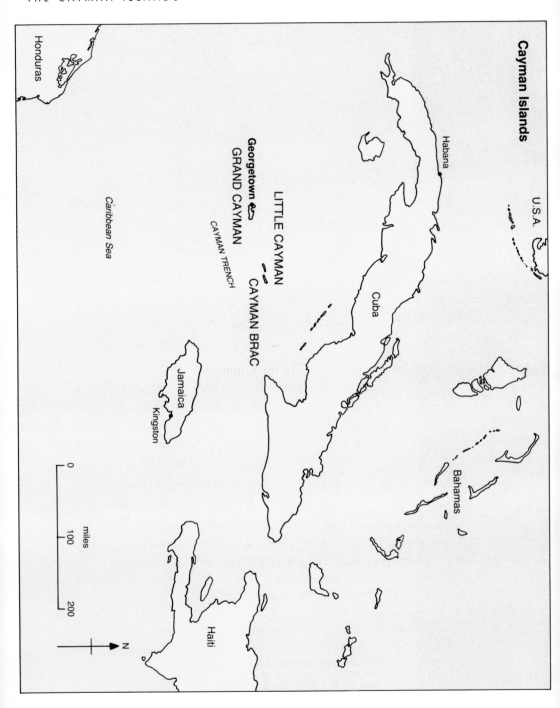

The Cayman Islands exude an atomosphere of exclusivity while boasting some of the best beaches in the Caribbean and the best underwater sights and sites. The three tiny islands are the furthest west of the Caribbean and are still relatively undiscovered by the British tourist. They have long been a favourite haunt of Americans, but only for those who could afford it.

The islands are a safe haven for tourist and businessmen alike, with their tax-free status, low crime rates and quiet location. Proud of the multi-racial, multi-cultural attitudes, the Caymanians provide one of the warmest welcomes found in the Caribbean. They are very choosy about who they allow to live permanently in the islands but are more than happy to make your trip the holiday of a lifetime.

Tourism is increasing steadily but is also carefully controlled to maintain the right atmosphere. Hotel development is also carefully planned. Buildings are not allowed to exceed 'palm-tree height' and are well spaced out, even along the most developed area of Seven Mile Beach. This is said by the locals to be the most beautiful beach in the Caribbean and it would certainly be hard to beat for its clear, blue waters. The water here is shallow and safe for swimmers, but there are spectacular reefs just metres offshore for snorkellers and divers.

Known as a mecca for watersports lovers, the Cayman Islands do have plenty of other attractions for tourists. Being such small islands, it is easy to 'do' the islands very quickly but longer, slower journeys are easily planned for visitors eager to soak up the history and romance of these Islands which have long been linked to pirates, tales of brave men and legends of fishing and diving experiences.

29

The Cayman Islands attract scuba divers from across the world to explore the vast coral reefs and sponge corals

Grand Cayman is usually the first stop for most visitors, although for some people the development of the recent years makes them rush straight off to the smaller Cayman Brac and Little Cayman where residents are few and tourists even rarer. The fourth, rarely mentioned island in the group is Owen's Island. Uninhabited, this tiny island nestles just 200 metres south of Little Cayman and is a favoured picnic and fishing spot.

Pre-Planning – How to get there

Flights The easiest way to Grand Cayman is via the USA, although there are regular flights from Jamaica.

The islands have their own airline, Cayman Airways, which connects Grand Cayman with Miami, New York, Tampa, Atlanta and Houston in the USA. It also flies to Jamaica, and its inter-island service connects the international flights with flights to both Cayman Brac and Little Cayman. Cayman Airways also runs a service between the two smaller islands.

Air Jamaica has flights from both Kingston and Montego Bay. Northwest Airlines has daily flights from Miami and there are season charter flights from the States and Canada. Eastern Airways also has a regular service.

Tour operators from the UK include Kuoni Travel, Dream Island Holidays, Peregor Travel, Twickers World, Page & Moy Holidays, Jetlife Holidays, Speedbird Holidays, Virgin Holidays, Harlequin Holidays, Frontiers Gogo Tours, Interline Tours, Elegant Resorts, Abercrombie & Kent, Christian Travel Services, Exotic Island Holidays, Tropical Magic, Bladdon Lines, Hayes & Jarvis and New Beginnings.

When to Go The high season, is from 15 December to 16 April. Prices are higher and accommodation more difficult to find. Temperatures average 25°C(77°F) in summer, when most of the rainfall occurs, running from May to October.

The hurricane season is from August through to October but Hurricane Gilbert in 1988 was the first major hurricane to hit the islands in over thirty years. If you are unfortunate enough to be there when a hurricane approaches, you will discover that the islands have a well-established and efficient emergency procedure and tourist safety is among the top priorities.

Passports and return tickets are required for everybody but USA and Canadian citizens. Americans and Canadians have to produce some proof of citizenship, either a passport, birth certificate or voters' registration and a marriage certificate for women using their husband's name. You will be asked for a departure levy of CI$6.00 or US$7.50.

Health There are not specific health requirements.

Getting About

Car Rental There are plenty of car rental agencies on Grand Cayman, including Avis (Tel: 9 2468) and Budget (Tel: 9 5605) and cars can be booked in advance in the UK. Care hire is very cheap and one day's hire can be cheaper than three average taxi rides. Car rental starts at about CI$18, insurance is an extra CI$6 and most companies offer free mileage. As the island is so small, one tank of petrol will probably be enough.

A valid British driving licence is needed to get a temporary local permit which will be issued by the police or car-hire firm, costing CI$2.40.

31

The Hyatt Hotel, Grand Cayman

Driving is on the left, and drivers have to stop behind stationary buses as the bus doors open into the centre of the road. There is a one-way system in the capital of George Town and yellow lines mean No Parking. Observe the speed limits as there are plenty of traffic police.

Taxis are everywhere. You can pick them up from all the hotels or just flag them down. They do have set fares and will accept either CI dollars or US dollars.

Buses There are bus stops, but they will stop anywhere. If you want to go off the bus route just ask the driver and he will take you. All stops on the set route cost you CI$1.00 however far you travel, but if you leave the main route the driver will charge you as if he was running a taxi service. Bus timetables do not really exist and if you are waiting at a bus stop, you will often find that someone will stop and offer you a lift.

Accommodation is split into hotels and self-catering apartments. From the UK, many travellers will have booked a package-style holiday with accommodation and flight all sorted

32

out by the tour operator. But if you are travelling independently, the Cayman Tourist Board office in London (Tel: 071 581 9960) will make the booking for you, saving you both time and money.

Many of the self-catering apartments will have a starter pack of food ready for your arrival. Most also have a maid service. *Kondo Kitchen* (Tel: 1 809 949 7430) will make up food and beverage parcels for delivery either as you arrive or during your holiday.

Electricity is 110 volts so British appliances need adaptors.

Money The official currency is the Cayman Islands Dollar. It is fixed against the US dollar and CI$1 costs US$1.25. Both currencies are acceptable, and most people will take a mixture of both as payment. Sterling is easily exchanged at local banks, and there are plenty to choose from because it is a tax haven. Grand Cayman is home to over 500 banks. American Express, Mastercard and Visa are all widely accepted.

Banks are generally open from 9 a.m. to 2.30 p.m., Mondays to Thursdays, and from 9 a.m. to 1 p.m. and 2.30 p.m. to 4.30 p.m. on Fridays. The Washington International Bank, West Bay Road Branch in 7-Mile Shops is open until 4 p.m., Monday to Friday.

Tipping is often left to your discretion. Restaurants may add a 10 or 15 per cent charge in lieu of tipping, and a Government tourist tax of 6 per cent will be added to your accommodation bill as will a 10 per cent gratuity.

Safety Do not worry about safety. The whole atmosphere on the islands is one of a safe haven, everyone is friendly and, while it is always unadvisable to walk around at night with a lot of cash and dripping with jewels, you will be surprised at the numbers of people strolling around after dark.

Food and Wine Tourism is one of the islands' major industries. Grand Cayman may only be a few kilometres long but it has a huge variety of restaurants, ranging from the very exclusive to a jerk pork stop. The smaller islands do not have such a choice, with eating out limited to the hotels on the islands.

All food has to be imported and most of it comes from the USA. Most major US brand names are available at the numerous supermarkets in George Town, such as *Comart* where there is a wide international selection, from escargots from Thailand to *foie gras* from France as well as chutneys from the UK. Another supermarket with a wide selection of groceries is *Foster's Food Fair* in The Greenery and on the Airport Road. For gourmet foods and international wines and spirits, try *The Wine Cellar* in Galleria Plaza, on the West Bay Road.

Shopping As a tax haven, Grand Cayman has plenty to offer the eager shopper. Among the best buys are gold and gold dubloons, crystal, fine china and photographic equipment. And among the many perfumes on offer, try the island's own Cayman Caress. Black coral jewellery is also widely sold if you are looking for an expensive but beautiful gift. Products from the world's only turtle farm are also on sale but these are banned from import into the USA, so watch out if your journey home means stopping over there.

Most of the duty-free shops are in George Town. The *Kirk Freeport Plaza* is devoted to jewellery and watches. Its newly opened *Waterford Wedgwood Gallery* is also on Cardinal Avenue. The Kirk Freeport Centre is home to the island's largest display of crystal and china. The *Cayman Camera Store* overlooks the harbour. All these shops are within easy walking distance of each other.

Slightly further down Harbour Drive is the *Soto Freeport*, which offers a range of less expensive china, crystal and linens. The Anchorage Centre is home to *Colombian Emeralds* and *Amazing China Turtle*, while *Pure Art Gallery and Gifts* is in a Cayman cottage just south of the capital.

Hairdressers: *Visage Hair Stylists* have two locations, offering hairstyling, manicures and facial services. The shops can be found in Treasure Island Resort and in The Greenery, next to Foster's Food Fair in West Bay Road.

Undersea Photo provides everything for underwater photographers as well as gifts from its outlets at Treasure Island Resort and in the Falls Shopping Centre. The Falls shop is next door to *Book Nook*, which contains a wide range of hard and paperback books. To learn more about the people, an excellent book is *The People Time Forgot*. It is a collection of black and white photographs of islanders past and present.

The main Post Office is in George Town and is open from 8.30 a.m. to 4 p.m., Monday to Friday. It contains a Philatelic Bureau. Postage back to the UK will cost 15 cents for a postcard and 50 cents for an airletter.

Local Colour

The People The Cayman Islands are still a British Crown Colony and are loyal to the Royal Family. English is the official language here but is spoken in a Caymanian dialect which can be confusing, often sounding more like singing than talking. It helps if you get the speaker to slow down and if you work on the basis that all the 'V's will probably be pronounced 'W'.

The people are a mix of English, Welsh, and Spanish, with some pirates and slaves among their ancestors, too. They pride themselves on their multi-racial, multi-cultural attitudes. Added to the natural Caribbean laid-back style is an island friendliness that is hard to beat. People will approach you on the street for nothing more than a chat, to find out if you are enjoying your holiday and where you come from.

The Country The Cayman Islands are approximately 770km(480ml.) south of Miami in the British Caribbean. Cayman Brac and Little Cayman are 11km(7ml.) apart and lie 142km(89ml.) north-east of Grand Cayman. Grand Cayman is

An old Caymanian enjoying the sun outside a typical island home

the largest, measuring 11 by 45km(7 by 28ml.) with a population of 23,000. Cayman Brac has less than 1,000 residents on its 19km(12ml.) long island and Little Cayman is the ultimate 'get-away-from-it-all destination with about 46 residents on its 17 square kilometres(11 sq.ml.).

Jamaica is about 320km(200ml.) to the south-east of the Cayman Islands and until 1961 the islands were a dependency of Jamaica. In 1961 they became a British Crown Colony and a Governor was appointed. The islands are determined to remain a colony and have sent an official delegation to the United Nations to tell them that the islands want to remain as they are. The islands came under British protection in 1670 under the terms of the Treaty of Madrid, in which Spain handed over both Jamaica and Cayman.

Columbus was the first to discover the islands. He found Cayman Brac when he got lost on his way from Panama to Hispaniola. After his visit, the islands remained virtually uninhabited until they were given to the British. Among the first to arrive then were deserters from Oliver Cromwell's army and refugees from the Spanish Inquisition. Pirates also lived on the islands and some of their treasure is rumoured to be still hidden in the island caves, while their shipwrecked treasure ships are among the favourite haunts of divers.

At one time there were almost 1,000 slaves living on the islands with the new settlers from Scotland, Wales Ireland and America. The mix of English dialects accounts for the local way of talking.

With an appointed Governor in control, the islands are ruled with the help of a twelve-man Legislative Assembly. These members are elected by the people. They also elect four of them to sit on the Executive Councill along with three members from the Civil Service. Each councillor has a particular part of the government to run.

The Cayman Islands is a famous tax haven but it has not always been that way. In 1788 a convoy of ten ships was on its way from Jamaica to England when the lead ship ran aground close to the islands. The other ships all followed their leader, but no one drowned thanks to the quick rescue work of the islanders. The Legend of the Ten Sails is that a member of the royal family was on one of the ships and that King George III was so grateful that his relative was saved, he ordered that no islander need ever face conscription and none of them need ever pay taxes.

Being a tax haven has made it a very attractive area for many financial institutions. The 500th bank opened recently on Grand Cayman but the island is careful not to allow too many to open, careful of possible failures or frauds. It is proud of the success of its licensing system, with only three banking failures in sixteen years.

Often referred to as a second Switzerland, it also stresses the need for confidentiality and has rigid laws, although it does have a Mutual Legal Assistance Treaty with Britain and the USA to allow limited disclosure for drug-related criminal investigations. It is the largest offshore centre in the world and, as well as the banks, there are 17,000 companies registered on the islands along with 350 offshore insurance companies. To help businessmen, communications from the island are excellent, with telex and fax machines standard and most business houses also having specialist wire services for up-to-the-minute information.

Tourism is of growing importance to the islands, providing about 35 per cent of jobs and about 70 per cent of gross domestic product. The number of beds available is also rising rapidly, the new Radisson Hotel doubled the hotel beds on Grand Cayman in 1990 and labour has to be imported to cope with all the new construction. Because everything has to be imported, the cost of living is fairly high.

Unlike many of the Caribbean Islands, Cayman is not volcanic. The islands rose from the sea when the North American tectonic plate was lifted by the movement of the Caribbean plate. Coral reefs grew in the shallow areas, eventually forming the three islands. The advantages of the coral islands across the region is that this is where you find the fine, white sand that everyone associates with the Caribbean. There are some of the stunning geological features on the islands, including Hell on Grand Cayman. This area of rock is an estimated 2.5 million years old. The 'Wall' has made the islands one of the world's best diving spots. There are four walls off the islands. Off Grand Cayman, the drop can be from just 11m(35ft.) of water down to 1,830m(6,000ft.) and visibility can be up to 60m(200ft.).

Events Calendar

Holidays include:

New Year's Day

Ash Wednesday

Good Friday and Easter Monday

Batabano (Grand Cayman) and Brachanal (Cayman Brac) in the last week of April

Discovery day, 21 May

Million Dollar Month (June)

The Queen's Birthday, 11 June

Constitution Day, 2 July

Pirates Week (the last in October)

Halloween, 31 October

Remembrance Day

Christmas Eve, Christmas Day and Boxing Day

New Year's Eve

Below
The winning marlin caught during a Million Dollar Month competition

Below right
Pirate's Week, held each October, ia a week of fancy-dress parties and a carnival in every village on Grand Cayman, culminating in the Grand Ball

Batabano is Grand Cayman's carnival weekend and Brachanal is a week later. Visitors are encouraged to join in the fancy dress parades and competitions. Dressing up is also required for Pirates Week, when many hotels offer special rates. Each day a different area of the islands has a carnival and parties. Firecrackers abound and even cars are dressed up with Jolly Rogers. Pirates take control of the islands on the first Saturday and are chased off a week later when Government forces regain control after the grand Pirates Ball.

Million Dollar Month in June is a mecca for fishermen the world over. They come to the islands to take part in the hundreds of contests to catch the largest marlin, tuna or yellowfin. During the fishing contest the islanders take time out to celebrate the Queen's Birthday with a full-dress uniform parade, marching bands and a twenty-one gun salute.

Grand Cayman To drive around the whole of Grand Cayman takes about three hours but if you want to take your time and soak up the history and natural wonders, there are plenty of places to visit and to stay at around the coast.

George Town is a delightful capital where the traffic moves slowly, gives way to pedestrians and where everyone has a friendly, smiling face. Most people visiting Grand Cayman will stay somewhere along Seven Mile Beach and will probably spend most of their time in the water or on the beach. But a trip down to the capital is well worth the effort.

Seven Mile Beach runs into George Town via West Bay Road and local buses or taxis will take you down to the waterfront at Hogaty Bay, where the cruise-ship passengers disembark. Cruise ships tend to come in on Tuesdays, Wednesdays and Thursdays so the town will fill up with shoppers for a few hours.

As you enter George Town from Seven Mile Beach one of the first buildings you will see is Tower Building, a Government office which houses the Department of Tourism (Tel: 9 7999). Just a few yards further down the road and you are into the main town. It is easy to walk around the whole town in less than an hour and not worth getting a taxi to take you round – you will only get stuck in the one-way system.

As you come in down North Church Street from West Bay Road, one of the first sights worth stopping at is the *Pirates World*

The Main Street in Cayman's capital George Town

and Treasure Museum. It is one of the island's newest attractions and has been set up to show off sunken treasure recovered from *Nuestra Señora de las Maravillas*, reputed to be the second most valuable galleon to sink in the New World. The Museum also has theatre shows and slide presentations and a gift shop which sells genuine artefacts.

From the Museum, you can travel down Fort Street past the Legislative Assembly Building down to the Town Hall. The Town Clock is the centrepiece of the roundabout opposite. Turning right at the roundabout down Edward Street, visitors can travel down to the Courts Building and along to the Main Post Office.

At the end of Edward Street, turn into Elgin Avenue to find the police station and Glass House, the Government Administration Building. The island's hospital is further down the road. Going back into town down Shedden Road takes you past the Old Courts, which are destined to become a Museum. Turning right along the waterfront takes you to George Town Docks and behind them the new Port Authority Building.

40

If you turn left at the waterfront to go down South Church Street you will pass the offices of the *Atlantis Submarine* (Tel: 9 7700) on the right. This is well worth a trip. The 28-seater submarine takes you on an hour-long trip off the Wall. Dropping to 46m(150ft.) along the coral reef, the sights are spectacular and an ideal way for those who do not want to get their feet wet to see what it is that makes the islands such a mecca for divers.

The submarine does day and night trips. Both trips are worth doing because of the different fish which can be seen. Lobsters and many crustaceans can only be seen at night, while many of the brightly coloured reef fish are daylight creatures only. The best photographs can be taken at night and the submarine crew give an excellent commentary on what is around you.

Shopping George Town is heaven for shoppers. Glitzy shops abound, offering duty-free bargains of every description. There are little courtyards everywhere, filled with yet more shops. It is difficult to miss the main shopping centre of Kirk Freeport Plaza. Walk up Cardinal Avenue from Hogaty Bay and you will be surrounded by perfume, china and camera shops. The Plaza continues around the corner in Albert Panton Street. Most of the islands have duty-free shopping centres to lure tourists, though some have become dilapidated as the type of tourists change and their requirements change with them. But in the Cayman Islands, the shops are new and clean and still very much up-market.

If you are a keen shopper, do not expect to get to Freeport Plaza too quickly as you will have wandered past shops such as *Colombian Emeralds* and the *Amazing China Turtle*. Tucked behind the main town on the Airport Road is the Elizabethan Square which houses the leatherwork shop of *Le Classique*, among others.

Jewellery made out of black coral is an island speciality and some of the best examples can be found at *Mitzi's* on North Church Street. Bernard Passman is world famous for his artwork. For the Queen and Prince Philip he fashioned a replica of the horse the Queen used to ride during the Trooping of the Colour. His main shop is *Black Coral And*, which is on Fort Street, but he also has outlets at the Treasure Island Hotel and in the Galleria Plaza on West Bay Road.

There are plenty of dive shops in George Town, including *Eden Rock Diving Centre* (Tel: 9 7243). It is located on South Church Street and may appear to be in the centre of town but just 46m (150ft.) away is a famous dive site, Eden Rock and the Devil's Grotto, which is considered one of Cayman's greatest natural wonders. Close by is another large watersports centre, *Parrott's Landing*, (Tel: 9 7884). Not only a centre for equipment, trips and tuition, it also has a picnic site complete with hammocks to lie back and enjoy the sun.

Restaurants After a morning wandering around the shops, there are plenty of places to stop off for a cooling drink and a bite to eat. *Daisy Queen* (Tel: 9 6311) is on Shedden Road, or you can continue further along Shedden Road and turn left into Edward Street to find *Coritas Copper Kettle*. For a waterfront view, try *Island Taste* (Tel: 9 4945) which offers both Caribbean and international cuisine. Open Monday to Saturday, it is located on South Church Street opposite the Atlantis Submarine office.

A short taxi ride out of town down South Church Street will get you to *Chef Tell's Grand Old House* (Tel: 9 2266). American TV personality, Tell Erhardt, will recommend the best food and wines of the day and settle you in for a gourmet treat in this waterside restaurant. Open both for lunch and dinner it is an experience not to be missed.

Still further out of town on South Church Street, you can enjoy the day at *Coconut Harbour* (Tel: 9 7468). Guests enjoy swimming and snorkelling on the sandy beach before sampling tropical drinks at the outdoor bar and then a buffet-style meal.

Going north out of George Town, back towards Seven Mile Beach, you can enjoy the underwater sights without leaving the restaurant at the *Almond Tree* (Tel: 9 2893). Tables are set out on the patio and under the thatch roof for diners to sample a wide range of seafood or local specialities while slide shows reveal the underwater world.

For a really quick snack try *The Pit Stop*. It offers jerk pork, chicken or fish. This is a Jamaican style of cooking which is a cross between barbecueing and smoking and is very tasty.

Seven Mile Beach This area is where most people will stay while on Grand Cayman and it links George Town with West Bay. Hotels and apartments line the beach, while on the other side of the road restaurants and bars provide entertainment for the guests. The idea of a long strip of hotels and bars may sound more like Spain than the Caribbean, but do not worry, the hotels are spaced out in well-laid-out-gardens, many with private beach areas.

Most of the hotels provide evening entertainment but it is quite safe to wander down the road in search of something different. Barefoot Man has a show most nights at the *Holiday Inn* and is famed in the Islands for his folk shows, while the *Ramada Treasure Island Resort* is better known for its country and western acts. Once owned by singing stars like Conway Twitty and Larry Gatlin, some big US stars still make appearances there.

During the day, most of the entertainment is geared towards the beach. Several of the hotels have dive shops and schools attached to their premises, such as *Aqua Delights* at the Holiday Inn and *Don Fosters* at the new Radisson Hotel. Diving and snorkelling groups are taken to the island's best spots, while for the less adventurous there are plenty of swimming-pools with bars alongside.

Deep-sea fishing trips also set off from the beach, along with evening cruises, glass-bottom boat trips, waterskiing, parasailing and just about every watersport you can think of. If you do not

43

want to get wet, most hotels have tennis courts and the Hyatt boasts the island's only golf-course. Playing golf on Grand Cayman is a one-off experience. Designed by Jack Nicklaus, the 9-hole course requires a special golf-ball. The Cayman ball floats – necessary when you realize that for some drives you actually have to hit the ball over inlets from the sea.

Hotels With such a choice of accommodation, it is easy to pick somewhere to suit both your pocket and your needs. Prices range from less than a hundred dollars a day to more than five hundred.

The top hotels include the *Hyatt Regency & Villas* (Tel: 9 1234). This not only has the island's only golf-course but a diving centre and a stretch of private beach. A night here costs upwards of US$150. The *Grand Pavilion Hotel* (Tel: 7 4666) has some slightly cheaper rooms but a suite in high season can cost around US$1,500 a night. The rooms are furnished in Louis XV-style furniture and it has its own swimming-pool and dive facilities. The new *Radisson Hotel* (Tel: 9 8088) is the largest property on the island with 310 bedrooms built around a central courtyard, close to the beach, complete with conference facilities, shops and a night-club. Another new hotel is the *Cayman Islander Hotel* which is close to Seven Mile Beach without being in the main strip. It has 68 bedrooms set in tropical gardens.

There are plenty of condominiums and villas, including *Cayman Islands Resort Club* (Tel: 7 4822), *Turtle Beach Villas* (Tel: 9 6347) and *Casa Caribe* (Tel: 7 4287). Cheaper hotels and guest houses include *Ambassadors Inn Resort* (Tel: 9 7577), *Grama's Bed and Breakfast* (Tel: 9 3798) at the West Bay end of the beach, and *Windjammer Hotel* (Tel: 7 4608).

Restaurants Some of the island's top restaurants are in the big hotels, such as *Hemingways* at the Hyatt's Britannia Beach Club (Tel: 9 1234), or *L'Escargot* at Ramada Treasure Island Resort (Tel: 9 7255). If you feel like a change from island cooking, try the Italian restaurant *Bella Capri*, behind Foster's Food Fair (Tel: 7 4755).

For the younger jet setters, a night out could end with a visit to *Monkey Business* night-club, which is located almost opposite the Holiday Inn, or to *Silvers Night Club* at the Treasure Island Resort. The newest club on the island is called *Faces*, just down the road from Treasure Island Resort.

Behind Seven Mile Beach on the eastern coast is the North Sound. This is an area of relatively sheltered water lined with inlets and small bays. The *Hyatt Golf-course* is in this area, taking advantage of the inlets to make the course more challenging.

A new development is springing up in this area, *The Cayman Islands Yacht Club* (Tel: 7 4322), which is being built next to Governor's Harbour. It houses up to 150 yachts of up to 12metres(40ft.) on three piers and a further thirty larger vessels at a jetty next to Governor's Harbour. The Club owns a 12-acre site and plans a 200-bedroom hotel as well as a range of condominiums. The focal point of the site is the Yacht Clubhouse itself but guests will also have access to swimming-pools, four tennis courts, a sports club and a selection of shops.

West Bay Tourists flock to West Bay, not just for its diving sites and excellent watersports facilities but for the island's large turtle farm. To get there, you just follow the road out of George Town along the coast, past Seven Mile Beach. The road forks, you take the left turning and the farm is another 3km(2ml.) further on. The journey takes you past the Governor's residence, perhaps most remarkable for its lack of guards, barbed wire or other security. The Governor has been known to invite tourists in for a drink after they have wandered on to the beach outside his house.

The view of George Town Harbour that cruise-ship passengers have as they arrive in the capital

The Green Sea Turtle farm, Grand Cayman, is breeding turtles to boost the wild population

Once at the *Turtle Farm*, the entrance fee is $5 and then you can wander past the tanks of tiny baby turtles and see the giant 270-kilo(600lb) Green Sea Turtles. The Farm was set up to preserve the turtle which once swarmed across the island. When Christopher Columbus first saw the islands, the waters were so full of turtles that the islands were called 'Las Tortugas', only changing to the Cayman Islands after false rumours that a crocodile had been sighted there.

Now the Farm returns many of the turtles bred there back to the sea. It keeps a large tankful of turtles for breeding purposes and the turtles' eggs are kept in the hatchery in the best possible conditions, ensuring that large numbers do hatch out. Some of the turtles are killed for meat which is served in many of the island's restaurants, including the one at the Farm, which has turtle sandwiches on offer. Other products from the turtle, such as the shell, are made into jewellery and other souvenirs. But turtle products can not be taken into America, so be careful if your return journey takes you into the US.

The West End is also home for the small community known as Hell. Hell is an area of ironshore, limestone and coral, an area of black jagged rock, where the temperature always seems to be higher than anywhere else on the island. The community boasts a Post Office and some souvenir shops, so that you can send postcards, postmarked Hell and with all the clichés like 'It's Hell here without you' or 'Go to Hell'. It is a tourist trap, but still worth the visit to marvel at the weird and wonderful rock formation.

West Bay is also home to most of the island's craftsmen, from thatchers to jewellers and painters. Unlike the modern concept of selling crafts in a shop, these people still sit on their porches and are happy to invite you in to watch them work. Many of them have the familiar Caymanian names of Ebanks or Bodden. Straw workers, Asnetta Bush, Anetta Jackson and Nin 'Cootsie' Rivers live and work just along the street from thatcher Laris Ebanks (Tel: 9 3447), all close to the town hall. At Boatswain Bay you can find Lorna, Greta and Francis Ebanks all working in their different houses on straw products, while nearby Garnal Ebanks works on black coral jewellery.

Just off the road to the Turtle Farm, you will find Mabel Smith (Tel: 9 1039) producing coconut oil, while *en route* to the Farm Carolyn Watson (Tel: 9 3778) is famous for her wompers and thatch. It is best to give them a telephone call to make sure they will be in when you call.

Deep-sea fishing boats moor up at Morgan's Harbour and you can book up on a trip from the nearby charter booking office. If you would rather stay on terra firma, the harbour is a nice place to take a walk.

Hotels There are plenty of places to stay at West Bay and good places to eat. *Villas Pappagallo* (Tel: 9 3568) are among the best accommodation at West Bay. Recommended for its peace and quiet, the villas are still within easy access of Seven Mile Beach and George Town and cost around $280 for a villa sleeping four in high season. *Spanish Cove* (Tel: 9 3765) offers everything for the diver and has a restaurant, oceanside pool and beach-front villas for those not so keen on diving. The *Beach Club Resort* (Tel: 9 2023) is at the West Bay End of Seven Mile Beach and again offers all watersports in a quiet location. Villas can be found at the *Caribbean Club* (Tel: 7 4099), which is run with the services of a hotel but with the privacy of your own villa. *Island House Resort* (Tel: 9 3017) is among the island's cheapest accommodation and is a good base for divers. West Bay has a wide selection of condominiums for rent in every price bracket.

Restaurants Among the best is the *Island House*, which specializes in local cuisine and is housed in a renovated Caymanian house which is over 100 years old. Also offering good local food is *Liberty's Restaurant*. One of the island's best restaurants is *Ristorante Pappagallo* at Barkers, West Bay (Tel: 9 1119), offering Italian cuisine in a lakeside setting. The lake is a sanctuary for many of the island's birds.

Bodden Bay Going south from George Town takes you around the South Sound and its quaint-named coves, such as Pull-and-Be-Dammed Point and Little Pedro Point. The road also shows you the contrasts of the islands from the old Cayman wooden homes to the most exclusive homes. Just off the main road is the island's oldest-standing building, *Pedro's Castle*. Originally called St James Castle, it was built by William Eden in 1780 but it was almost destroyed in 1877 when it was hit by lightning. Now it has been rebuilt and is used as a restaurant and bar. Legend has it that the pirates Blackbeaard and Morgan used to visit the castle. Others claim that it was built for protection against pirates.

Sports abound in South Sound, with three squash courts at the *Cayman Islands Squash Racquets Association*, six tennis courts at the next-door *Cayman Islands Tennis Club* and rugby is played every Saturday from September to May at the *Cayman Rugby Football Club*.

Bodden Town itself was the first capital of Cayman and had developed as the half-way point between two settlements, Prospect at South Sound and Old Isaac's in East End. Prospect has all but disappeared after its destruction by a hurricane in 1846. As you arrive in Bodden Town, the first sights are the *Guard House* and two cannons. The original guard house was built in the late eighteenth-century to protect the town against pirates.

Also used as protection against pirates was *Slave Wall* which, as the name suggests, was built by slaves. You can wander around Gun Square and then view the monument to Queen Victoria which was only erected in 1981. Confirming the links between the islands and pirates are the *Pirate Caves*. Large enough to walk through, you used to be able to walk under the road to the beach. The walk takes about ten minutes and, watch out, cannonballs and bones have been found in the caves. The entrance to the beach has now been blocked but the caves are still fun to walk in. There is a public beach at Bodden dedicated to former governor, Thomas Russell.

As you leave town towards the East End, the road runs alongside *Meagre Bay Pond Bird Sanctuary*. The islands' national bird is the white heron. There are a total of 45 different bird species resident on Grand Cayman, with more than 100 migratory species spotted at the sanctuary. Further down the road towards East End is the small community of Breakers. There is not much in the village except for a good local restaurant, *The Lighthouse Club*.

Hotels Places to stay in Bodden include *Beach Bay* (Tel: 7 2166) which is on the beach and also has a saltwater lagoon. From the complex you can book deep-sea, bone, tarpon and snorkelling charters. *Tradewinds* (Tel: 7 3435) has a private beach with a pier as well as hammock cabanas.

East End The road to East End takes you past ironshore blowholes from which water sprays 9 metres(30ft.) into the air as each wave hits the shore. The road continues into East End, which was once known as Old Isaac's, named after Isaac Bawden who was the island's first recorded settler. East End and Gun Bay are firm favourites with divers because it is here that the most famous wrecks lie. The Wreck of the Ten Sails is credited with the island's tax-free status after the islanders rescued the crew of ten ships floundering on their way from Jamaica to England.

After absorbing the history of the area, you can relax at the *Tortuga Club* (Tel: 7 7449). This has recently been rebuilt on the site of the first ever hotel on the island. With 46 bedrooms, it is geared up towards watersports with a full dive operation, freeform pools and sailboats. Just off the coast there is plenty of marine life if you want to try snorkelling or diving.

The Northside To get to the Northside from East Bay, you drive along the Queen's Highway which was opened in 1983, at the time of her state visit to the island. Before the road existed, people could travel along a trail across the cliffs, worth doing if you are feeling adventurous. Old Man Bay to the end of the road at Cayman Kai is the location for luxurious American-owned condominiums. Many local people will come up to the area with picnics for lazy days by the sea but there are some good restaurants, too.

Hotels *Ville Caribe* (Tel: 1 809 947 9627) includes snorkelling equipment in its price and also has scuba diving and fishing trips available. It has an excellent restaurant offering a different selection of fondues and turtle. *Cayman Kai* (Tel: 1 809 947 9055) also has an excellent restaurant concentrating on seafood caught from the waters just outside the restaurant and is in a very peaceful location. The *Rum Point Club* (Tel: 7 9059) has beach parties, barbecues, live bands and good food. While there is plenty to do without watersports, it is for diving that the Cayman Islands have become such a popular location. Rated alongside the Great Barrier Reef off Australia and dive sites in Indonesia, Grand Cayman has some unique features. Sting Ray City is reputed to be the only place in the world where stingrays will take food from divers. There are 26 dive operations catering for tourists as well as submarine trips, including the 28-seater *Atlantis* submarine (Tel: 9 7700) costing US$50 for an hour's dive at 46metres(150ft.) or *Research Submersibles'* three-man *Pisces* submarine which will take you down to 244metres(800ft.). This trip costs US$245 and for more information call 9 8296. Around Grand Cayman alone there are 23 dive sites, some just a few metres offshore.

Diving If a submarine or snorkelling trip makes you want to take the plunge, there are lots of dive schools to help you learn. They will lend you all the equipment and have experts on hand to teach you. Certification courses include PADI NAUI, NASDS and SSI. *Don Foster's Dive Grand Cayman* (Tel: 1 809 949 7025) and *Bob Soto's Diving* (Tel: 1 809 949 2022) both offer holiday packages, including flights, for divers from keen learners to experienced mariners.

Useful Telephone Numbers

UK Tourist Office: Knightsbridge House, 197 Knightsbridge, London SW7 1RB. Tel: 07 581 9960.

Department of Tourism. Tel: 9 5358

Post Office. Tel: 9 2474

Library. Tel: 9 5159

George Town Hospital. Tel: 9 2121

Ambulance. Tel: 555 999.

Fire. Tel: 500 999

Police. Tel: 999.

Diver's decompression chamber. Tel: 9 4235.

Edmar's discount drugs. Tel: 9 6085.

Directory inquiries. Tel: 118.

Operator. Tel: 100.

Overseas operator. Tel: 119

Cayman Airways.

    Reservations, Tel: 9 2311/2/3;

    Flight info., Tel: 9 8272/3.

Cayman Brac If you are looking for an unspoilt island paradise, then the two smaller Cayman islands will delight you. Cayman Brac is the larger of the two. About 130km(80ml.) from Grand Cayman, Cayman Airways flies a regular daily service out to the island, which is only 24 square kilometres (15 sq.ml.).

The 19km(12ml.) long island is dominated by the bluff which rises to 42 metres (140ft.) at the east end of the island. The craggy bluff looks much higher than its 42 metres and is a challenge for visitors to climb. Steps have been carved in the side of the bluff in Spot Bay to make it easier, and most people climb this east-end route where the cliffs are honeycombed with caves, famous as the hiding places of pirates and their treasure. Earlier this century, the caves were used as safe havens for settlers in the hurricane season. There are reported to be 170 caves on the island.

Many of the caves are easy to get at, but if you are feeling more adventurous you can attempt to get to the *Great Cave*. However, be warned, the climb involves scrambling over jagged limestone rock and using vines to heave yourself up. Once inside, the climb is worth it for the stalactites and weird rock formations. Harmless fruit bats abound in the caves and one is actually called *Bat Cave*.

Cayman Brac has a resident population of 2,200, made up of islanders and, more recently, Americans who have built retirement homes on the island. Islanders are known as Brackers and are happy to welcome visitors. Most people who go to the island are divers and fishermen but Cayman Brac is also a haven for the tourist wanting to escape the 'bright lights' of Seven Mile Beach on Grand Cayman.

Hotels Most of the entertainment is based around the island's three hotels: the 40-room *Brac Reef Beach Resort* (Tel: 1 809 948 7323), the 59-room *Tiara Beach*, a Divi Hotel (Tel: 1 809 948 7553) and the 39-room *Buccaaneer's Inn*, which is on the north-western tip of the Brac while the Brac Reef and Tiara Beach Hotels are on the south-west tip of the island. They are all close the tiny airport and all have restaurants and offer full diving and fishing facilities. The Tiara Beach has a wooden pier with a bar on it that is a really peaceful spot. In fact, it is so idyllic that some people have been married on it. It may be a secluded island paradise but the Brac is not without its creature comforts. The hotels are well-furnished, air-conditioned and have most of the facilities you would expect in a large city hotel, including satellite television and conference facilities such as fax and telex, with conference rooms at the Brac Reef.

You can either use a local taxi guide or hire your own vehicle but all tours around the country take much the same route as there are only two main roads, one along the north coast and one on the south coast. Most inhabitants are on the north coast where many of them live in the traditional Brac homes. The north side is also the location for the island's three primary schools and one high school, the 12-bed Faith Hospital, the District Administration building which houses government officials, and the Museum.

The Museum is well worth a visit, even if you are just on a day trip from Grand Cayman. It shows you how life has developed on the island since it was inhabited, with a display of photographs, household items and even kitchen utensils. Until recently, the island economy relied on all the men leaving home to earn enough to support their families. Most of them went into the world's merchant navys or were deep-sea fishermen. It is said that their nomadic lifestyle has taught the Brackers the importance of a warm welcome in a strange country, which they now return to visitors to the Brac.

Although the hotels are on the southern side of the island, there is little other development and it is easy to drive along the southern road and spend a day without seeing anyone else. The south side of the island is a good place to go walking and explore the lush vegetation in the hope of catching a glimpse of the

Pointers to all over the world from Cayman Brac where traditionally the men took jobs in the world's navies

island's unusual birdlife. The island is home to green, red and blue parrots as well as the national bird, the white heron. The more unusual plant life includes rare orchids, aloe, jasmine, several different palm-trees, and papaya and mango trees.

53

Diving Divers the world over know about Cayman Brac because of its spectacular, unspoilt reefs. Just a few metres into the water, the coral begins, making it an ideal place for snorkelling, and then the deep water starts just 400metres from the shore with the 1,830m(6,000ft.) wall. There are two dive operations on the island: *Brac Aquatics* and *Peter Hughes Tiara Divers*. And divers say the real beauty of the Brac is that no one knows how much more there is to discover. They have already found some stunning sites, but each time they visit they see different fish and, sometimes, fish they had not even realized were in those waters. On the north coast, divers can find good examples of collar coral and many other photogenic sights.

Fishing The fringe reef which is 30metres(100ft.) out into the water makes the Brac Reef Beach an ideal spot for fishermen who can just wade out into the water. And to make sure that no one can claim it is hard work, the hotel bar staff will keep you supplied with cooling drinks as you stand fishing. Most of the waders are fishing for bonefish, something that the locals will use as bait for the big game fish, such as marling or tuna, which are caught just off the Wall.

The Brackers take their fishing very seriously but are happy to help the less experienced to learn. Most of the fishermen on the island compete in Million Dollar Month each June. The tournament is so named because of the staggering US$1,000,000 that goes to the first angler to break the existing IGFA All-tackle record for Atlantic blue marlin in Cayman waters. The winner would also get a condominium, a sports car, sport-fishing boat and a lifetime of free trips on Cayman Airways. No wonder there are hundreds of fishermen ready to compete. If the main prize eludes you, there are still the US$100,000 for the person to beat the existing Cayman record of 265kilos(584lb.) or US$20,000 for the largest catch of the month. Fish of under 90kilos(200lb.) in weight have to be returned, yet the anglers still manage to catch and keep hundreds of marlin during the contest.

If fishing contests do not appeal, the Brackers have their own festival earlier in the year. Brachanal is a weekend of costumed carnivals. It follows a similar festival on Grand Cayman, called Batabano, which is always in the last week of April. The Brackers celebrate the following Saturday. Visitors are encouraged to dress up, join in and compete for the prizes.

If you do not have enough time to stay on Cayman Brac, Cayman Airways runs day trips, a package which includes the return flight, a drink and lunch at either Brac Reef or Tiara Beach Hotels and a half-day sightseeing tour. It is well worth the trip, just to experience what the islanders say Grand Cayman was like about twenty years ago, before it became more popular.

Useful Telephone Numbers

Faith Hospital. Tel: 8 2243.
Cayman Airways:
    Reservations, Tel: 8 3235;
    Flight info, Tel: 8 7221.
Brac Reef Beach Resort. Tel: 8 7323.
Tiara Beach Resort. Tel: 9 7553.
Brac Aquatics. Tel: 8 7429.
Peter Hughes Tiara Divers. Tel: 9 7553.

Little Cayman The third island in the Cayman group is by far the smallest, most remote and to some people the most attractive. Here is the real get-away-from-it-all island. It only has three telephones, no restaurants, no petrol stations and no central electricity supply. Little Cayman has just a handful of permanent residents but they will all have a warm welcome for visitors.

Flights to the island connect from Cayman Brac 8km(5ml.) away. The runway is grass rather than tarmac and not designed for high heels. You will probably be met by a welcoming party, not just to say hello to the new faces, but to collect their mail and groceries from the plane. The other way to travel to Little Cayman is by boat and people often visit for a day, catching their lunch on the way .

Once there, they discover an island of just 16 square kilometres (10 sq.ml.) but with plenty of places to hide away from the rest of the world. One of the most popular spots is East Point where there is a barbecue pit, but it is easy to find a more secluded picnic site if you prefer. There is plenty of birdlife and marine life to watch around the island's lakes or you can visit the Cayman's fourth island, Owen's Island, which nestles in the lagoon opposite one of Little Cayman's three fishing lodges. The tiny island is uninhabited but is a popular picnic site.

Hotels The three lodges are the *Southern Cross Club*, which is opposite Owen's Island, *Pirates Point*, which is also on the south side of the island, and *Sam McCoy's Fishing Lodge*, which is 8km(5ml.) away on the north side. All three lodges can offer up to fifteen divers full facilities as well as fishing charters. Since there is nowhere to buy anything except T-shirts at the lodges, they are also happy to make up picnics for you. Each of the lodges has its own characteristics, not least because of the owners. Sam McCoy's and Southern Cross both offer big-game fishing trips, while Pirates Point is where divers go for a gourmet experience. A group of anglers started the Southern Cross Club over twenty-six years ago and it is the oldest lodge on the island. For a really local experience, Sam McCoy is one of the island's oldest inhabitants – he moved from Cayman Brac in 1962 – and knows all the island tales. He can recount the day when the island's only two vehicles met in a head-on collision or regale you with pirate legends or fishing stories that could become legends.

Some of the islanders rent out their homes to visitors, such as *Sefton's Cottage* (Tel: 8 3255). Most of the accommodation will have beautiful beachfront settings in which to sit and admire the spectacular sunsets across the water.

There is nowhere to hire cars or mopeds and very few vehicles on the island. Everyone drives at the same laid-back pace of island life. They stop for wildlife to cross the road – the only road on the island, it goes almost all the way round the coastline. If you want to go inland, then you can walk the plank – literally. The main island trail is on planks balancing on stilts. If that sounds too much like hard work, there are plenty of hammocks strung between palm-trees on the beach ready for you to lie in and soak up the atmosphere.

Like Cayman Brac, Little Cayman is the frequent haunt of fishermen and divers. Some anglers claim that Little Cayman has the best bonefishing in the world. The founders of the Southern Cross Club were among the first to fish the South Sound Hole. Large tarpons can be spotted leaping in the water of Tarpon Lake, a large lake bordered by mangroves just inland from East Rocky Point on the South Coast Road.

**Opposite
Bone fishing, a popular
pastime on the tiny island of
Little Cayman**

Part Two: **The Dominican Republic**

**An aerial view of Mount Isabel
and the north-coast town of
Puerto Plata, Dominican Republic**

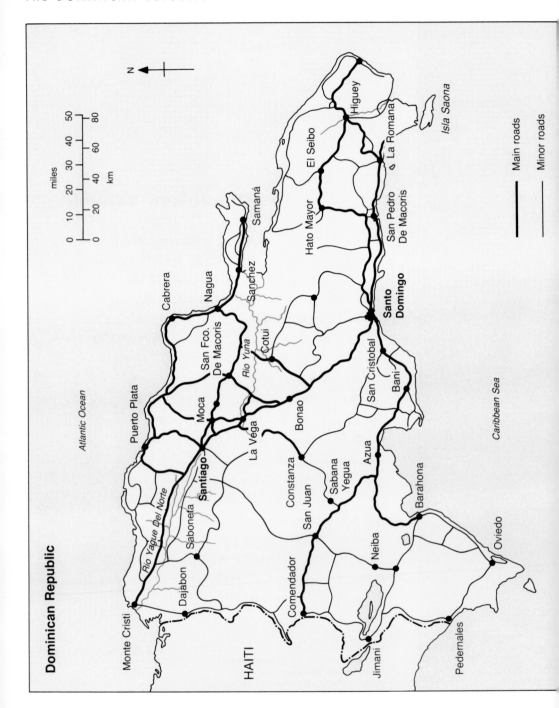

Dominican Republic

The Dominican Republic was a virtually undiscovered Caribbean destination by the British until 1989 and it is easy to see why other tourists kept the place a secret. Its miles of golden sand lined with palm-trees, cheap living and luxurious accommodation make it a place worth visiting.

But there is far more to the country than its beautiful beaches. It shares the island of Hispaniola with Haiti and is one of the largest islands in the Caribbean, second only to Cuba. The mountainous interior is vastly different to the coastal plains. Surrounded by the Atlantic to the north and the Caribbean to the south, many of the beaches are protected by coral reefs alive with colourful tropical fish.

For many visitors the trip to the Republic is made by its people. Everyone is friendly and eager to help. Although they are Spanish speaking, they are very proud of their attempts to speak English and always want to try out their language skills. If you get lost there is always someone on hand to help, they will stop and chat at any opportunity, and service in restaurants and hotels is superb. Although there are plenty of new developments, they are mostly concentrated in resort areas and within five minutes you can be in the heart of Dominican life, while enjoying the luxury of your hotel.

There is a huge gap between the rich and poor in this country. There are enormous problems with unemployment and Haitians coming across the border to provide cheap labour. They live in huts that can hardly rate the term shanty town and their poverty is extreme. Water and electricity are a luxury for many Dominicans, and the government has a clear policy of providing services to the resorts at the expense of local people. But they do not seem to mind, realizing that tourists mean jobs. The resorts are heavily guarded by security men with guns and are fenced in by barbed wire. Many people think this is because it is unsafe but this is not true. Guns are a way of life in a country that only emerged from harsh dictatorship twenty years ago and which still feels threatened by its Haitian neighbours. Travelling around the country you will go through many police road blocks, set up for the same reason. They normally wave tourists through and will only stop you if they have not realized you are in a hired car.

Although there are shanty towns, there are wealthy areas, too. High in the mountains you will come across towns where everyone looks affluent. There are some large ranches which obviously belong to some very rich people and much of the land looks well cared for. In the towns, the old centres are being carefully restored and maintained and expensive-looking shopping areas are being developed. The island has been used as a location for numerous films, the latest being *Havana*, starring Robert Redford.

Black, white, old and young get on together in the Dominican Republic

The Dominican Republic offers visitors a little of everything they could want on a holiday, from history and culture to good food and beautiful beaches. It is still a relatively undiscovered place where many tourists stay within the resort areas and miss out on the wealth the country can offer. So be adventurous and explore as the island has a lot to experience.

Pre-Planning – How to get There

Flights Most flights come from the USA and from Canada but increasing numbers of European operators are starting to fly into the country's two international airports, one at Santo Domingo and one at Puerto Plata. Airlines operating flights are Air France, Iberia, Dominicana-Viasa. They all fly from Continental Europe. From the UK, there are flights connecting through Puerto Rico with American Airlines and Lufthansa. Pan American has connecting flights from the USA, as does American Airlines. Other airlines serving the country include Air Florida, ALM, Avianca, Capitol Air, Eastern Airlines, Prinair and Varig.

An old man and his donkey sweep the beach daily to keep it clean for visitors in the Dominican Republic

63

LIAT has flights direct from Puerto Rico to La Romana every Thursday and Sunday and twice daily flights every other day of the week from Puerto Rico to Santiago. On Mondays, LIAT operates a non-stop flight from Santo Domingo to Antigua.

UK tour operators include Intasun, who use their own airline, Air Europe, for direct flights, Airtours, Club Med, Cosmos and Thomson.

When to go The climate is fairly even with year–round average temperatures of 25 °C(77°F). August is the warmest month and January the coolest. Temperatures in the mountains tend to be slightly lower. Rainfall is spread fairly evenly through the year with the heaviest occurring from May to August and in November and December. The rain tends to fall in short, sharp showers so there is not really a best time to go, although, like the rest of the Caribbean, mid-December to mid-April is the peak season. It is best to take lots of light, cotton clothing with some smarter clothes for evenings.

Many of the UK operators only go there from May to September when prices are lower. There are fewer people around at that time of year as well so it can be more pleasant. It is very hard for the Dominicans to get a passport. They need to own their own house and business as well as have a certain amount of money in the bank so many of them holiday at home. Cubans, too, are frequent visitors. They tend to visit in the cheaper winter time and so much of the hotel entertainment can be geared to them rather than to the British. Hoteliers are realizing the importance of the European trade and this is gradually changing.

Passports British and other European passport holders need a valid passport and to buy a US$10 tourist card on arrival. If you are travelling with a tour operator this will be bought for you, along with the departure tax which is another US$10. Spanish, Italian and German citizens are exempt from the US$10 tourist card fee. USA and Canadian passport holders only need some form of identity, although taking a passport is a good idea as it will be needed to change travellers cheques.

It is illegal to import or export the Dominican peso but there is no limit to what foreign currency you take into the country. You are limited to leaving with less than US$5,000 or its equivalent. All drugs are illegal in the Dominican Republic. There are large signs warning you of this on arrival and anyone caught with illegal drugs faces fines, a prison sentence and then deportation.

Health It is worth getting full insurance cover, particularly for health as it can be expensive. No vaccinations are needed except if you have travelled from certain countries where diseases like typhoid are prevalent. It is worth checking with your doctor before travelling. He may well recommend you having typhoid, tetanus and polio protection. It is best not to drink the water when you first arrive to acclimatize your stomach. Bottled water is easily available. Be careful of the midday sun; the cooling winds can be deceptive and many people suffer from heat-stroke. One symptom of this is an upset stomach and it is advisable to take medicine with you to settle a bad stomach because so many people seem to suffer.

Getting About

Car Rental Tour operators may well warn you against hiring a car or bike because the roads are dangerous. But if you are careful, driving can be fun and is definitely the best way to reach the areas off the tourist routes.

Car hire is relatively easy. Booking the car is no problem, actually getting the car is something different. There are not many hire cars available and the roads are bad so a lot of checks have to be done when each car is returned. So although you may book a car, if it is returned late or damaged you may well have to wait several hours or even days to get it. The best policy is to check every day and then be very insistent that you need the car immediately. The car-hire operators will collect and return you to your hotels from the shop. It is worth booking a car with air conditioning as it can get very hot on the road. And make sure the insurance covers damage done by the rough roads as well as accidents or else you could face a repair bill.

British driving licences are valid for 90 days and international licences are also acceptable.

Once you have the car, the rest is easy. Petrol is ridiculously cheap. Filling the tank will only cost a couple of pounds and will give you enough petrol virtually to get around the island. It is worth filling up while in the major towns before heading off into the mountains or along the more remote coastal roads. Garages are usually open until 10 p.m. but some are open 24 hours a day.

One of the hotels in the Playa Dorado complex, Dominican Republic

The roads have to be experienced to be believed. Tarmac is a relatively new thing and the local subsistence farmers have taken full advantage of it. They use it for everything from sunbathing to drying crops on it. Animals roam at will and people seem to have no road sense at all – and that is without the other cars.

Driving is on the right. On a two-lane road, people will overtake on either side of you on the brow of a hill. It is not unusual to go over the top of the hill to face three vehicles in your path. Drive either side of them, that is what everyone else does. The other major hazards are scooters. Up to six people can hang precariously on to a bike as it weaves in and out of cars.

At night the hazards are worse as few cars have rear lights and even fewer people bother to dip their headlights as you approach. It is definitely safer to drive during daylight and avoid night-time driving. If you do drive at night, have someone else in the car to keep a look-out for other vehicles and pedestrians. Many drivers will completely ignore traffic lights once it gets dark. Even during the day, the numerous potholes and rough roads keep the speed down and you will be lucky to get up to 55kph(35mph).

The roads in the towns are much better and there are dual carriageways where you can pick up speed. The official speed limit is 80kph(50mph) on highways, 60kph(37mph) in suburban areas and 40kph(25mph) in cities.

In city areas, one-way systems and parking areas are not well marked. Many of the crossroads should have give-way signs, called *Pare*, but a shortage of signs leads to problems, with the biggest or bravest winning. The narrow streets can be confusing and there are few road signs. It is often easier to stop at a garage on your way into town to ask for directions than to rely on maps. *Rotundas* – or roundabouts – are equally poorly signed and you will often find people parked in the middle and having a conversation. Again, confidence is the key to success.

Public Transport for tourists is really limited to taxis. There are *publicos* and minibuses that run along a set route with a set fare. You will recognize the buses because of the conductor who hangs out of the side door touting for business as the vehicle moves along the road. It will pick up and set down passengers anywhere along the route. The *publicos* pick people up until the vehicles is full.

Taxis are safer for visitors, mostly because the driving is more reliable. The taxis are usually large old American cars that can fit up to six people. There are usually plenty around the hotels but otherwise the porter will quickly find one for you. They are cheap and reliable and are identified by the tax disc which they have to display on the windscreen or on the roof. Negotiate the fare before you set off. Most hotels will advertise the taxi rates to set destinations but other routes must be negotiated. It is not necessary to tip taxi drivers, although you should tip drivers if they also give you a tour of the local town or sights.

Many people want to cross the border into neighbouring Haiti for a day trip but land crossings in hired cars are illegal. Tour operators have stopped crossings because of the unstable situation in Haiti, so the only way across is by air. Pan Am has four flights a week from Santo Domingo to Port-au-Prince costing about US$50.

Accommodation Most of the hotels are restricted to tourist areas. Many are new and have all the modern comforts you would expect. Air-conditioning, colour TV, restaurants and swimming-pools are standard in the new hotels. But, be warned, electricity does go off several times a day. Most of the new hotels have generators which come on automatically so the power cuts tend to be short, and a lot of work is being done by central government to improve the situation. The voltage for the electricity supply is the same as the USA, 110volts. Water supplies can also be haphazard, particularly in the older hotels or in resort areas where they have built too many hotels for the reservoir serving the area. Again, this is being remedied.

Apart from the five-star tourist hotels, there are plenty of smaller, local hotels in all the major towns, and guest houses are common in the smaller beach resorts. There are also many apart-hotels. These apartments are usually privately owned but are run like hotels for guests, who have the advantages of their own apartment but with a daily maid service and with good hotel restaurants and swimming-pools close by.

Money The currency is the Dominican peso with 100 centavos to one peso. It is a fluctuating currency and it is illegal to import or export any local money. It is much easier to change US dollars than sterling, although some of the banks will make the change. The hotels, which will happily change dollars, are not allowed to accept sterling or any other currency.

Banks There are banks in all the major towns. Many only stay open until 2 p.m. although some will open until 6 p.m. Hotels will usually change money up to 9 p.m. All the banks offer the same exchange rate. Travellers cheques are widely accepted and it is easy to cash money with all the major credit cards.

Some hotels have a system of cards. You will often be given an identity card to prove you are staying at that hotel, and this needs to be produced at the watersports shop, some of the restaurants and for beach towels. A second card will allow you to put everything on account, and the hotel will usually take a credit card imprint before giving you a card. Otherwise, everything has to be paid for in cash, which can be a nuisance, particularly in the beach areas.

Tipping All hotels add a 5 per cent room tax to your bills. Restaurants and hotels will add a legal mandatory 10 per cent service charge. If you get exceptional service you are expected to add something extra – Americans usually do this, so many of the waiters expect it. On top of that there is a 6 per cent sales and consumption tax added to the service charge. So when ordering at a bar or restaurant, remember to add at least 16 per cent to everything. Porters and tour guides should be tipped but do not worry about taxi drivers unless they give you a tour.

Safety Like any third world country it is not a good idea to wander the streets carrying a lot of cash and dripping with jewellery. But the Republic is much safer than many Caribbean islands and, so long as you are sensible, there is no risk, even at night.

Food and Wine The food is influenced by the country's Spanish heritage, blended with the tropical tastes of the locally produced fruit and vegetables. Seafood is also cheap and popular in the many beach resorts and towns. Here are some things you might come across on the menu:

Asopao de pollo.	Chicken stew.
Barbacoa.	Barbecue.
Bija.	Annatto seed, often used in paellas.
Casabe.	Manioc bread.
Catibias.	Manioc fritters stuffed with meat.
Centolla.	Crab.
Jugo.	Juice.
Lambi.	Conch shellfish.
Locrio.	The Dominican version of Spanish paella.
Longaniza.	Spicy pork sausage.
Mangu.	Purée of green plantains.
Mani.	Peanut.
Moro.	Rice cooked with red beans.
Morcilla.	Blood sausage.
Papas.	Potatoes.
Sancocho prieto.	A black stew containing seven different meats.
Tiburon.	Shark.
Tostones.	Plantain chips, often served as a pre-meal snack.

In the resort areas, there will be a wide range of restaurants offering everything from hamburgers to gourmet feasts. Chinese restaurants are intermingling with local restaurants and there are beach bars, barbecue pits and swim-up pool bars to visit. They will

69

nearly all be of a very high standard with good service, although that is in the usual laid-back Caribbean style and so can be slow.

For really good local food, you are best to leave the resorts and wander around the nearby towns where there will be a mass of bars and restaurants tucked away down the narrow roads. These will be an awful lot cheaper than the resort restaurants, although some in Puerto Plata and Santo Domingo do catch the tourist trade and charge accordingly.

Some of the best places are the most unlikely looking huts. The smaller villages will often have local restaurants on the beach where the fresh fish is unloaded from the fishing boats straight into the kitchen. Small boys will run up the nearest coconut tree to pick you some fresh fruit, and charge about 10p for it, and they will all give you good food served with a smile. It is a good way to meet the local people who will soon be telling you all about their family and village problems. Their problems are never told with long faces but always with a good deal of humour. The British are particularly popular because we tend to be more polite and more patient than other tourists and you can get much better service as a result.

There are plenty of supermarkets and small shops, as well as fresh food markets in all the towns to buy supplies for picnics or for self-catering apartments. But with prices among the lowest of anywhere in the Caribbean, it is often as easy to eat out most of the time.

The food, even in the resort areas, is cheaper than in the UK. But alcohol can be expensive. Wines, in particular, can cost six times what you would pay in the UK and they will not all have travelled that well. Many wine lists contain European names rather than local Caribbean or American wines. Other drinks tend to cost about the same as in England, although cocktails are slightly cheaper. Outside the resorts, prices drop to about a third of the resort prices.

The best beer is Presidente (also most expensive) but you have to ask for it or else they will serve you something cheaper. There are plenty of different rums but most popular are Brugal and Bermudez. Imported spirits are very expensive. Cocktails will vary according to what fruit is in season and watch out for language misunderstandings creeping into the menus. Some cocktails said to be suitable for children really mean you will sleep like a child after drinking just one.

Shopping Like many of the Caribbean islands, shopping is split into two sectors, that for tourists and that for locals. The tourists can select from a large variety of arts and crafts at shopping centres and craft markets across the country. There are duty-free shops or roadside stalls where you can haggle fiercely, and there are modern shopping facilities in all the major towns. But in some of the resort towns there are few shops except for those attached to the hotels.

In Santo Domingo, the craft shops are mostly in the old colonial city along narrow, quaint streets. Tobacconists and wine shops are hidden away among the art and craft shops. Some of these are full of cheap souvenirs but there are plenty with worthwhile goods. Most shops are open from 8.30 a.m. to midday when they close for a siesta until 3 p.m., closing again at 7 p.m. The duty-free shops mark up prices in US dollars.

Amber and larimar are both native to the island and both are fashioned into jewellery. *Muneca sin rostro* are china Dominican ladies. In hundreds of poses and sizes, all the dolls are without faces. The story is that the artists were asked to give the dolls a typically Dominican face but, with such a melting pot of nationalities in the population, no one could come up with a single typical face so the dolls remain faceless. Other products worth buying include pottery and basketware. Some of the artwork is superb. Much of it is influenced by Haiti but with a distinctive Dominican style. There are plenty of galleries across the island in the resorts and tucked away in the mountains. You can also pick up some excellent pieces from the roadside stalls.

If you need a pharmacist they are found in most large towns and you can get most generic drugs. If you need a doctor, most of the resort hotels will have a doctor on call and then will collect your prescription for you. But make sure your insurance fully covers you as the cost of medicine and doctors' fees are high.

Telecommunications in the Republic are good. There are nearly 200 radio stations, eight television channels as well as American cable and satellite services and good communications internationally. The telephone system is run by Codetel which has offices in all main towns, offering fax facilities along with

71

Stopping for a chat while working on a north-coast beach in the Dominican Republic

telex and telegram services. There are also Post Offices in all major towns. Do not bother posting anything in post boxes as collections are unreliable. Most hotels will sell stamps and postcards or letters.

There are five morning newspapers and three evening papers. There are two English weekly papers, and *Touring* concentrates on information for tourists.

Local Colour

The People The population of about seven million (at the last count in 1987) is a complete mixture. About 76 per cent are of mixed race, 16 per cent are white and 11 per cent are black. There is no racial discord of any kind. Most people speak Spanish with a few Taino Indian words but there are regional differences. In the border area many people speak a form of Creole, a mixture of French and Spanish. Around Sabana del Mar, many people speak English. In the resort areas, the Dominicans speak Spanish, French, English and Italian.

The Spanish heritage shines through in their customs and manners. They tend to dress up in the evenings and it is not a good idea only to wear swimming costumes anywhere except in the resort areas. Almost everyone is Roman Catholic although other religions are happily accepted. There are many churches and cathedrals to visit but women must wear a skirt with a hemline below the knee and men should wear trousers rather than shorts.

The Dominicans are very musical, again influenced by their mixed heritage from Spain and Africa. The most common music is the *merengue*, which is also a dance. Derived from Sevillanas and West African tribal dances, it takes over the capital Santo Domingo for much of July when there is much dancing in the streets. The merengue music is played on three instruments, the *guira* – a sort of hollow grater with sharp prongs – a tambora drum and an accordion.

There are regional variations, most notably in San Pedro de Macoris, an area where other Caribbean islanders were imported

to help with the sugar-cane harvests. They have developed the *guloyas* dance based on the old English mummers drama.

The Dominicans find plenty of excuses for singing and dancing. There are several national festivals but each village and town has its own annual patron saint festivals. Many have developed their own style, complete with strange traditions of fancy dress. All these parties add to the feeling that this is a land of happy-go-lucky people.

The Country The Dominican Republic occupies two-thirds of the island of Hispaniola and was originally inhabited by the peaceful Taino Indians. Christopher Columbus landed on the island on his first trip in 1492 and the Dominicans claim that his remains are buried in the Cathedral in Santo Domingo. The Spanish quickly colonized the island and began its turbulent history. Columbus arrived on the north coast and established a colony there, leaving his brother Bartolomé in charge. He quickly discovered that the north coast was unhealthy and fever ridden. The settlement was uprooted, moved south and Santo Domingo was founded in 1496.

A statue of Christopher Columbus stands outside the cathedral in Santo Domingo

The Spanish used the native Indians as slaves and within two decades almost the entire population had been wiped out.

The Spanish originally controlled the whole island and, in 1508, the King of Spain, King Ferdinand, named the island Santo Domingo. But the island was quickly under attack from other European countries who saw the potential of its central site in the region. Drake gained control of Santo Domingo for a few days in 1586 before the Spanish forced him back. Drake left behind a cannonball which still rests in the city's cathedral roof where it landed during the battle for the city. The French were more successful in their attempts to gain a foothold, and in 1697 had won the western third of the island, which became Haiti. France was officially given Haiti under the Treaty of Ryswick and it named the new country Saint Domingue.

75

Since then, the Dominicans have been invaded countless times by the Haitians, who have sometimes controlled the whole island for over twenty years at a time. This constant fighting through history accounts for the Dominicans' fear of invasion which grows every time Haiti becomes politically unstable. In 1809, Spain won back control of the Republic with the help of the British Navy. Spain showed little interest in the colony and it became the Independent State of Spanish Haiti in 1821. A year later the French Haitians were back in control, and it was only in 1844 that it gained independence again to become the Dominican Republic.

Even the Americans have occupied the island. In 1916, the USA controlled the Republic, only handing it back in 1924 when Rafael Leonidas Trujillo Molina headed the army. He took control in 1930 and started a vicious dictatorship which lasted 31 years.

Thousands of people were killed or tortured by Trujillo. The Haitian immigrants were particularly vulnerable but so was anyone else who caught his attention. Horror stories still abound, and people will point out shrines built to honour his victims. There are stories of whole families being wiped out because he took a fancy to a daughter who refused to succumb to him. Political adversaries lived dangerous lives and many were shot. One story is that he used to line up his political prisoners after church on Sunday and choose a few to be shot before he went home for Sunday lunch.

His assassination in 1961 did not end the troubles. Governments came and went, often with the help of the military, and gradually peace has been restored. There are still general strikes and riots associated with Government policies but there is a much greater stability.

There are three main political parties, and elections are held every four years. Joaquin Balaguer was actually in power during Trujillo's reign but has led his party, the Partido Reformista Social Cristiano (PRSC) during five terms in office. The country is run by a bicameral Congress, a 27-seat Senate and with a 120-seat Chamber of Deputies. The President is elected every four years, along with the rest of the Government. The President selects regional governors while the Senate chooses the judiciary.

The Dominican Republic now occupies two-thirds of Hispaniola, which is the second largest island in the Greater Antilles, second only to Cuba. It has a surface area of

48,280 sq.km.(30,000 sq.ml.). There are three mountain ranges, including the highest in the Antilles. Duarte Peak reaches 3,175m(10,414ft.) above sea level. And, dropping to the depths, Lake Enriquillo is about 30m(98ft.) below sea level where huge colonies of crocodiles reside. There are five large national parks and 4.8 million hectares divided between arable land, forest and pasture.

Almost half the population are employed in agriculture, with sugar-cane dominating the farms. Haitians are brought in to harvest the crops because they will work for very low wages. Tobacco is also grown widely and the Marlboro factories across the Republic produces 18 million cigarettes a day – all for home consumption. Other exports are cocoa and coffee. Rum is produced locally and some is exported. Gold, silver, nickel and bauxite are all mined and are becoming increasingly important as the demand for sugar changes.

Tourism is another industry that is growing in importance. It is the largest foreign exchange earner and the numbers of hotels are growing rapidly. The traditional market has been from Canada with a high number of Americans, too. But now the hoteliers are looking to Europe because tourists tend to stay longer and spend more money. The European holiday season tends to be from June to September when it is relatively quiet in the Caribbean, and the British, in particular, are being encouraged to fill in the quiet months for the resorts. Most of the new resorts are along the coastal areas although one or two are springing up in the mountains.

Events Calendar

National holidays are:

New Year's Day

Epiphany, 6 January

Feast of Our Lady of Altagracia, 21 January

Juan Pablo Duarte's birthday (the founder of the Republic), 26 January

Independence Day, 27 February

Good Friday

Labour Day, 1 May

Corpus Christi Thursday

Restoration of the Republic Day, 16 August

Feast of Our Lady of Mercy, 24 September

Christmas Day

The Dominicans are fond of celebrations, and the whole of July seems to be one long party. They follow the Catholic calendar of feast days; each town honours its patron saints with festivals, and brings in the New Year with a series of year-end parties between 22 December and 2 January.

Another important week is at the end of February, which is the culmination of Carnival. The festival is marked by parties and street fairs across the country. *Diablos cojuelos*, colourful devils, fill the streets of La Vega every Sunday afternoon during February. Santiago is reported to observe the carnival traditions better than most with its colourful parades. Each region has its own distinctive masks; famous mask-making towns are Santiago, Le Vega and Monte Cristi, and all the major towns hold parties where masked men, women and children roam the streets. Carnival is a good time to visit the country because everyone is in a party mood. The month ends with a grand parade through Santo Domingo on 27 February; the parade usually travels along George Washington Avenue through the centre of town.

Late in February there is an annual crafts festival at Altos de Chavon in the Casa de Campo resort, La Romana. The whole centre is dedicated to crafts but the festival draws all the different works together.

Easter is another busy festival time. A mix of the Dominicans' Christian and African heritages results in the singing and dancing to religious music in towns such as Higuey and Cabral. On the African side, *Ga-Ga* rituals dominate. Masked dancers crack their whips and often frighten the onlookers. But don't worry, it is only acting.

July is *merengue* month. Merengue is the national music and dance. It has distinctly Latin rhythms combined with a Caribbean feel. The dance is quite an art but beginners are always welcome to have a go. Many of the discos play merengue music rather than European pop music. And guitar players who serenade guests in many resort restaurants will always ask what you want played but will always end up playing the music they love best – merengue. During July there are street parties in Puerto Plata to celebrate the merengue festival. The main festival, however, is in Santo Domingo. The last week of July and first week of August are dedicated to the merengue. The festival also celebrates the anniversary of the founding of Santo Domingo on 4 August.

There are more carnival festivities in August to celebrate the Restoration of Independence Day on the 16th. Again, each region has a slightly different festival. These are well worth seeing. With such a friendly atmosphere towards tourists on a normal day, you will be given a special welcome on festival days.

The Feast of Saint Barbara is celebrated in Samana during October when the locals dance the Bambula.

In December, there is a crafts festival at the Artisans Craft Centre in the colonial sector of Santo Domingo.

Santo Domingo Most people know very little about this city, which is one of the oldest in the Caribbean. The secret of the Republic's beautiful white beaches has escaped but the secret of its culture and history has remained intact. It comes as a shock to find streets virtually unchanged since the days of the Spanish *conquistadores*. In many ways, the colonial sector of Santo Domingo is similar to Old San Juan in Puerto Rico, but this area is slightly older and can claim many firsts for the region, and it was from here that Juan Ponce de León set out to colonize Puerto Rico.

Christopher Columbus arrived on the north coast on 5 December 1492. He is supposed to have preferred Hispaniola to any other Caribbean island and to have wanted to make his home there. In fact, he spent little time on the island, leaving it to his brother Bartolomé to colonize the area. The north coast was unhealthy and many of the Spanish died of fever. Bartolomé moved his tiny colony south and founded Santo Domingo on 4 August 1496.

Many of the first buildings survive along with some of the original city walls. The city had to be well fortified as it suffered hundreds of years of attack from the British, French, Haitians and even the Americans, who took control earlier this century. Founded in 1496, it is the oldest capital city in Spanish America and so it is home to the oldest cathedral, church and university. The country is already gearing up for the Columbus celebrations in 1992 and much of the old city is being restored by the Government. Santo Domingo was the focal point for much of the Spaniards' exploration of the region. It was the launching point for Hernan Cortes' attack on Mexico, for the trip to settle Puerto Rico by Juan Ponce de León and for sailings into the Pacific and to South America.

Now the city is divided into two parts, the modern city and the colonial sector. Most of the hotels and shops are in the modern

79

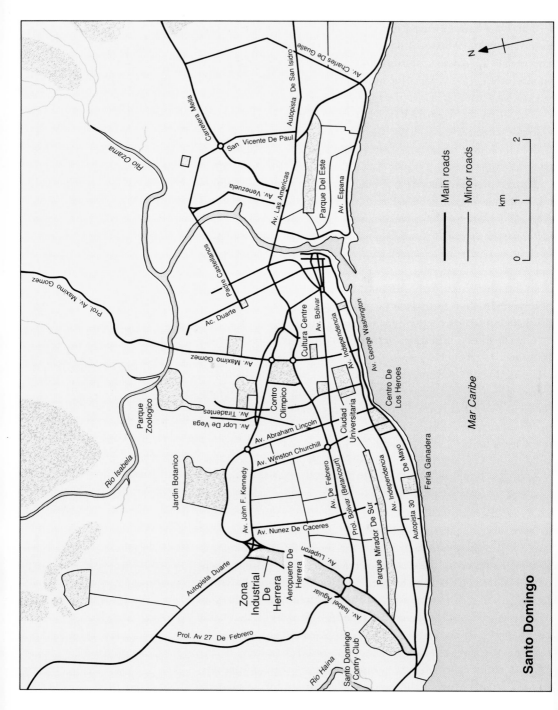

Santo Domingo

Main roads

Minor roads

km

Mar Caribe

Río Ozama

Carretera Mella

San Vicente De Paul

Autopista De San Isidro

Av. Charles De Gualle

Parque Del Este

Av. España

Av. Las Americas

Av. Venezuela

Prol. Av. Maximo Gomez

Padre Castellanos

Ac. Duarte

Av. Maximo Gomez

Cultura Centre

Av. Bolivar

Av. Independencia

Av. George Washington

Parque Zoologico

Río Isabela

Centro Olimpico

Av. Tiradentes

Av. Lopr De Vega

Ciudad Universitaria

Centro De Los Heroes

Av. Abraham Lincoln

Jardin Botanico

Av. Winston Churchill

Av. De Febrero

Prol. Bolivar (Betancourt)

Av. Independencia

De Mayo

Feria Ganadera

Av. John F. Kennedy

Av. Nunez De Caceres

Parque Mirador De Sur

Autopista 30

Autopista Duarte

Zona Industrial De Herrera

Aeropuerto De Herrera

Av. Luperon

Av. Isabel Aguiar

Prol. Av 27 De Febrero

Santo Domingo Contry Club

Río Haina

sector, along with the business districts. But the colonial city is not just a museum: it has hotels, shops and restaurants as well as museums and art galleries. It is easier to explore the colonial sector on foot as the narrow winding streets are difficult to drive around and the one-way systems do not make it any easier.

Santo Domingo also has some spectacular natural wonders to visit, such as the *Three Eyes Caves*, and some white, sandy beaches within a short distance. Most visitors stay in resorts along the north coast and take a day trip or a short overnight stay in the capital. But it would be easy to spend your holiday here and travel elsewhere around the island.

The Colonial Sector When you walk around this area you will be approached by tour guides and by little boys selling souvenirs. It is well worth employing a guide. Many of them speak English and they know all about the history of the area. Make sure you agree on a price first, usually dependent on the length of the tour and, if they take you to any shops, remember they will be getting their cut so the prices are likely to be higher than average. It is not a good idea to buy from the street sellers. Most of their goods are poorly made and some have been known to fall apart even as they display them. The guides are also quite useful for keeping the souvenir sellers at bay. There is so much to see in the colonial sector, with well over 300 churches, monuments and historical houses and it would be easy to spend several days wandering around. But you can get a feel for the place in just an hour or two. Remember that men must wear trousers and women skirts below the knee if you want to go into any of the churches or the Cathedral.

The Cathedral The Cathedral square is a good place to start a tour. The Cathedral is on Columbus' Park and is lined by the Callejon de los Niches (Lane of the Niches). The Cathedral is dedicated to Our Lady of the Annunciation and is called Cathedral Basilica Menor de Santa Maria, Primada de America. Work on the Cathedral began in 1512 and took thirty years to complete. Christopher Columbus's son, Don Diego Columbus, laid the cornerstone of the Cathedral. Inside is the *Mausoleum of the Great Admiral of the Ocean Sea*, Christopher Columbus. A number of other Caribbean countries also claim to have the remains of Columbus and, so far, no one has proved who is right.

There are letters from the Royal Court of Spain giving Don Diego's wife permission to bury the remains of her father-in-law in the Santo Domingo Cathedral. But the original markers were lost after a Bishop ordered them wiped clean in fear that the British might seize them. Sir Francis Drake did come close to destroying the Cathedral when he attacked the city in 1686. A cannonball fired from one of his ships landed on the Cathedral roof and is still there today. Once in control of the city, the Cathedral was made safe by Drake using it as his headquarters.

When the French gained control of the island in 1775, the Cubans decided that the remains of Columbus should be on Spanish soil, and unearthed an urn from the Cathedral and took it away. A century later, the Spanish were surprised to discover another urn in the same spot and this one actually had Columbus' name carved on it. The argument rages on but, in the meantime, you can see the square, dark box in the Cathedral.

Back outside the Cathedral in Columbus Square, or Main Square, there is a monument to Columbus sculpted by French

Casa de Ovando has been converted into a hotel in Santo Domingo's colonial sector

artist, E. Gilbert. Opposite is the *Borgella Palace*, built by the Haitians during their occupation in the 1800s and used by the Government. Behind the Cathedral is the Callejon de los Niches, a pedestrian street which belongs to the city's colonial past. Virtually every house was once inhabited by someone closely involved with the development of the country and the New World.

The Tower of Homage At the end of the street there is a small alley leading down to Calle Las Damas, which in turn leads to La Fuerza or Ozama Fortress. The area has several buildings, the most prominent being the Tower of Homage. Built in 1503, it was the city's first fortification and was later added to by other defences. Your guide will tell you that this is where Trujillo, the dictator who rules with a rod of iron for more than thirty years, kept his political prisoners. The church where he went for Sunday services is alongside the Tower. The Tower is open daily from 8 a.m. until 5 p.m. and entrance is free. Inside the Fortress and in front of the Tower of Homage is a statue of Gonzalo Fernandez de Oviedo, a famous historian, who was once

Calle Las Damas in the colonial zone of Santo Domingo is one of the oldest streets in the New World

Governor of the Fortress. At the entrance to the fort is the Santa Barbara powder house which was built during the reign of King Charles III of Spain.

Casa de Bastidas Across the Plaza is the former home of Rodrigo de Bastidas. The interior courtyard gardens are well worth a visit. Full of beautiful, tropical flowers, this must have been a peaceful haven from the bustling fort outside. The old house is a cultural centre and there are many art exhibitions and Government functions held there. It is also home to some permanent craft exhibitions and art galleries, including Planarte, a craft centre sponsored by the Government.

Nicolas de Ovando was one of the most influential men in the early life of Santo Domingo. He was appointed Governor of the Colony in 1502 and was responsible for much of the city's design. He is said to have chosen the spot to build the Tower of Homage and to have been responsible for the design of many of the houses in the surrounding streets. A few short steps along from the Casa de Bastidas is his house. It has been carefully restored and is now used as a hotel. A hotel for romantics or historians, it has views

A statue of Gonzalo Fernandez de Oviedo stands in front of the Tower of Homage inside the Ozama Fortress, Santo Domingo

across the Ozama River and picturesque inside courtyards. It is one of the cheaper hotels in the city costing about US$60 (Tel: 687 7181).

Further down Calle las Damas is a 200-year-old sundial, *Reloj de Sol*. Built on the order of Governor Francisco Rubio y Peñaranda in 1753, local people are proud that it has never had to be repaired but still manages to tell exactly the right time. The sundial is outside the *Capillo de los Remedios*. This recently restored chapel was built by the Davila family for use as their private chapel. The Davila family house is next door to the house built for Nicholas Ovando.

The National Mausoleum Opposite the Davila family house is the National Mausoleum. Also called the Convento de San Ignacio de Loyola, it was built in 1743 as a Jesuit church. Since then it has been used for many different purposes including a tobacco warehouse and a theatre. It was restored in 1955 when it became a monument to national heroes. Trujillo ordered an ornate tomb for his own remains to be built there but his body was never laid in it. The Panteon Nacional is open daily from 10 a.m. to 5 p.m. and admission is free, but men do need to be wearing long trousers and women wearing skirts falling below the knee.

Museo de las Casas Reales On the corner of Calle las Damas and Calle las Mercedes is the Museo de las Casas Reales. It started off life in the sixteenth century as the Palace of the Governors and Captains-General and on some maps is still marked as the Palace of the Captains or Palacio de los Capitanes. It was also used as a Court of Appeals, and judges used to be able to look out of the windows at the sundial opposite to keep their eye on the time cases were taking. It is now a colonial museum and is a treasure trove of artefacts from the days of the grand Spanish galleons. Many items have been found on sunken wrecks of ships departing for and coming from Spain. It is open every day except Monday from 9 a.m. to midday and from 2.30 p.m. to 5.30 p.m. Entrance costs about US$1 (Tel: 682 4202).

The Alcazar At the north end of Calle las Damas is the Alcazar, or the Prince's House. This square, squat stone building was home to Christopher Columbus's son Diego. He brought architects across from Spain to direct the building of his home in the New World. Employing 1,500 Indians, work started in 1510

Christopher Columbus's son Diego built this house, known as the Alcazar, in Santo Domingo, Dominican Republic

and in the entire building of 22 rooms not one nail was used. The building cause great consternation at the time because Diego's enemies feared he was building a fort, but investigators sent from Spain ruled that a fort would not have had such large windows and wide doors and so pacified the critics. The house was home to Columbus's family for the next 67 years and it became the centre for the New World governments. Expeditions to explore other islands, Mexico and South America were planned from here until 1586 when Sir Francis Drake sacked the house. The building was restored in 1955 and is now open to the public. It contains the Museo Virreinal and they are both open daily from 9 a.m. to midday and from 2.30 p.m. to 5.30 p.m. The Alcazar is closed on Tuesdays and the museum is closed on Mondays; the entrance fee is US$1. Bilingual guides are available until 5 p.m.

Next to the Alcazar is Calle la Atarazana, an area of former colonial warehouses, customs houses and an arsenal. Now it is the start of the commercial part of the colonial zone and houses souvenir shops, restaurants and art galleries. It is worth browsing through the shops in this area.

After wandering down Calle la Atarazana, you can travel down Calle Restauracion to *Las Ruinas del Monasterio de San Francisco*. This was the first St Francis monastery in the New World and dates back to around 1510. It was destroyed by Drake's forces in 1586, and then in the nineteenth century was used as a lunatic asylum. The monastery has also been hit by natural disasters. Earthquakes have shaken the ruins twice but enough remains for it to be the stage for some cultural evens throughout the year.

Close by is the *House of the Cord* which is the city's first stone house, and nearby is the sixteenth-century *Coin House* where the island's money was first minted. The House of the Cord was built in 1503 by Don Francisco de Garay and later lived in by Christopher Columbus's son, Diego. It is also believed to be here that the city's leading ladies gathered in 1586 to pool their jewellery to pay the ransom demanded by Sir Francis Drake.

If you head back down Calle Hostos from the San Francisco Monastery you will pass the *Altagracia Church* and, next door, the ruins of the *Hospital-Iglesia de San Nicolas de Bari*. This hospital was the first to be built in the Americas. Work on it was started by Nicolas de Ovando in 1509 and it was completed by 1552. But it did not survive for long and was one of the buildings to be attacked and destroyed by Drake and his men. The ruins then had to survive earthquakes across the centuries before much of it was taken down earlier this century and its timber taken away to be used elsewhere.

Turning off Calle Hostos down Calle las Mercedes at the junction of this street with Calle Jose Reyes you will find the *Iglesia de las Mercedes*. On one side of the church is the Chapel of Christ's Solitude, dating from 1555. Tirso de Molina lived here when he wrote his famous novel *Don Juan*.

It is worth going down Calle Jose Reyes to Calle El Conde. The street is full of little shops and is one the busiest commercial streets in the colonial zone. This street leads to what was originally the city boundary at La Puerta del Conde. This gate is where the country's independence was declared and the first Republican flag unfurled. There are a series of old gates around the former city boundaries, along with small fortresses.

If you prefer to stay within the old city limits, return to the city centre down Calle Arzobispo Nouel, passing the Carmelite Church and St Andre's Church, or wander along Calle Padre

Bellini and pass Regina Angelorum Convent, the Chapel of the Third Order and the Dominican Friar's Convent. On the corner of Calle Padre Bellini and Calle Arzobispo Merino is the *Casa de Tostado*. This was once the Archbishop's Palace and boasts a Gothic double window. Now it is home to the *Museum of the Nineteenth-Century Dominican Family* and its collection of furniture and mementoes of that era. The Museum is open every day except Wednesday, from 9 a.m. to 2.30 p.m. Admission is about US$0.50.

Shopping The Colonial Zone is not just museums and old houses. It is liberally scattered with shady parks and shopping areas. If you are looking for locally made crafts, this is one of the best areas to come to. There is a wide selection of both goods and prices. There are expensive galleries but, if you are a keen bargain hunter, there are plenty to find. Obviously the shopkeepers will not haggle with you but, if you are buying a number of items, they will sometimes give you a good price. If you want to try your hand at real haggling, you are best to wait and shop at the numerous roadside stalls.

If you hire a guide for the day, he will probably take you to shops where he will earn a commission. But if you are wandering around on your own, make sure you go down Calle las Mercedes or Avenida Mella to the *Mercado Modelo* where you can definitely haggle – but, watch out, they are real experts here. The *Planarte* is in the Casa Bastides on Calle las Damas and is well worth a visit, although the craft pieces are more expensive than those at the MAI Centre on Calle las Mercedes.

Some of the art galleries in this area include *Galleria de Arte Naive*, on Calle Isabel la Católica, open daily, except Tuesday, from midday to midnight; *Galeria Ulloa*, Calle Hostos, open 10 a.m. to 7 p.m. Monday to Saturday; and *Galeria Commander*, Calle El Conde, open 8.30 a.m. to midday and from 2.30 p.m. to 7 p.m., Monday to Saturday.

Restaurants There is plenty of choice for eating out in Santo Domingo. In the colonial zone there are a good selection of Spanish and local restaurants, many in old colonial buildings. For a cheap and cheerful seafood meal, try *America* on the corner of Calle Nouel and Santome (Tel: 682 7194), or *El Buren* on Padre Billini for local food and also a small display of native artefacts

(Tel: 685 7636). A romantic atmosphere is one of the highlights of sampling the Creole and international cuisine at *Fonda de la Atarazana* on Calle Atarazana (Tel: 689 2900).

Eating out in the Dominican Republic is generally much cheaper than in many other Caribbean islands and trying local restaurants is even cheaper for excellent food.

The Modern City Travelling between the old and new cities is like travelling between two countries. There is a totally different atmosphere in the modern city, but there is just as much to see here and it is just as attractive as the colonial zone. Most of the large international hotels are in the modern sector, along with many of the large businesses. It is an area of wide, tree-lined avenues with grand monuments. The city has a friendly, comfortable feel. You can wander around day or night without fear and, in fact, some of the roads are the setting for large open-air parties that just seem to happen out of nowhere. There are very few high-rise buildings and most buildings are just spread out across a large area. This gives the impression of a very spacious city and adds elegance.

There are several main thoroughfares of special note. Avenue George Washington runs along the coastline into the colonial zone. This is where many people meet friends or family and is often where spontaneous parties are sparked off. It is the main site for the Merengue Festival when you will find everyone dancing in the streets – and foreign tourists are not excluded. The street is also called the Malecon. At the eastern port end of the 33km(20ml.) long road you will find a statue of Friar Anton de Montesinos. He was a defender of human rights during the island's colonial days. There are two other monuments along the Avenue, built during Trujillo's regime.

There are some large parks which provide welcome relief from the constant traffic and noise of the city. If you are driving around the city, beware of the one-way systems and also of the locals' habit of stopping in the middle of roundabouts. Parking in the city is quite easy and all the major hotels have their own car parks.

Museums There are several museums worth visiting but remember to take your Spanish dictionary – the exhibit captions are all in Spanish. These include the *Juan Pablo Duarte Cultural Plaza*, and *Hall of Prehistoric Art* and the *Instituto de Investigaciones Historicas*.

The *Cultural Plaza* is off the Avenida Maximo Gomez and houses six museums, the national theatre and the national library. The *Museum of the Dominican Man* (Tel: 687 3622) houses an exhibition of Taino Indian artefacts, art and culture along with a display of Dominican life today. The museum is closed on Mondays. The *Museum of Natural History* (Tel: 689 0106) covers the flora and fauna of the island with videos of the national parks, while the *National History and Geography Museum* (Tel: 687 5337) has a collection of the former dictator Rafael Trujillo's personal belongings. *The Gallery of Modern Art* (Tel: 682 8280) has displays depicting the evolution of Dominican art. It is open from 9 a.m. to 5 p.m. and entrance is about US$0.50. The other two museums in the complex are the *Cinemateca Nacional* and the *Museo de la Familia Dominicana*.

The Plaza is worth a visit even if you do not actually go into any of the museums. The *National Library* has a good selection of books. One building you can not fail to miss is the *National Theatre* at the west end of the Plaza. With a completely marble façade, the inside of the building is lined with Dominican mahogany. Opened in 1973, it has two auditoriums and organized tours are taken backstage every morning. (Box office, Tel: 682 7255). You can also take a tour of the whole Cultural Plaza from Tuesday to Sunday from 10.30 a.m. to 5.30 p.m.

The National Palace Among the other buildings to visit is The National Palace on the corners of Boliver Avenue and Dr Baez Street. Built in the 1940s, it is used as the seat of the Executive Power and can only be visited with the permission of the President's public relations office. Call 686 4771, ext. 340 or 360, to make an appointment. Tours are taken on Mondays, Wednesdays and Fridays.

The Numismatic and Philatelic Museum is on Pedro Henriquez Urena Street and is open from Tuesday to Saturday from 9 a.m. to 5 p.m. for visits to the stamp and coin collections. The Museum of Pre-Hispanic Art is on Avenida San Martin and is open from 8 a.m. to midday, Monday to Saturday. Entrance is free (Tel: 565 6691).

Art Galleries Santo Domingo has many art galleries. The native Hispaniola art varies from Haiti to the Dominican Republic and from rough roadside stalls to elegant galleries. Some of those galleries featuring local artists include *Galleria Arteresa* on Lea de Castri Street, open from 10 a.m. to 12.30 p.m. and from 4 p.m. to 7 p.m. Monday to Saturday; *Nouveau Centro de Arts*, Avenida Independencia, open from 9 a.m. to 8 p.m. Monday to Saturday; *Galeria de Arts Deniel's*, also on Avenida Independencia, open from 9 a.m. to 1 p.m. and from 3 p.m. to 9 p.m., Monday to Saturday; the *Galeria de Arte Nader* also includes Haitian art and is open from 9.30 a.m. to 1 p.m. and from 3.30 p.m. to 7.30 p.m. Monday to Saturday.

Parks The city's parks are also worth seeing. The large *Parque Mirador del Sur* is 8 km(5ml.) long and runs parallel to the ocean south of Anacaona Avenue, and is also known as the Paseo de los Indios. The *Central Olimpico* has a sports centre, and *Parque Independencia* is on the borders between the modern city and the colonial zone. Both the national zoo and the botanical gardens are worth visiting.

The Zoo, to the north of the city, covers 10 square kilometres (6sq.ml.) and features native species as well as an African plain. A train takes you for rides around the grounds. Entrance is US$0.20 and the zoo is open from 9 a.m. to 5 p.m. daily. *The Botanical Gardens* are to the west of the main city and cover almost two million square metres. Again, a train takes you around the park, or you can walk; with over 300 species native to the island, there are plenty on show in the gardens, which costs US$0.20 to enter and which is open Tuesday to Sunday from 9 a.m. to 5 p.m.

A little further out of town but still within the city boundaries are *Los Tres Ojos*. The three caves are close to the road to the airport on Las Americas Avenue. But it is worth going there for a little longer than for a few minutes before you fly off. There are two caves which you can walk into and admire the lake. A small boat takes you across the second lake into the third cave, which is rumored to have two crocodiles living there. Guides will give tourists a scare by diving into the pools, which look extremely shallow but are in fact, quite deep.

Shopping in the modern city is made easy by the equally modern shopping malls. Although most people will head to the colonial zone for crafts, there are also centres in the modern sector. *Plaza Criolla*, in front of the Olympic Centre, houses Handicrafts Fairs. This is a modern shopping centre designed like a Spanish village and is full of little shops and restaurants. There are duty-free shops where you can buy crystal and jewellery in the *Centro de los Heroes*. A flea market operates at the Centre on Sundays.

Hotels There are plenty of good-quality hotels in Santo Domingo, from the international names like the *Sheraton* to high-quality locally-run hotels like the *Gran Lina*. Among the more expensive properties are the *Sheraton* (Tel: 685 5151) and *Jaragua* (Tel: 686 8161), which are both on Avenida George Washington and both of which start at around US$140 a night. The *Gran Hotel Lina* (Tel: 689 5185) is slightly cheaper at around US$110. The older *El Embajador* (Tel: 533 2131) costs just under US$100 a night. A hotel on the borders of the old and new city is the *Commercial* (Tel: 682 8161) on Calle El Conde which costs around US$20 a night and which is popular with business travellers.

Restaurants The major hotels all boast good restaurants like the *Jade Garden* (Tel: 533 2131), a Chinese restaurant at El Embajador Hotel, or *Lina's* (Tel: 689 5185), next door to the Gran Lina. Lina originally came from Spain and was once the dictator Trujillo's cook. It is worth booking to make sure of a table.

But, if you prefer to leave the main hotels behind, there are plenty of local restaurants to find. A stroll down the Malecon will take you past a wide range of restaurants. Most seem to be either Spanish or Dominican cooking, but for something slightly different, try *Vesuvio* (Tel: 689 2141) on the Malecon. This Italian restaurant has developed into a small chain with another outlet, *Vesuvio II*, on Avenida Tiradentes (Tel: 562 6060). Or, for a setting with a difference, go to a cave for a night out. *Meson de la Cueva* (Tel: 533 2818) is in the Parque Mirador and specializes in steaks, but is on the expensive side. It is also very popular with the locals, so book ahead. For cheap seafood dishes, try *La Bahia* (Tel: 682 7585) near the docks on the Malecon. For snacks or light meals, try *Café Atlantico* on Avenida Mexico (Tel: 565 2841), or *Café Galeria* in the Galeria shopping centre (Tel: 567 4059).

Night Clubs There are numerous night clubs, usually playing the local merengue music. Again, most of the major hotels have a disco but other clubs are scattered along the Malecon and several have nude shows, coyly promoted as 'popular with unescorted gentlemen'. There are also casinos attached to many of the major hotels.

Useful Telephone Numbers

Emergency Ambulance, Police and Fire. Tel: 711.

Chemists:

   Los Hidalgos. Tel: 565 4848;

   San Judas Tadeo. Tel: 689 6664.

Clinic Abreu, good for tourists needing medical treatment.
   Tel: 686 8784.

Airport Information. Tel: 549 0226.

Botanical Gardens, Avenida Botanico. Tel: 565 2860.

British Embassy, Avenida Abraham Lincoln.
   Tel: 562 5262/562 5010.

Ministry of Tourism, Avenida George Washington. Tel: 682 8181.

Tourism Information Office, at Las Americas International Airport.
   Tel: 542 0120.

Modern Art Gallery, Cultural Plaza. Tel: 682 8280

Museum of Natural History, Cultural Plaza. Tel: 689 0106.

Museum of History and Geography, Cultural Plaza. Tel: 687 5337

Museum of Royal Houses, Las Damas. Tel: 682 4202

Numismatics Museum, Pedro Henriquez Urena. Tel: 688 6512

Museum of Dominican Man, Cultural Plaza. Tel: 687 3622.

National Parks Office, Calle Las Damas. Tel: 685 1316.

Main Post Office, is at Isabel la Católica while its usual home at
   Calle Emiliano Tejera is renovated for the 1992 Columbus
   celebrations.

The South-West This area is another relatively unexplored
region of the country. There is a main coastal road from Santo
Domingo but it is 188km(117ml.) to the region's main town of
Barahona, so it is best to spend a few days in the area rather than
rush around – the roads generally are not that fast anyway.

The first large town out of Santo Domingo is San Cristobal,
about 20km(12ml.) out of the capital. The town's *Fort* was
planned by Christopher Columbus and the country's first
constitution was signed in the town in 1844. It was also the
birthplace of the dictator Trujillo, and two of his homes are
being restored to open to the public. His home, *Casa de Caoba*,
is open from 9 a.m. to 5 p.m.; a luxury home at El Cerro was
built for him but never lived in.

Other places to visit include the town's church. *Iglesia de
Piedras Vivas*, and the church and caves at *Santa Maria* where there

is a festival from 6–10 June. This festival celebrates the patron saint with African-style stick and drum rituals. The dancing is typical of the region and is known as *carabine*. The caves at nearby *El Pomier* have Taino Indian petroglyths, and at *La Toma* there are natural springs with swimming-pools.

Continuing west to Bani, you can visit the birthplace of Maximo Gomez, one of the fighters for the liberation of Cuba in the 1800s. Other things to see include the parish church of *Nuestra Señora de Regla*, with its patron saint festival on 21 November.

Just to the west of Bani is the small village of Arroyo Hondo where there is an *Orchid Garden*. There are about 300 varieties of orchid grown on the island, and this garden is owned by prize-winning gardener Gretchen Vallejo de Barcelo (Tel: 567 1351). Further along the coast, the town of Azua is best known for being burnt to the ground. It has had the misfortune to be destroyed three times from 1804 to 1849 during invasion attempts by Haiti.

Barahona is a good base for travelling around the region, and the town itself is a pleasant place surrounded by beautiful white beaches. There are few tourist sights or museums to visit but the scenery more than makes up for a lack of buildings.

Hotels in town include *Hotel Barahona* and the rather basic *Hotel Guarocuya* (Tel: 685 6161), but the sea views are spectacular.

From Barahona it is easy to drive along the coast and discover unspoilt beaches. Development will come to this area but it is still a few years off. *Lake Enriquillo* is one of the most popular spots in the region. It lies 30m(98ft.) below sea level and is home to the largest number of American crocodiles in the world – probably not a good spot for swimming. The lake contains three small islands, one of which is used by the crocodiles for nesting. The islands are also home for flamingos and iguanas. You can visit the lake with permission from the National Parks Office in Santo Domingo. Around the lake there are numerous fresh water and sulphur springs.

South of Barahona town there is a small village of Polo. There is nothing special about the village but the road leading to it is said to be very unusual. The road goes over the Magnetic Hill and the story is that if you turn the car engine off and put it into reverse gear, it will be pulled up the hill by the strong magnetic forces – not many people actually give it a try or even find it as it is not marked on any map.

Puerto Plata The Silver Port is the place that most visitors see first as they fly in to this northern town's international airport. The northern coast is the main resort area and its beautiful beaches are lined with hotels. Sugar-cane plantations dominate the agriculture but tourism is becoming increasingly important to the economy.

Puerto Plata is the tourist hub but, unlike so many Caribbean tourist towns, it has managed to retain its charm and character. The tourists are still very much secondary to ordinary life for most of the town's inhabitants, and the latest hotel developments have tended to be self-contained and a short distance away rather than being imposed on the old town.

Puerto Plata got its name after the Spaniards sailing towards the natural harbour saw what looked like a lake of silver. The scenery is dominated by Mount Isabella which towers above the town. A cable-car links the gardens at the peak to the main town and there are spectacular views of the island and coastline from the gardens.

The Puerto Plata region is a place for spectacular views. The beaches literally stretch for miles and there are plenty of secluded spots. Most hotels confine beach and watersports activities to a small area in front of their properties, leaving huge tracts of coastline untouched. Fishing villages dot this coastline and many have small, fresh seafood restaurants where small boys will run up the nearest coconut tree to pick the fruit to provide you with dessert. These places may look rough and dirty but you are as likely to get an upset stomach eating in the major hotels as in these cafés.

Puerto Plata is squeezed between the mountain and the Atlantic Ocean but its outlook is to the sea rather than the land. Most activity in the town is along the wide, elegant waterfront boulevard and in the narrow Spanish-style streets behind. To the west of town is the port area which is all set for a major overhaul. Few yachts come into port, leaving it to industrial tankers, but this could change once a marina is developed.

The tourist town really begins a little to the east of the port at the west end of the Malecon (the waterfront road), with the *San Felipe de Puerto Plata Fortress* which is the only building left from the original town founded in the days of Christopher Columbus.

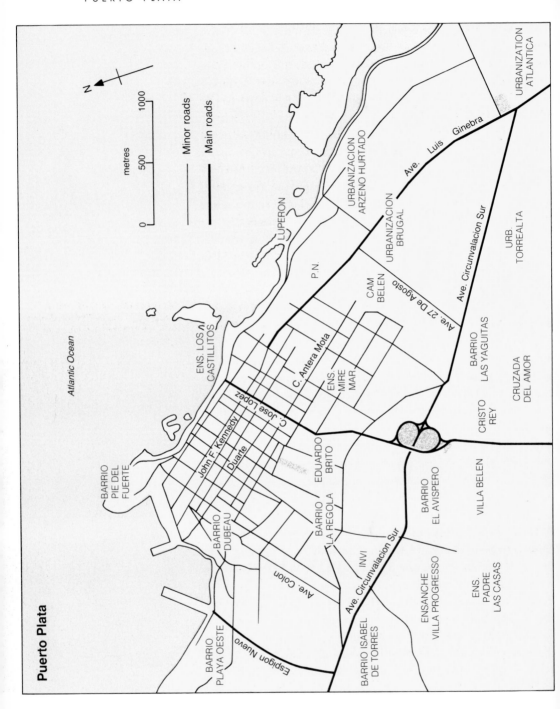

Puerto Plata

Columbus first arrived on the north coast in 1493 and a settlement was established to the west of Puerto Plata, at Isabella. This was quickly abandoned because of fever and the Spaniards moved south to found Santo Domingo. But ten years later the town of Puerto Plata was founded on the order of Nicolas de Ovando. Even then the town was not secure. A hundred years later it was destroyed by government order because of the numerous pirates operating on this coastline.

It took settlers from the Canary Islands, who arrived in 1742, to establish the town as an important agricultural centre and port. Somehow the Fort managed to survive all the upheaval of the town and is worth a visit to see the small museum and the cell where one of the country's liberators, Juan Pablo Duarte, was once held prisoner. But the Fort is probably more worth while for its size. If you arrive in Puerto Plata it will really be the first major building that you will see remaining from the colonial era and, if you do not get a chance to go to Santo Domingo, it will give you some idea of the massive structures of the Ozuma Fortress and the city walls.

The San Felippe Fortress marks the end of the Malecon in Puerto Plata, Dominican Republic

One of the unusual features are the 1.2m(4ft.) high doors. The story is that the waiting soldiers used to hide behind the doors and hit invading troops on the head with clubs as they bent down to go through them. More likely is that the doors were low because the people of that era were not tall men. The Fort is open daily from 8 a.m. to 5 p.m. and admission is RD$5.

The Fort is at the west end of the 4km(2¹/2ml.) Malecon which is lined by flats and houses overlooking the ocean. Many local people take a stroll along the road to meet family and friends and you will often find artists selling their pictures on the pavements. It is quite a good place to find Haitian artists and to haggle for some bargains. As you stroll along you will see a tiny island just off-shore. The large statue on it is a bronze of Neptune.

At the eastern end of the Malecon are the hotels, restaurants and the main beach. Long Beach is a fairly narrow piece of sand protected by rock breakers. There are much better beaches along the coast in either direction and this stretch can also get fairly crowded, particularly at weekends when all the locals are relaxing, too.

Hotels The *Puerto Plata Beach Resort Hotel* is opposite Long Beach. This is a good, quality hotel with a series of cottages in pretty gardens. This is a busy area but the cottages are secluded and offer a peaceful haven. It is also a good base for wandering around town from. There are cheaper hotels just behind the beach, such as the *Jimesson* on John F. Kennedy or the *Caracol Hotel* on the Malecon. But it may be worth paying extra to ensure a more reliable power supply.

Other sights in Puerto Plata are also tucked away behind the Malecon. It would be easy to drive through Puerto Plata and miss out on the quiet, green squares and narrow, quaint streets. Unfortunately, many of the locals have discovered that pestering tourists does result in getting money for nothing and they will converge on you, wanting to give you a conducted tour of the town. It is worth getting a taxi and getting the driver to give you a tour; he also helps in fending off the other 'guides' and most drivers will be genuinely helpful.

The main town square is called Central Park and is surrounded by Victorian wooden structures. These include the *Church of San Felipe* and the *Commerce Club*. The Church holds

General Gregorio Luperon sits astride his horse in Puerto Plata

Catholic services at 6.30 a.m. and 5.30 p.m. on weekdays and at 5.30 a.m., 7 a.m., 9 a.m. and 5.30 p.m. on Saturdays. The Protestant service is held at the *Asamblea de Dios* on Calle El Moro at 5.30 a.m., 7 a.m., 9 a.m. and 5.30 p.m. on Saturdays. There is also a Catholic service in the Manzanda Room of *Hotel Playa Dorado* at 11.30 a.m.

Amber Museum Just around the corner from Central Park is the Amber Museum on Calle Duarte. Even those not keen on museums will enjoy this tiny building. It is stuffed full of the most incredible pieces of amber. An upstairs room holds an exhibition of amber and of how it forms, with examples of insects and creatures trapped in tree sap literally millions of years ago. Some of the examples seem perfectly formed. Downstairs there is a shop selling larimar and amber. Larimar is also known as Dominican turquoise, a stone unique to the islands and found in the Bahoruco mountain range. The Museum is open from Monday to Saturday, from 9 a.m. to 5p.m. (Tel: 586 2848). Admission is RD$3.

The Amber Museum in a quiet side street of Puerto Plata, Dominican Republic

**Opposite
A view of Mount Isabel from the beach at Playa Dorado, Dominican Republic**

Brugal Rum Distillery A day trip for those who hate museums could be to the town's rum distillery. The Brugal Rum Distillery is on Calle Duarte near to the port and is the largest distillery in the country. The Dominican Republic is a large producer of dark rum, and at this warehouse visitors are encouraged to conduct their own rum survey and, of course, to buy a bottle to take home. While many wines and spirits are expensive because they have to be imported, rum-based cocktails are often cheaper than beer, and rum is one of the bargains worth taking home.

Botanical Gardens A visit to Puerto Plata is incomplete without a cable-car ride to the Botanical Gardens at the top of Mount Isabel de Torres. Standing (2,565ft). high, the mountain is a good place to spend a quiet afternoon strolling through the gardens admiring the views inland and along the coast. A short cable-car ride takes you to the top. It starts from the edge of the main highway out of town towards Santo Domingo and is open

daily (except Tuesdays) from 8 a.m. to 5 p.m. Admission is RD$3 for adults. Once at the top, there is a small gift shop and snack bar.

Shopping Close behind the Amber Museum is the town's market which sells locally produced fruit and vegetables. The town also has a small industrial zone on the road to Santo Domingo and there you can visit *Mink America*. The fur outlet allows visitors around the factory to admire the craftsmen at work and to learn how to tell the difference between the furs (Tel: 586 4396).

There are plenty of small souvenir shops in Puerto Plata but there are also roadside stalls along the road towards the airport and Playa Dorado. The stall holders are fiercely competitive but very friendly. A good tip is to expect to pay about half their original price but the haggling will be hard and, once they have hit their true price, you will be lucky to budge them. Items to watch out for are Haitian and Dominican art.

Dominican art can often be identified by a red flame tree. For some reason, most Dominican artists will feature the tree while the Haitians do not. Local art is usually slightly more expensive than the Haitian. Other good buys are silver and larimar jewellery and the native, faceless dolls. The stalls also have the usual T-shirts and cheap souvenirs. Ask for *Los Managuitos* if you hire a taxi, to get to the roadside stalls.

The main tourist shops are in the *Plaza Tourisol*, which is between Puerto Plata and Los Managuitos and offers visitors a chance to shop in air-conditioned surroundings rather than haggling in the heat and dust of the open stalls. And closer to Playa Dorado is the *Plaza Isabela*, with a similar range of shops as Plaza Tourisol.

On your way from Puerto Plata to the resort area of Playa Dorado 6km(4ml.) away, your taxi driver may well point out a bench at the side of the road. This has been put there in the memory of three daughters of a local man. The story is that the dictator Trujillo took a fancy to the eldest girl but she rejected him. In a fit of pique he ordered the execution of both the girl and her two sisters.

Restaurants Puerto Plata has a very active night life, beginning with a wide selection of restaurants, bars and then night-clubs. Many people staying in the nearby Playa Dorado resort travel into town to experience the local cuisine. Seafood restaurants dominate, with chefs using the catch of the day and there is always plenty of cheap lobster. *Jimmy's* (Tel: 586 4325) is one of the more expensive at US$30 a head for a lobster meal but is popular with visitors and does serve excellent meals. *Aqui Norma* is famous for its creole cooking, while *De Armando* (Tel: 586 3418) is another good fish restaurant, *Los Pinos* (Tel: 586 3222) is a café run by a Canadian and opens for a North American-style breakfast. Later in the day, the menu changes to steaks and pastas, which are particularly popular. *The Victorian Pub* specializes in seafood dishes served in the old-world surroundings of a Victorian seafront building or in the intimate atmosphere of an open courtyard complete with fountain (Tel: 586 4240).

Playa Dorado Many visitors to Puerto Plata are actually staying in the nearby resort complex of Playa Dorado. This is a group of about fifteen hotels and part-hotels on 18km(11ml.) stretch of beach. The idea of so many hotels together might conjure up pictures of tower blocks and fish and chip shops but the whole area has been carefully planned and landscaped. Most of the hotels are five-star and are divided up by a golf-course and by beautiful gardens. They all have their own swimming-pools, tennis courts and a selection of restaurants and bars. Some are on the beach, while others are a short walk away with views of Mount Isabel. The beachfront hotels tend to offer a wide variety of watersports to their guests.

The main advantages of the complex is that it was purpose built, and further developments are controlled so that supplies of water and electricity can cope with demand. There are still power cuts, but the hotels do have their own generators and have air-conditioning. Many of the older hotels do not have reliable air-conditioning systems and it can get unbearably hot and stuffy in the summer.

Playa Dorado offers visitors so many different restaurants and activities during the day that it would be easy to stay in the resort and never leave. In fact, some people do not leave, put off venturing further afield by the armed guards at the gates to the resort. These guards do give you a feeling of security while in the resort, but the guns are not really needed and should not put you off from leaving the resort.

The sports available within the resort include golf on the Robert Trent Jones designed 18-hole course. It is open to non-players but the club insists on sending a caddy around with anyone who does not have a handicap. Tennis courts can be booked at most hotels, and horse riding can also be booked, although many of the horses look like they could do with a good meal rather than trekking in the hot sun. The watersports vary from deep-sea fishing, scuba diving, snorkelling and water-skiing. There are also a couple of small sea-planes that take people on flights around the bay for about US$30.

In the evenings, attention turns to the casinos and discos. The local merengue music dominates many of the entertainments. Several of the hotels have Happy Hours – but, watch out, half-price drinks actually means they give you two for the price of one, and the second one has usually melted before you get to it.

Hotels Some of the better hotels are the *Eurotel* (Tel: 586 3663) which costs around US$110 a night. The *Radisson* (Tel: 586 5350) costs about the same, while the cost of the *Playa Dorado Hotel* rises to nearer US$200 in the high season (Tel: 586 3988). The *Villas Dorados* (Tel: 586 3000) are cheaper at around US$70, and the *Montemar* (Tel: 586 2800) is also cheaper, at around US$60. The only disadvantage of staying in this area is the proximity to the airport. Flights start arriving at 8 a.m. and the planes pass over the coastline just a few miles from Playa *Dorado* and can be heard from most of the hotels. This could become more of a problem as the tourist industry in the area picks up dramatically.

Restaurants Many of the hotel restaurants are excellent, such as *Elaine's* at the Jack Tar Village where reservations are required (Tel: 586 3800), the *Comida* at the Eurotel or the *Flamingo* restaurant at the Dorado Naco Suites (Tel: 586 2019) and it is worth booking ahead. There are also some good restaurants elsewhere in the complex. These include *Valentino's* for pasta or pizza under the stars (Tel: 586 2019) or the *Jardin de Jade* (Tel: 586 3000) where, for one night a week, there is a buffet of their excellent Chinese cuisine, but you need to book early for a seat.

Opposite
An aerial view of the Playa Dorado beach resort, Dominican Republic

Useful Telephone Numbers

Hospital. Tel: 586 2210

Doctor, Centro Medico. Tel: 586 2342/3542. Take your holiday invoice and passport to sort out insurance paperwork.

Police. Tel: 586 2328.

Fire. Tel: 586 2312.

Post Office. Tel: 586 2368.

Airport. Tel: 586 0219.

The North Coast Glorious white, sandy beaches fringed with palms line the north coast, which borders the Atlantic Ocean. This means that surfers love it, while swimmers battle. Most developments are around the sheltered beaches, with coral reefs just off-shore to protect the beaches. One of the most famous north coast resorts is Sosua.

Sosua This little town is dominated by its long, curving beach. The town really took off in the 1940s when Jewish refugees fleeing from the war in Europe were made welcome in the community. Most of the refugees had been professionals but

The Dominican Republic's north-coast beaches are reputed to be among the best in the world

once in the Dominican Republic they turned to agriculture. The community formed a co-operative and successfully marketed dairy products and raised cattle. The co-operative is still one of the most successful in the country and the town has become a prosperous centre. The Jewish community has shrunk down to about twenty families, but there is still a synagogue in the town which holds occasional services.

Now the town is also developing fast as a tourist centre. It still has its small-town charm and is a delightful place either to visit or stay. It is within easy reach of Playa Dorado and Puerto Plata, and many people catch a taxi down to the beach for the day. The taxis will drop you off on the main road, with no sign of the beach, but there are paths through the trees down to the beach, or you can ask to be taken around to the edge of the beach in the centre of town. There is a taxi stand there to catch a ride back.

The town is split into two sections, either end of the long beach. On the west side is Los Charamicos where the locals live in crowded, narrow streets, while on the east is El Batey where

most of the hotels are set out in landscaped gardens, and a mass of bars and restaurants cluster around the beach.

Los Charamicos contains the town's theatre as well as the Post Office and police station. The Anglican church and the bus station are on the east side of Los Charamicos close to the main beach. El Batey is probably the area that most visitors will explore first, as many will stay there. The clinic is on Calle Dr Alejo Martinez which leads from the point to the town's park. On the other side of the park, the road continues past the synagogue and, if you turn right down Calle de Ayuntamiento, you will come to the City Hall. To reach the beach car-park, take the first turning left after the beach, turn left on to Calle Pedro Clisante and then left again to the car-park.

The town's market attracts as many visitors as the beach. It actually lines the beach, with stalls hiding away in the shade of the palms, and it is well worth browsing through the many stalls. There are plenty of local arts and crafts. Haggling is the order of the day and those right on the beach are often more expensive than those slightly further away. There are also bars and cafés scattered amongst the craft stalls, which, although they do not look too hygienic, provide welcome breaks from the beach.

But, if you prefer not to move off the beach, do not worry, the drinks and food will come to you. The moment you arrive on the beach, little boys will rush up and offer to be your 'secretary' for the day. For just a few RD dollars they will get you sunbeds and then collect drinks or snacks throughout the day. They will also get you snorkels, collect coconuts or just sit and watch your belongings as you swim. It is worth appointing one just to stop the others approaching you non-stop all day.

From the beach, there are plenty of watersports, from scuba diving and snorkelling to jet-ski rides or water-skiing. The coral reefs fill the bay, and tiny, tropical fish can be seen just a metre or so into the water. The water is very calm and shallow, making it safe for children. There are stakes marking the reefs to keep boats and skiers clear of both the coral and the divers.

Some of the reefs are very close to the surface and at mid-afternoon you can usually see at least ten or twelve divers standing knee-deep in water, way out in the bay. There are also glass-bottom-boat rides for those who prefer to see the fish while getting a tan. The ticket usually includes a free rum punch and entrance to the town's disco that night. But the trip is worth it for itself: the number of fish are enormous and, if you are lucky, you will catch a glimpse of something large, like a sting-ray or some of the larger groupers.

The main beach at Sosua is popular and can get quite busy at peak holiday periods but you can hide away just around the corner. Most of the hotels are just to the east of the main beach and there are tiny, sandy coves in front of them. These get less crowded as most people head to the main beach where there are plenty of watersports. On the smaller beaches, the watersports and sunbeds tend to be for hotel guests only, but you get more privacy.

Restaurants Once you have had enough of the beach, there are a selection of bars and restaurants to try. Many of them are attached to hotels but welcome other customers. *Hotel Sosua Sol* (Tel: 571 2334) is a good place to eat or stay. It has a pleasant beach in front of it and a swimming-pool, with a restaurant set in gardens. Or for a lunchtime snack and rest in the shade, try the *Wet Spot Bar* at Sosua-by-the-Sea (Tel: 571 3222).

Hotels *Playa Chiquita Hotel* (Tel: 571 2800) is 3 km(almost 2ml.) out of town on its own beach; it has a free shuttle service into town. Costing around US$100 a night, it offers visitors a chance to enjoy the local town without the hustle and bustle, and is recommended for families.

The *Ocean Place* (Tel: 571 3131) is slightly cheaper, at around US$80 per night, and is within easy walking distance of either the main beach or the quieter Casa Marina beach. There are a number of new hotels, either recently completed or under construction in the town centre. It is a hot and dusty area with all the usual noise of a building site, so staying slightly further afield would be a good idea if you are looking for some peace and quiet.

Nightlife At night, the town is full of life, with both local people and tourists frequenting the many bars. The best way to enjoy the area is just to wander around and stop at wherever takes your fancy. Many of the restaurants offer local Dominican cuisine and there are night clubs to dance away the effects of the good food.

Useful Telephone Numbers

Hospital. Tel: 571 2332.
Pharmacy. Tel: 571 2350.
Fire. Tel: 571 2301.
Police. Tel: 571 2233.

Cabarete From Sosua it is a short, ten-minute drive along the coast eastwards to Cabarete. This is a windsurfers' paradise with constant, strong winds providing good conditions. The wind tends to pick up in the afternoons, giving the sportsmen the perfect opportunity for lazy mornings waiting for the best conditions after lunch. The wind does mean that sunbathers get chased off the beach pretty quickly, too, because of the stinging sand that gets whipped up.

The beach is a long, sandy stretch that, so far, has escaped the mass tourism that has descended on some of the other beaches. Cabarete is also close to Goleto Beach – another favoured spot for windsurfers.

Cabarete has developed a few small guest houses and beach bars. It also has a number of windsurfing schools and is very much a young town, full of athletic surfers. If you want to try out the sport, there are plenty of shops which will hire out the equipment and give you tuition. It is a wonderfully colourful place, with the white beach lined with the brightly coloured sails of the windsurfers.

Hotels Because it has attracted so many young people, the guesthouses and restaurants are also cheap and cheerful. The best way to find somewhere to stay is to turn up and drive down the road looking for signs outside the houses. There are one or two major hotels in the town and, no doubt, more will follow as people discover this delightful spot.

Camino del Sol (Tel: 571 2858) costs up to US$140 per night for a three-room apartment with all-inclusive facilities. At Costa Azul, developers have built a golf and beach resort. The villas are privately owned and are close to the sea, with a 9-hole golf-course behind the properties. *Punta Goleta* (Tel: 571 0700) has a windsurfing school together with tennis courts and a swimming-pool.

Continuing east along the coast, you will pass endless golden beaches and secluded coves. The road deteriorates the further you travel from Puerto Plata. If you are driving yourself allow plenty

Well-laden donkeys do much of the carrying in the Dominican Republic

of time for it could well take twice as long as you would expect. It is also worth keeping the petrol tank filled up – there are garages along the road but opening hours vary. Many of the hotels and tour companies organize day trips along this coastline to Rio San Juan and those coaches hurtle along – knowing the road obviously helps. If you stop anywhere along the road you will find lots of friendly people eager to talk or point you in the right direction.

Rio San Juan is included in many tours because of its lagoon. Boat tours of the Gri Gri lagoon take you through the mangrove swamps. The town's main hotel is the *Rio San Juan Hotel* (Tel: 589 2379) or 589 2211) from where you can book boat tours. Most of the tours include a visit to one of the hidden beaches in this area.

Cofresi To the west of Puerto Plata is the Cofresi resort. Like Playa Dorado, it is a self-contained resort area. Five kilometres (3ml.) out of town, the hotels are perched on the hills overlooking the beach and the north coast. *Club Cofresi* (Tel: 586 2898) has its own restaurants, discos and watersports facilities, but there are some steep steps to climb to reach some of the rooms so it is not recommended for the elderly or for those with very young children.

Luperon Travelling further west of Puerta Plata you come to the small town of Luperon. Hidden away on the edge of town there is a large hotel resort, popular with both the British and the Canadians. The *Luperon Beach Resort* (Tel: 581 6262) has all the modern facilities you would expect, including tennis courts and a golf-course, but it is a long way from anything else. The town of Luperon does not have much to recommend it except for the friendly people. There are a few shops and bars but hotel guests really need to travel to Puerto Plata to find much of interest.

Monte Christi An equally small and remote town, close to the border with Haiti. Behind the town is the peak of El Morro which is one of the country's national parks. There are several wildlife centres in this area, including seabird nesting grounds on the small offshore islands. This is a good area for fishing and there are some good beaches.

The Mountains Most of the holiday resorts are along the Dominican Republic's beautiful coastline, but for those who prefer a holiday away from the sun and sand, the mountains provide welcome relief. Popular with the locals is the area known as the Little Alps around the inland town of Jarabacoa.

Many of the wealthier Dominicans have a second home up in the mountains to which they escape during the hot summers. These homes are often built with timber in the style of Swiss chalets, adding to the impression that you are in Europe rather than the Caribbean. The weather is much cooler than on the coast and there is more rainfall. Pine forests abound and the rolling hills invite long walks, while for the more athletic there are steeper hiking trails up the higher peaks.

The emphasis is on the gentler pastimes and there are golf-courses, horse-riding and tennis courts. It is also a popular area for artists, both visitors and locals who have galleries hidden away in the small villages. The main inland city is Santiago, which was the first place to be called Santiago in America, it is full of history and culture as well as modern industrial zones.

Santiago This area is dominated by the surrounding agriculture. Tobacco is the main crop, and Santiago is the centre for much of the country's cigarette and cigar production. If you are looking for a good cigar to buy, the locally produced La Aurora is reported to be among the best. Rum is also produced in large quantities in the city and daily tours of the factory can be taken.

You can fly to Santiago with LIAT from Puerta Rico twice a day every Monday, Tuesday, Wednesday, Friday and Saturday.

Historically, the city was originally founded in 1495 because of its good position on the banks of the River Yaque del Norte, with the building of a fort. There was another town built at the same time called Santiago but it was destroyed in an earthquake in 1562, so the settlers moved to the fort and renamed it Santiago de los Caballeros. Santiago has been the site of numerous battles in the many wars that have raged across the country since the 1500s.

The Monumento a los Heroes de la Restauracion dominates the skyline and can be seen from any point in the city. It stands 67 metres(220ft.) tall and contains a small museum. It was built in the 1940s by Trujillo as his monument to peace. The interior murals were painted by Spanish artist Vela Zanetti.

Other things to see in the city include the *Catedral de Santiago Apostol* which was completed in 1895 and has stained glass windows painted by Rincon Mora. The Cathedral faces Duarte Park which is where the taxi drivers gather. Duarte Park is also home to the new *Cultural Plaza* built on similar lines to the one in Santo Domingo and which contains the *Museum of the City of Santiago*.

The Tobacco Institute is opposite the Cathedral and contains a museum outlining the development of the crop, its farming and its current importance to the country. Marlboro produces 18 million cigarettes a day in the Dominican Republic and every one is sold for domestic consumption, with no exports. The city also has the large campus for the Universidad Catolica Madre y Maestra which was founded in 1962.

The *Tourist Office* is in the Town Hall on Avenida Juan Pablo Duarte, which is one of the main streets in the city and is just behind the Monument.

Shopping Apart from shopping at either the cigar or rum factories while on a tour, there is also a good market on the corners of Calle del Sol and Avenida Espana in the centre of the city. The market sells both fruit and vegetables as well as a selection of crafts. More crafts are available in the many roadside stalls that line the highway leading south to Santo Domingo. A few miles out of the city, these stalls sell more pottery and basketware than paintings but are a good place to pick up a bargain. Speaking Spanish automatically cuts the price but most things are very cheap to start with.

Hotels Many of the hotels in Santiago are used by businessmen, such as the *Camino Real* (Tel: 583 4361) with its roof-top restaurant and piano bar. *Matum* (Tel: 582 3107) has a casino and is well patronized by the Dominicans, while the *Don Diego* (Tel: 582 7186) has a night-club and a Chinese restaurant.

Restaurants The hotel restaurants can be recommended, but also worth trying is the *Don Miguel* (Tel: 583 3996) for local specialities or Cuban dishes. For pizzas and ice-cream, try *Restaurant Pizzeria Olé* (Tel: 582 0866), or for French cuisine try *L'Elysée* (Tel: 582 1243).

Useful Telephone Numbers
Hospital. Tel: 583 4311.

The Surrounding Areas Travelling south from Santiago takes you into the most mountainous area of the country and into the Little Alps. The main towns in this area are Jarabacoa, Constanza and La Vega. With its mild climate, the area attracts many Dominicans and there are a number of holiday homes in the villages as well as country-style clubs.

Jarabacoa is a pleasant little town without much of the poverty of the coastal towns or sugar-cane areas. There are some large properties in secluded gardens and a general feeling of affluence. Wandering along the roads in this area you will also pass art galleries, worth stopping at if you want to find true Dominican art.

The Constanza Valley region is an important producer of vegetables and flowers, and the gardens are very pretty and colourful. It is a good area to walk around and there are plenty of sports on offer, from tennis to golf.

In Jarabacoa, the main hotel is *Pinar Dorado* (Tel: 574 2820), which is quite reasonable at about US$25. There are some new developments under construction and this area is probably set to become more accessible to tourists.

Constanza is even prettier than Jarabacoa; it is slightly further off the main road from Santiago to Santo Domingo but is worth the trip. It would take a whole day from either Santiago or Santo Domingo to get there and back but, to date, there are few hotels in this area. One with breath-taking views is the *Hotel Nueva Suiza*, costing around US$25. In town, the local market sells really fresh tropical produce. There is also the former summer residence of dictator Trujillo and the old houses where Japanese and Spanish migrants first lived when they first settled in the country in the 1940s and '50s. The town's church is in front of the central plaza.

The highest peak in the Caribbean is the Pico Duarte at 3,075m(10,086ft.), but you need the permission of the army before you can go walking on the mountain. It is also advisable to hire a guide.

La Vega is actually on the main road between Santiago and Santo Domingo and makes a good place to have a break in the journey and stop in one of the roadside cafés for a coffee. Just outside the town is the site of the first cross to be planted in America; Christopher Columbus placed a cross there in 1492. The story is that during a battle with the Indians they tried to

115

burn the cross but it would not catch fire, and the Virgin of Mercy was said to appear on one of its arms. Now there is a monument dedicated to Our Lady of Mercy on top of Santo Cerro and a piece of the cross is on show.

The East Coast Leaving Santo Domingo, you come to some of the most built-up tourist areas in the country. If you are visiting this south-east stretch of coastline, it is worth making it a weekday visit, as hordes of people flock to these towns from the city at weekends. The further from the capital the less congested it becomes.

The international airport is along this coast. Next door to Las Americas airport is *La Caleta Park and Museum*. This free museum has a collection of pre-Hispanic ceramics on the location of an old Indian cemetery.

Boca Chica One of the first stops is at Boca Chica. Just 25km(16ml.) east of Santo Domingo, it is within easy reach of the weekenders who regularly crowd this area. The town is on the edge of a shallow lagoon, making it a safe place for families. The beach quickly becomes crowded with sunbathers, hawkers and fishermen. The village was originally a fishing port and the locals still sell their fresh catches on the beach immediately after landing their boats. A roving market has also developed with craftsmen wandering along the beach offering their wares.

Hotels A new hotels is being developed in town. Millions of pounds are being spent on the 220-bedroom *Hamaca Beach Resort* which will replace the derelict Hamaca Hotel built in Trujillo's reign but then neglected. The *Don Juan Aparthotel* (Tel: 523 4511) has apartments on the beach and costs around US$75.

There are two tiny islands just offshore. You can actually wade through the lagoon to *La Matica* but you will have to resort to a boat or swim to its neighbouring island, *Los Pinos*. People make their way to the islands to sit and watch the sunsets. After sunset the beach life continues as people come out to parade, listen to the merengue music or just to watch everyone else.

Continue eastwards to the equally popular beaches of Guayacanes and Embassy. The next one along is Juan Dolio-Guayacanes, which is about to be transformed into a large resort. Hotels are springing up, including a new 276-bedroom *Sheraton*. Hotels that have been in existence on this coastline for some time include the *Playa Real* (Tel: 529 8471), costing around US$50 and the *Decameron Hotel* (Tel: 685 0151), which costs around US$150 for all-inclusive facilities.

Sugar-cane is the major crop in the area and contributed to much of the wealth of the region. Towns were developed to process the cane, and old mills are everywhere. While sugar is still important, other factors have contributed to the growth of some towns.

San Pedro de Macoris has become famous for its university. The Universidad Central del Este attracts students from across the world to its medical and dental schools. The student population gives the town a young feel, which is enhanced by its baseball-mad residents. The town's boast is that it has turned out more major league baseball players than any other town in the world. Several of the major American clubs keep baseball camps in the town. The baseball season, from October to January, is a busy time in town and, if you want to watch a match, see the local team Estrellas Orientales at the *Tetelo Vargas Stadium*.

The Church of St Peter faces the Macoris River and is close to the town's main bus terminal. One of the best times to visit the town is at the end of June. The 29th is the town's patron saints' day: St Peter and Paul. Workers for the sugar-cane plantations were imported from other Caribbean islands and have brought their influence to the festivities. The dancers are known as *Guloyas* and have produced their own sounds. Its origins apparently came from the English mummers drama and the dance is split into three types. On Saints' day the dancers parade in all the different costumes sending the crowds wild with their music.

La Romana San Pedro de Macoris is just along the coast from the Dominican Republic's oldest resort area of La Romana. There are direct flights into the resort twice a week from Puerto Rico. Again, it was built up because of the sugar-cane and was one of the country's major ports. The *Batey Central sugar mill* is worth a visit and, for art enthusiasts, the *Altos de Chavon* should be visited. This is a replica of a fifteenth-century Italian village that is home to 100 local artists. There is also a small church, a Taino Indian museum, bars, restaurants and shops. The 5000-seater amphitheatre was opened by Frank Sinatra and is still used for major concerts. The whole village is set on a hilltop above La Romana and a regular, free bus service runs from the Casa de Campo resort area to the village.

Casa de Campo resort covers 7,000 acres and includes hotels and villas. There are three golf-courses, one on the coast and the others inland, designed by Pete Dye. There are four polo fields which have international tournaments, thirteen tennis courts, horse-riding, and watersports on Minitas Beach. There is also a shooting range. The resort has eight restaurants as well as numerous bars lining its three beaches. Prices for accommodation at the resort vary from US$95 up to US$600 in the high season (Tel: 523 3333). There is a small island offshore called Catalina which can be reached for day trips by boat.

Higuey Heading eastwards the next major town is Higuey which has great religious significance for the Dominicans. The town is about 12km(7ml.) inland and was founded in 1494 by Juan de Esquival who later moved to Jamaica. Then Juan Ponce de León led the settlers from 1502 to 1508 before he moved on to colonize Puerto Rico. He lived at a castle in San Rafael del Yuma, close to Boca de Yuma where there is an annual fishing tournament.

Back in Higuey, there is the modern *Basilica de Nuestra Senora de la Altagracia* to which people make a pilgrimage every 21 January. The old sixteenth-century church still stands alongside, and people visit the churches in search of cures for both physical and spiritual ailments. Our Lady of Altagracia is the patron saint of the whole country.

Punta Cana East of Higuey, on the coast, is the resort of Punta Cana which has recently undergone some major development, including the construction of a Robert Trent Jones designed championship golf-course and a marina. Like Casa de Campo, the resort covers a large area, including long stretches of beach. Sports are well catered for, from scuba diving to horse-riding. The emphasis is on privacy, although the resort contains several major hotels.

Hotels The *Bavarao Beach Hotel* (Tel: 682 2161) is where many of the charter packages send their clients and costs around US$60. There is also a *Club Med* complex which caters mainly for French tourists. These hotels are for guests only but visitors can buy a day ticket to use the facilities. For those seeking true privacy, try the *Punta Cana Yacht Club* (Tel: 541 2714) which is just to the south of Punta Cana and costs anything from US$95 to US$190, including some meals.

The Samana Peninsula Travelling around the east coast on your own does require some knowledge of Spanish because relatively few people travel along this stretch of coastline. At the moment there are no roads connecting the Punta Cana region with the major eastern town of Samana. To reach this town you need to travel out from the north coast. You can make the crossing by boat.

The peninsula was first seen by Christopher Columbus, who tried to land there in 1492 but was kept back by the fierce fighting Indians who lived in the region. Columbus named the area Golfo de las Flechas – the Gulf of Arrows. It was the first recorded battle between Europeans and the Indians. It was over 250 years before Santa Barbara de Samana was founded in 1756 by the then Spanish governor of the island, Francissco Rubio Peñaranda, but none of the original buildings survives.

Like much of the Caribbean, the peninsula became a haunt for pirates but by the eighteenth-century it was home to former slaves who travelled to the area from the United States, resulting in many English-speaking people still living there today. A hundred years later, in 1870, the islanders tried to sell off the peninsula to the USA for use as a strategic naval base but Congress turned down the offer.

Samana town is very modern and full of noise and bustle. The area is dominated by its coast: humpback whales come to this coast every year to mate, and to the south of the southern bay is *Los Haitias National Park*. Unreachable except by boat, this is an area of caves, complete with Indian drawings. Also reached by boat are the small cays just offshore from Samana in the southern bay. Cayo Levantado is a popular picnic spot with nice beaches.

The best hotel to stay in Samana is the former Bahia Beach Hotel which used to have cabins out on Cayo Levantado. It is now called the *Cayacoa* (Tel: 687 5307) and is perched on a hill overlooking the bay. It costs around US$80 per night.

At the western end of the peninsula is the small town of Sanchez where you can head north to the amazing beaches of Las Terrenas and El Portillo. The beaches stretch for over 30km(19ml.) and have been used in films because they are so deserted. There is one hotel in their region, the *El Portilla Beach Club* (Tel: 688 5715), which costs around US$130, including meals, and has small cabins on the beach.

Further Information - Sports

Baseball One of the most popular sports in the country, with five professional stadiums across the country. The season is from October to January and the country is very proud of having produced nearly 300 players for the major American leagues from one town alone, San Pedrol de Macoris. This is the undisputed capital of baseball and several of the American clubs, including the Los Angeles Dodgers, have training camps there. Local clubs are very competitive and any town with a stadium will have regular matches.

Basketball Another popular sport but only played at amateur level. The main practice area is the Olympic Centre in Santo Domingo.

Cockfighting The arenas are known as Galleras and are found in all the rural communities and in many of the larger towns and cities. Fights are held virtually every Sunday and are enthusiastically supported by the locals.

Diving Scuba diving is popular at the resorts, with plenty of opportunities to explore the many coral reefs around the island. Many tour companies offer scuba diving or snorkelling tours around the reef areas off beaches like Sosua or Playa Dorado. *Actividades Acuaticas* will give you local details. Santo Domingo, Tel: 688 5838, Puerto Plata, Tel: 586 3988, ext. 7479.

Fishing Deep-sea fishing is organized at the major resort hotels. Ask front desks for local information. An annual sports fishing contest is held at Boca de Yuma for blue marlin, dorado and bonito. Samana Bay is one of the best-known fishing spots, and local boats will take charters for the day. They will also organize tours to see the humpback whales which come into these waters to mate. The *Actividades Acuaticas* offices have further information. Santo Domingo, Tel: 688 5838, Puerto Plata, Tel: 586 3988 ext. 7479.

Golf Most of the courses are in the major resorts as well as at the *Santo Domingo Country Club* (Tel: 532 9521). There is a Robert Trent Jones designed 18-hole course at Playa Dorado, Puerto Plata. Pete Dye has designed the three 18-hole championship courses at Casa de Campo in La Romana. Punta Cana has another Robert Trent Jones designed 18-hole course, while at Costa Azul on the north coast a 9-hole course is under construction.

Greyhound Racing Races every Wednesday to Sunday starting at 7 p.m., La Yuca race track, Santo Domingo (Tel: 565 8333).

Hiking Most walking is done in the mountainous area of the Constanza Valley where the temperatures are cooler. There are also trails in some of the National Parks. (Call their office in Santo Domingo on Tel: 685 1316.)

Horse-Riding There are stables at many of the major resorts, such as Playa Dorado at Puerto Plata, Casa de Campo at La Romana, and Bavaro Beach at Punta Cana. But many of the horses do not look too fit and healthy, obviously needing a good meal rather than a hot and dusty trek. For good-quality horses, there is a polo ground at Casa de Campo with five playing fields. This ground attracts international competitions.

Sailing and Windsurfing The beach hotels nearly all have small boats for hire, often free to guests. Winds on the north coast tend to pick up in the afternoons, and often sailing, windsurfing and parasailing can only be done before lunch. Beaches such as Cabarete and Goleta are most popular for windsurfers and an increasing number of competitions are being held on this stretch of coast. There are numerous hire shops and sailing schools in the villages.

Tennis Most hotels have tennis courts, including those hotels in the mountain regions. Public courts are at the *Olympic Stadium* in Santo Domingo and there are numerous tennis clubs within the city, including at the *Santo Domingo Country Club* (Tel: 532 9521).

Water Sports Water-skiing, jet skis and glass-bottom boat rides are available in many of the major resorts but can be quite expensive because of the difficulties in obtaining spare parts. Facilities are often cheaper or free to hotel guests. Most inland and coastal hotels have swimming-pools and many of the hotels organize games and competitions for both adults and children.

Children There are few places of interest designed specifically for children but most of the large hotels have organized sports and games. They also have baby-sitting services.

There is a *zoo* in Santo Domingo covering 10 square kilometres (6sq.ml.). Open daily until 5 p.m., it has a train to carry visitors around the site and through the African Plain where the animals are free to roam. The *Paseo de los Indios* park is 8km(5ml.) long and full of caves to explore, along with play areas for children. It also has picnic areas and restaurants close by.

Los Tres Ojos is an area of three underground lakes, one only reached by boat across the second lake. Guides will dive into the seemingly shallow waters to thrill the tourists. The Three Eyes Park is on Avenida Las Americas towards the international airport heading out of Santo Domingo.

Many of the country's beaches are protected by coral reefs and are shallow and safe for children. *Sosua* is particularly good, although it can get crowded. Along the south coast, *Boca Chica* is a well-known family resort and there are plenty of safe beaches along this stretch.

Flora and Fauna The Dominican Republic has lost much of its native woodlands to agricultural lands but there are five national parks in which some of the natural habitat has been saved. There were fears that all the native forest would disappear but the Government hopes that the national parks will prevent this from happening.

Orchids abound on Hispaniola and over 300 varieties have been identified; one of the most common is the lilac-coloured May Flower found along the coastline. Before you can take any orchid out of the country, you have to get a certificate from the National Botanical Garden in Santo Domingo proving there is no danger of extinction. The country's national flower is the brightly coloured hibiscus which is found all over the island, along with the bougainvillaea.

Among the trees common on the island is the Traveller's Palm, named because no matter where it grows, its leaves point north, south, east and west. The Traveller's Palm is one of 25 varieties endemic on the island. The wood of the native mahogany trees is used for export and another common tree is the silk cotton tree.

Los Cabritos Island The smallest of the National Parks is Los Cabritos island in the middle of Lake Enriquillo which is about 30m(98ft.) below sea level. With its unusual location is has developed its own eco-system of plants, and over 100 have been identified on this one island alone. It is also the nesting ground of the American crocodiles which live in the lake. This is the largest colony of these crocodiles in the world and they use the island for breeding. You need the permission of the National Parks office to visit the island, which is also home to an endemic species of iguana.

Hispaniola is a safe haven for many birds where 62 species have been identified. Of these, 45 are native to the island. Among the birds to be found in the country is the national bird, La Cotica. This particular breed of parrot is one of the most talkative and among the quickest to mimic the human language. Humming-birds are also common, while the white-headed dove is nearing extinction.

Los Haitises National Park There are colonies of turtles living in the protected area south of Samana Bay at Los Haitises National Park. The jutias is an endemic rodent, which is now considered an endangered species.

Humpbacked whales migrate annually to just off the Samana coast from the Arctic to give birth to their young. You can hire boats from Samana to go out and see the annual migration.

There is a botanical garden in Santo Domingo along with the national zoo. The *Museum of Natural History* in Santo Domingo has full details of the flora and fauna on the island. The *National Parks Office* is in Santo Domingo (Tel: 685 1316).

Essential Addresses
Medical

All the *emergency services* are on Tel: 711.
Air ambulance. Tel: 533 0593.
Blood Bank. Tel: 689 7337.
Hospitals: Clinic Abreu, Santo Domingo. Tel: 686 8784.
Clinic Gomez Patino, Santo Domingo. Tel: 685 9131.
Centro Medico, Puerto Plata. Tel: 586 2342.
Hospital Ricardo Limardo, Puerta Plata. Tel: 586 2210.
Hospital Dr Simon Striddles, Azua. Tel: 521 3283.
Hospital Nuestra Señora de Regla, Bani. Tel: 522 3207.
Hospital Jaime Sanchez, Barahona. Tel: 524 2441.
Hospital Nuestra Señora de la Altagracia, Higuey. Tel: 554 2386.
Hospital Central Romana, La Romana. Tel: 687 7787.
Hospital Dr Morillo King, La Vega. Tel: 573 2442.
Centro Medico Moratin, Samana. Tel: 538 2233.
University Hospital, San Pedro de Macoris. Tel: 529 6111.
Hospital José ma Cabral y Beaz, Santiago. Tel: 583 4311.

Take your holiday invoice and your passport to help with insurance claim paperwork.

Information

The British Embassy, Saint George School, Avenida Abraham Lincoln, Santo Domingo. Tel: 562 5262/5010.

The Ministry of Tourism, Avenida George Washington, Santo Domingo. Tel: 682 8181.

Tourist Information Offices: The international airport, Las Americas, Santo Domingo. Tel: 542 0120;

Boca Chica, Avenida 27 de Febrero; Jimmani, Palacio del Ayuntamiento;

Puerto Plata, Malecon 20. Tel: 586 3676; Samana, Malecon, 2. Tel: 538 2350;

Santiago, Palacio del Ayuntamiento. Tel: 582 5885.

International Offices are at Madrid, Nuñez de Balboa, 37, 4 to Izquierda, Madrid 1, España. Tel: 431 5354;

USA, 485 Madison Avenue 2da Planta, New York NY 10022. Tel: 826 0750;

2355 Salzedo Street, Coral Gables, Florida 33134. Tel: 444 4592/93.

For further information you can call toll-free from the USA on 800 752 1151.

Language The Spanish spoken in the Dominican Republic is flavoured with Taino words and reflects its Indian heritage.

Gua gua	Bus or coach
Hamaca	Hammock
Huracan	Hurricane
Huespedes	Guest
Mercado	Market
Merengue	Music and dance influenced by Sevillanas and West African tribal dances.
Pare	Road sign for pause
Publicos	Taxis
Rotundas	Roundabout.
Telefrico	Cable-car

Opposite
Music is an important part of the Caribbean way of life

Part Three: **Haiti**

**Bougainvillaea grows
everywhere in the Caribbean,
adding a mass of colour to the
scenery**

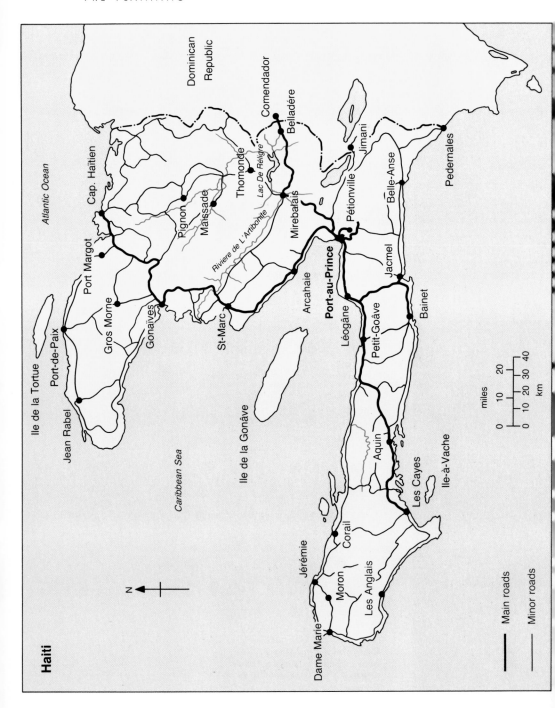

Haiti

Main roads
Minor roads

Haiti is known the world over for two things: voodoo magic and constant upheaval. The western part of Hispaniola, Haiti has been through wars ever since it was first split from the Dominican Republic. It occupies roughly a third of the island but contains about the same population as the Dominican Republic.

It is not a common holiday destination because of the political traumas, although some areas are visited by cruise ships and there are some holiday resorts. The instability does create a few problems. The general population is wary and extremely poor. Many sugar-cane cutters earn just one dollar a day and often travel into the Dominican Republic for the harvest to earn better money. There they live in extremely bad conditions but even those are better than many experience at home.

Haiti is extremely mountainous, making much development difficult and there are still numerous subsistence farmers eking out a living from a tiny patch of land. Coffee is the main export crop while products like maize, bananas, tobacco and cotton are for domestic consumption. About 80 per cent of the land is mountains and the land arcs around the Gulf of Gonave in two pincer-like shapes. The island of Gonave is just offshore.

With three mountain ranges, Haiti is one of the most mountainous countries in the region. It also used to be virtually covered by forest but this is disappearing rapidly as people cut it down indiscriminately for fuel and housing.

Pre-Planning – How to Get There

Flights You have to fly via the United States to get there, or via one of the other Caribbean islands. Air France, Eastern, American and ALM fly from the USA, while you can fly with BIWA from many other Caribbean islands either direct or via Puerto

Rico. Pan Am flies between Port-au-Prince and Santo Domingo in the Dominican Republic four times a week. Keep a close check on your flight bookings as there is sometimes confusion over bookings and you might end up missing your flight.

You cannot cross the land border between the two sides of Hispaniola with a hired car, and tour operators in the Dominican Republic have cancelled day trips across the border because of the recent unrest in Haiti.

The British Government has warned all potential travellers against going to Haiti. The warning was issued in March 1990 and was still in place at the time of writing. A Foreign Office spokesman said that the warning was in force following the unrest and the appointment of Ms Pascal-Trouillet as interim president. He advised potential travellers to check with the Foreign Office before considering any travel.

When to Go Like the rest of the Caribbean, the winter months of December to April are the most popular because the temperature is slightly lower and there is less rain so less humidity. As you travel higher up the mountains the temperatures drop and more rain falls.

Passports A British passport holder does not need a visa to go to Haiti but you need a valid passport and a return ticket. It is a good idea to keep your passport with you when travelling around the country in case you meet any road blocks. US and Canadian citizens do not need a passport but just some form of identification. You have to pay a US$15 departure tax.

Health It is a good idea to have good health insurance cover. There are hospitals and chemists in all the major centres but you have to pay quite high prices. Check with your doctor before you travel but you should not need any injections. A typhoid injection might be recommended, however. Do not drink the tap water and make sure you take tablets to protect yourself against malaria. AIDS is rife in Haiti and there is a general warning against casual sex.

Getting about

Car Rental You can hire cars in Port-au-Prince, either in town or at the airport, but it is quite expensive. Petrol is really only available in the main towns so make sure the tank is full before setting off on any trips. Driving around the capital is a haphazard affair. It is busy and there seem to be few traffic rules.

A British driving licence or any foreign licence is valid for three months in Haiti.

Taxis Taxi drivers are virtually the first people you will meet. At the airport they crowd around visitors offering to 'guide' them through airport formalities before getting a taxi. You can either take a *publico* which travels on a set route or pick a chauffeur-guide whose vehicle you can hire by the hour, day or for a tour.

Accommodation Hotels are mostly limited to the capital and the smarter suburb of Petionville or in the northern town of Cap Haitien. Tour operators in the UK do not use any Haitian properties, and Club Med, who used to have a property near the Point of Montrouis, have closed it (at the time of writing) because of the latest unrest.

Money The Haitian currency is the gourde which has a fixed rate against the US dollar. The rate is 5 gourde to US$1. Both currencies are accepted but other currencies can not be used.

Banks The banks will accept sterling but the exchange rate varies from bank to bank and you will be charged commission for any exchanges other than from the US dollar. Banks are generally open from 9 a.m. to 1 p.m., Monday to Friday.

Tipping Credit cards are widely accepted. The hotels will add a 10 per cent service charge and a 5 per cent government tax to all bills. You are expected to tip constantly, although they welcome cigarettes or sweets instead of money. Taxi drivers are not tipped.

Safety Haiti is not known for its safety but most of the unrest is internal and visitors are generally left alone. If there is any political upheaval it is advisable to stay in your hotel after dark and ask before venturing too far during the day. Pick-pocketing is rife in Port-au-Prince so keep valuables out of sight and safe. Money belts are a good idea and do not leave anything on view in parked cars.

Food With the country's French influence, there are some excellent restaurants. Many places have closed because of the unrest but there is still a good selection specializing in locally produced foods and seafood.

The food is a mix of French and Caribbean. Some of the Creole dishes worth trying include:

Griot.   Spicy pieces of deep-fried pork.
Lambi.   Conch seafood dishes.
Riz au djon djon.   Rice with black mushrooms.

Many restaurants serve excellent seafood, and lobster is the highlight of many menus. The local rum is Babancourt and the local beer is Prestige. The bakeries also have a French flavour and the many pastries are extremely tempting.

Shopping Haiti has some excellent markets. Produce is very cheap by British standards and can be bartered for. Haitian art is everywhere and you can pick up quite large pictures for just a few pounds. The Iron Market, or *Marché de Fer*, has become more tourist-orientated in the past few years but is still worth a visit to bargain hunt. Arts and crafts abound. The colourful paintings are the most common but other items include baskets, pottery and wood carvings.

There are many souvenir shops in Port–au–Prince but these are expensive. In general, shops are open from 7 a.m. to 4 p.m. Hours do vary in the busy winter season.

Local Colour

The People The vast majority of residents are black and are descended from former slaves. About 20 per cent are mulattos and have generally been the group to hold power within the country. There are a few whites, known as *blancs*, and visitors will also be called *blancs*. This is not necessarily a racist term although sometimes it can sound like it as you get hassled by street vendors.

Haiti is known world-wide for its voodoo traditions which came across to the Caribbean with the slaves from West Africa. Voodoo is still a powerful force in the country and was recently used by the Duvalier family to control the population. The resort hotels do have voodoo shows for guests but you are unlikely to experience the real thing unless you have good local contacts. Christianity exists side by side with the voodoo culture, influenced by the Catholic French colonists.

Like many Catholic countries, it is not a good idea to wear swimming costumes anywhere other than on the beaches. Women wearing skirts above the knee will attract a lot of attention and men are expected to wear shirts in the evening, not necessarily with a tie or jacket.

The Country Like its close neighbour, the Dominican Republic, Haiti has had a turbulent history. But, unlike its neighbour, it has often been the aggressor and frequently tries cross-border incursions. In the past, these have happened

132

whenever the country is relatively settled. But Haiti does not have a record of many settled times.

The most recent upset was the turning out of military leader General Prosper Avril and the appointment of a temporary president – for the first time a woman has been selected. Ertha Pascal-Trouillet was a member of the Supreme Court and was selected after the country rebelled against the army for breaking a promise of democratic elections at the beginning of 1990. Elections should have been held as soon as possible

Haiti's history started with the arrival of Christopher Columbus in 1492. He left a few settlers, including his brother Bartolmé, to build a new colony on the island. But they soon abandoned the north-coast site, which is now part of Haiti, and moved to set up the Dominican Republic capital of Santo Domingo. The whole island remained in Spanish control for many years and was used as a base for many expeditions into South America and other Caribbean islands.

The French and English both had their eye on the island because of its importance as a staging post between South America with its goldfields, and Europe. The English, under the leadership of Sir Francis Drake, gained control of Santo Domingo for a few days but it was the French who really gained a foothold on Hispaniola.

The French sprung an attack on the Spanish and gained control of the western portion of the island. The conquest was ratified under the Treaty of Ryswick of 1697. Haiti then went through an extremely prosperous period based on its sugar-cane plantations. But these were only successful because of the use of slaves imported from West Africa. After the French Revolution, the plantation owners lived in a state of unease, fearing a similar rebellion on the island. The French Government ruled that all those with a white parent should be allowed to vote. This sparked troubles between the white community and the growing mulatto community. While this was being sorted out, the slaves seized the opportunity to stage their rebellion, led by Francoise-Dominique Toussaint. Thousands of whites were killed and there followed years of fighting.

The English also saw an opportunity and invaded. They remained for four years before withdrawing, leaving Toussaint firmly in control. He then turned on the mulattos, killing many thousands. Toussaint led a raiding army into the Dominican Republic and captured Santo Domingo before the French Government intervened and imprisoned Toussaint, where he died.

The French intervention sparked off another slave rebellion, this time led by Dessalines who declared himself Emperor in 1804. Two years later he died, leaving the country in total disarray. His main achievement had been to name the country Haiti. For many years the country was split between black and mulatto rulers. It was in this period that the plantations were split up and small parcels of land given to peasants, ending the economic strength of the country.

This unhappy state of affairs lasted into the twentieth-century when the United States decided to intervene, having plans for the island because of its strategic location. The Americans invested heavily in building up an infrastructure for the country but were not welcome and were constantly attacked by the Haitians. The Americans withdrew in 1934. The mulattos continued to control the country until 1957 and the arrival of 'Papa Doc' Duvalier. A black nationalist, he kept control with the use of the Tontons Macoutes – a network of secret police who became synonymous with torture and terror throughout the world.

Hundreds of thousands of Haitians were killed during his rule and the upper class mulattos were crushed. No one knew who the informers were and everyone lived in an atmosphere of mistrust and despair. By the time that 'Baby Doc' Duvalier inherited the title President-for-Life from his father in 1971, the mulattos were gathering their strength and began to regain power with the marriage of one of them to Duvalier. Unrest around the country started a swell of discontent that ended in the unexpected fleeing of Duvalier to Europe in 1986 – but not before his police killed hundreds more. After he fled, the Tontons Macoutes were left to face the wrath of the people. Many of them were killed by mobs in revenge attacks.

Since then, the country has been ruled by the army, helped by civilians. Elections have been planned and then cancelled because of violence, and the people are still waiting for a new chance of democracy. The secret police are still active, and financial aid from the USA and France was cut in 1990 because of the army's poor record of human rights. This financial cut and the killing of a schoolgirl by the army provoked the latest uprising. Now everyone is waiting to see if the civilians can form a government and to see whether the army will truly relinquish control.

Since the days of the French sugar-cane plantations, the country's economy has gone downhill and it is now the poorest country in the Caribbean. There is mass unemployment, and, although many men travel into the Dominican Republic to harvest sugar-cane, those who do work earn a pittance of a wage. The country has received millions of dollars in foreign aid but it appears to have made little difference to the majority of Haitians.

Most people live in the country, despite the fact that 80 per cent of it is classified as mountain, and survive on subsistence farming. The destruction of the forests has caused problems of erosion and the land is deteriorating rapidly. The major export is coffee. The cooler climate in the mountains allows farmers to grow a range of crops but most are for home consumption with some being sold locally. The village markets vary enormously across the country because of the climatic conditions.

Tourism had been providing an amount of hard currency for the Government. This mostly came from Americans but the past few years of unrest has unsettled that market. Many of the hotels have closed, cruise ships which used to dock at Cap Haitien have stopped arriving and the numbers of tour operators using Haiti have dropped.

With its French background, it has never been a large tourist market for the UK. The Foreign Office in London issued a warning last year (March 1990) advising British travellers not to go to Haiti unless the travel is essential. The American Government and several other European Governments have issued similar warnings and this is likely to affect the tourism market in Haiti for some time to come. It is difficult to get up-to-date information in Britain and visitors really need to have some personal contacts on the island to make sure of hotel bookings.

The geography of the country has contributed much to its economic plight. The forest cover on the three mountain ranges has all but disappeared, giving much of the country a denuded look, with erosion on the open farmland. The mountains are among the highest in the Caribbean. The Massif de la Hotte on the southern peninsula has several peaks over 2,000m (6,560ft.), as does the neighbouring Massif de la Selle. To the north of these mountains there is a dramatic drop down to the lakes. Lake Enriquillo is just over the border in the Dominican Republic but is 30m(98ft.) below sea level. There are more mountains to the north, including the Massif des Montagnes Noires and a number of smaller ranges along the north coast.

Events Calendar Haiti used to have an annual carnival on Ash Wednesday. They do not have the money for exotic floats and huge parties but the atmosphere is usually lively, with everyone in good spirits. Over Easter, the acrobats take over with parades along the streets, showing off their athletic feats. Independence Day is celebrated on 1 and 2 January.

Port-au-Prince The first thing to strike a visitor to Port-au-Prince are the ramshackle gingerbread houses which seem to be propping each other up in every street. These quaint old houses are everywhere and give the city a picturesque quality despite the extreme poverty. The city is extremely dirty, particularly around the waterfront and dock areas.

Marché de Fer The old town is centred around the busy port. One of its most famous landmarks is the Marché de Fer, or Iron Market, which has become the tourist centre for cheap art and crafts. The true Haitian artists sell their paintings for thousands of dollars in the city's many art galleries but the market contains hundreds of cheaper versions that still evoke the colourful masters. It is also home to many other craftsmen selling baskets, pottery, jewellery and trinkets. You can barter the prices down but the traders are used to tourists and it can be hard work. The narrow, crowded market can also be a bit intimidating in times of unrest so it is worth checking with friends or at the hotel before venturing down there. And, while there watch out for pick-pockets.

Museums If you want to see some of the better art, a good place to go is the Musée d'Art Haitien, or Le Centre d'Art, just off Rue Capois on Rue 22 Septembre. Open from 9 a.m. to 5 p.m., Monday to Friday, and from 9 a.m. to 1 p.m. on Saturday, it has exhibitions, a shop and café (Tel: 2 2018). Another museum worth visiting is the Musé de Pantheon National (Tel: 5 5647). This is the former presidential palace on the Place des Heros de l'Independence. It contains many artifacts from Haiti's past, including paintings, historical documents and the anchor from

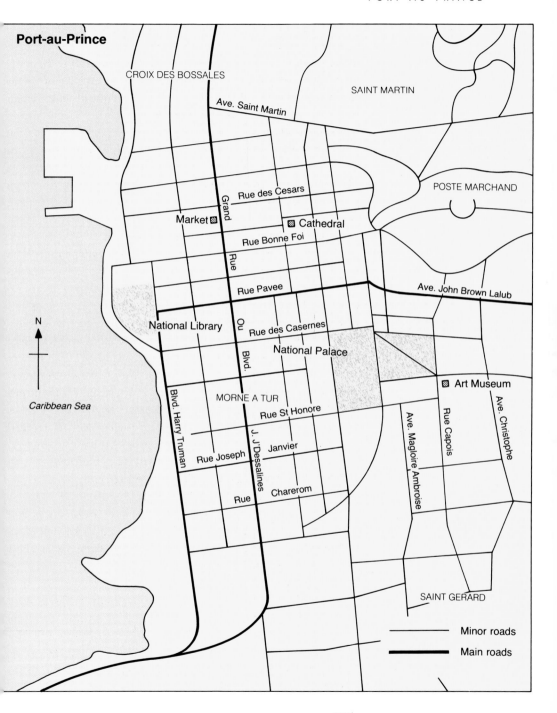

Port-au-Prince

CROIX DES BOSSALES

SAINT MARTIN

Ave. Saint Martin

POSTE MARCHAND

Rue des Cesars

Market ▣

Grand

▣ Cathedral

Rue Bonne Foi

Rue

Rue Pavee

Ave. John Brown Lalub

N

National Library

Ou

Rue des Casernes

National Palace

Blvd.

▣ Art Museum

Caribbean Sea

MORNE A TUR

Rue St Honore

Blvd. Harry Truman

J. J'Dessalines

Janvier

Ave. Magloire Ambroise

Rue Capois

Ave. Christophe

Rue Joseph

Rue

Charerom

SAINT GERARD

——— Minor roads

━━━ Main roads

Christopher Columbus's ship *Santa Maria*. The museum is open 8.30 a.m. to midday, Monday to Friday.

Cathedrals The city has two Cathedrals. The most interesting of these is the Protestant Episcopal Cathedral of Sainte-Trinité, which dates from the eighteenth-century and contains biblical murals painted in the Haitian style. The Catholic Cathedral is close by on Rue Bonne Foi.

The National Library is also in the old town centre on Boulevard J.J. Dessalines just to the south of the Iron Market.

Hotels Probably the most famous hotel in Haiti is the *Grand Hotel Oloffson* (Tel: 3-4000), forever remembered from Graham Greene's novel *The Comedians*. The gingerbread hotel has closed in the past because of the unrest but, if open, it is not only a good place to stay but a must to visit the mahogany bar and meet some of Haiti's most interesting residents.

It is difficult to recommend hotels and restaurants because of the unrest and the daily changing situation. The best thing to do is to check with the Haiti Tourism Office on Avenue Marie Jeanne (Tel: 2 1729). There is also a helpful Tourist Office at the airport.

Surrounding Area Petionville is 10km(6ml.) from the city centre and is considered to be one of Port-au-Prince's suburbs. Many of the wealthier have homes here where the cooler breezes blow across the mountainside. The Baptist church is in the centre of town and is a short distance from Fort Jacques with its excellent views across the Port-au-Prince harbour. A further 5km(3ml.) from Petionville is the Jane Barbancourt Castle. Barbancourt is the best known of the Haitian rums and is distilled here. You can take tours of the distillery, try samples and buy a bottle.

Continuing up into the mountains, you will come to Kenscoff. This is another town where the rich have their holiday homes and it is best known for its market. The most interesting day to visit is on Tuesdays when the market is at its busiest.

Back to the coast, Haiti is not renowned for its beaches, many of them have dull grey sand and some have black volcanic sand. But some are much nicer than others and there are also interesting reefs. One of these is just a few kilometres out into the bay from Port-au-Prince, at Sandy Cay, which locals claim is one of the best sites in the world. You can take boat trips out there, have a picnic and admire the reef.

Ibo Beach is to the north of Port-au-Prince on the mainland and is often crowded. The problem with Haitian beaches is that, although you have to pay a dollar or two to use them, no one bothers to clear up and they can get very dirty. Another well-known beach is at Jacmel to the south of Port-au-Prince. Congo Beach has black sand and is free of charge, but again is dirty. The town of Jacmel is full of old buildings which were being restored before the latest uprising.

Cap Haitien This northern town used to be one of the wealthiest in the whole Caribbean. Originally called Cap Francias, today it is know locally as Le Cap. Many of the old French colonial-style homes disappeared in the earthquake of 1842 but there is still a colonial ambience to the town and still quaint old streets to wander down.

More recently, it has been used by cruise ships as a stop on their Caribbean tours, but many have stopped since the most recent unrest. There were also several resort hotels in this region. There are several good beaches in this area, including Cormier and Labadie Pointe St Honoré, an area developed for cruise-ship visitors. To get to the best beaches, ask locally and many of the boatmen will row you to secluded coves for a small fee – negotiated first but paid after.

Most people come to Le Cap for just one reason: to see the Citadelle. Famous throughout the region as a madman's folly, it took 200,000 slaves to build it and 20,000 of those died in the attempt. It was a giant monument to Roi Henri Christophe. Originally from the Leeward island of St Kitts, Henri Christophe came to Haiti and declared himself King of the north in 1806. He ruled through fear with the island's first secret police force until his suicide in 1820. All he left behind were the Citadelle and his palace, Sans Souci, but both these are magnificent monuments, however dilapidated.

Sans Souci The first one you come to on leaving Le Cap is Sans Souci in the small, muddy village of Milot. Styled and named after a similar palace in France, Rio Henri Christophe lived in style with marble and cooling fountains filling his palace. Artists were brought from Europe to add elegance to his court. The palace was shaken by the earthquake of 1842 but it is still worth the visit. Admission for both Sans Souci and the Citadelle is US$1.25 and both places close at 5 p.m.

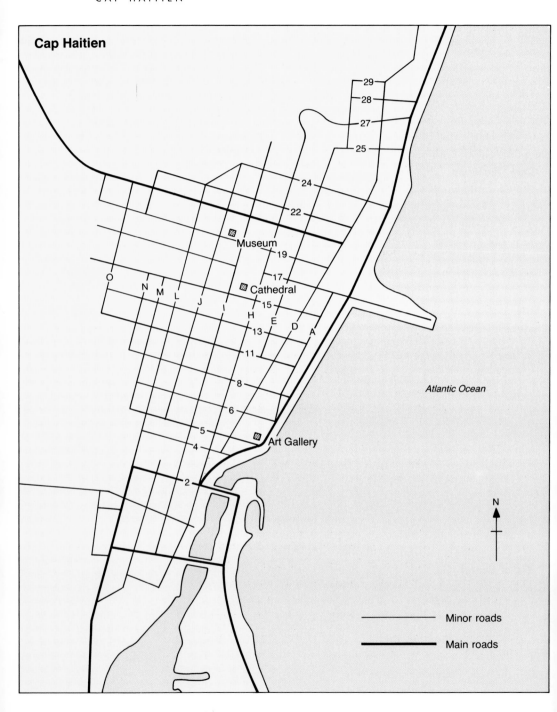

Cap Haitien

The Citadelle Security-conscious Roi Henri needed to feel safe from both the French and the mulatto Petion who ruled southern Haiti and so he ordered the construction of what many feel is the greatest modern monument in the world. Standing high on a mountain top, even now it can only be reached by a combination of four-wheel drive and a donkey ride. The donkeys can only make the climb in dry weather so if it has been raining, wear some good, comfortable shoes and be prepared to climb. Some people prefer to walk anyway rather than trust the donkeys. The climb is really only for the fit and healthy.

Once there, you can marvel at the monstrous fort that could never have been used efficiently to defend Roi Henri's kingdom and which must have been a nightmare to build. Walls several metres thick stretch for kilometres around this impenetrable castle, and the views overlooking the mountains and the coast are worth the climb. It is best to visit both places on days when there are no cruise ships in harbour to avoid getting caught up in the throng of visitors.

Further Information

Essential Addresses If you become ill while in Haiti, ask either your hotel or friends where they recommend going. The best hospitals are in Port-au-Prince, such as *Hospital Français de Haiti*, Rue de Centre. Tel: 2 2323; or *Canapé Vert*, Rue Canapé Vert. Tel: 5 1052.

The *British Consulate* is also in Port-au-Prince where you will be able to get advice if unrest starts up while you are visiting the country. It is at Avenue Marie Jeanne, 21, P.O. Box 1302. Tel: 2 1227.

Haiti does not have many sports facilities and those are mostly in the resort hotels. It is not a country for children to visit; there is little for them to except visit the beaches and it is not safe. Staying with friends is obviously slightly different but is still not recommended by the British Foreign Office. It is not a country to go to find any flora and fauna because the land has been virtually destroyed by the poor farming methods and nowhere except the impossibly remote areas has escaped.

Part Four: **Jamaica**

Negril

Montego Bay, Jamaica, from the Top O'Bay

Jamaica A land of trees and water, beautiful beaches, secluded bays, friendly people and steeped in history, Jamaica has long been a popular romantic holiday destination. First named Xayamaca, meaning Land of Wood and Water, by the Arawak Indians it has been colonized by Europeans since Christopher Columbus first set foot on the north coast of the island in 1494. It is now the largest English-speaking island in the Caribbean and is split up into countries and parishes with familiar names, such as Middlesex, Surrey, Manchester and Kingston.

The island has five main resort areas but there are plenty of other places to explore. With so many contrasts, from beaches to spectacular mountain scenery, most people will find somewhere to suit them within the island. Even those who prefer cool temperatures will enjoy staying in the hills around the very British town of Mandeville, while sun-lovers will head for the coast of Montego Bay or Ocho Rios.

144

Jamaica

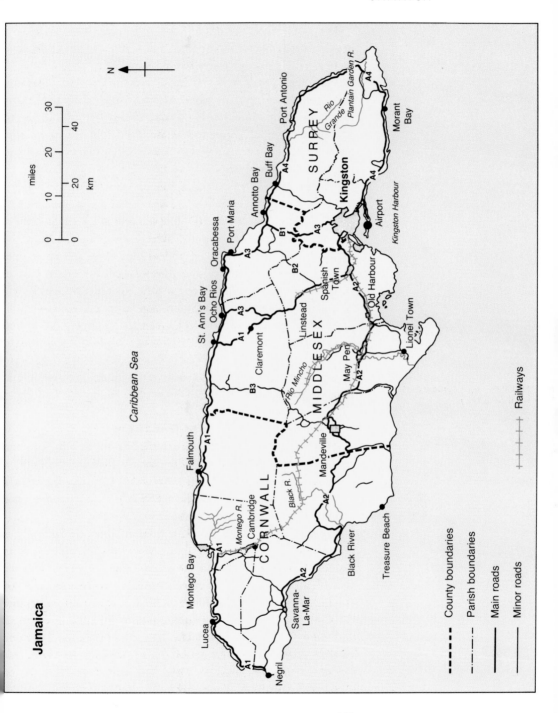

Legend:
- County boundaries
- Parish boundaries
- Main roads
- Minor roads
- Railways

Caribbean Sea

CORNWALL
MIDDLESEX
SURREY

Montego Bay, Lucea, Falmouth, Negril, Cambridge, Savanna-La-Mar, Black River, Treasure Beach, Mandeville, May Pen, Linstead, Claremont, Spanish Town, Old Harbour, Lionel Town, Kingston, Airport, Kingston Harbour, Morant Bay, Port Antonio, Buff Bay, Annotto Bay, Port Maria, Oracabessa, Ocho Rios, St. Ann's Bay

Montego R., Black R., Rio Minho, Rio Grande, Plantain Garden R.

A1, A2, A3, A4, B1, B2, B3

miles / km
0 10 20 30
0 20 40

N

Long-time favourite of the rich and famous, Jamaica has now become affordable for most people, but if you are after exclusivity, there are still plenty of places to hide-away. Most people head for the northern coast, which is lined with resorts, but the south coast, too, has many attractions. A much larger island than many might imagine, Jamaica is 233km(146ml.) long and up to 82km(51ml.) wide. To see the whole island in detail would take many weeks, but even a few days' travelling around can leave you with wonderful memories.

The majority of the island is mountainous, with the highest, the Blue Mountain, reaching 2,258m(7,402ft.). It also has 120 rivers, helping to create a green lushness that is unique to Jamaica among the Caribbean islands. The rivers that run from the mountains to the north coast tend to be shorter and faster than those in the south but all the rivers play an important part in Jamaican life, and visitors, too, will be invited to travel slowly down river on a banana boat or to scramble up waterfalls.

Sports enthusiasts will also enjoy Jamaica. Golf players will find several championship courses to take, while horse-riding is available in most areas, with places like Chukka Cove devoted to the sport. Tennis courts and most water-sports are available at nearly every large hotel. Cricket grounds abound and soccer is also a firm favourite.

Pre-Planning – How to Get There

Flights Jamaica's international airports are at Kingston and Montego Bay. There are flights four times a week from London with Air Jamaica and British Airways. Charter flights are increasing and now operate from Newcastle, Manchester and Stanstead during the summer season.

From the USA flights connect from Atlanta, Baltimore, Los Angeles, New York, Miami, Memphis, Detroit, Fort Lauderdale, Orlando, Philadelphia and Tampa. Airlines from the USA include American Airways, Northwest Airlines and Air Jamaica, Air Canada also flies to Jamaica. Connections around the Caribbean include Cayman Airways or Air Jamaica flights to and from Grand Cayman, BIWA flights from the southern and eastern Caribbean, BIWA or Air Jamaica flights to Haiti, Air Jamaica flights to Curaçao and to San Juan, Cubana flights to Cuba, and Copa to Panama City.

Tour operators from the UK include:

Airtours	Tel: 0706 260000
Airwaves	Tel: 081 780 2552
Alternatives	Tel: 071 589 3400
Caribbean Connection	Tel: 0244 41131
Caribtours	Tel: 071 581 3517
Elegant Resorts	Tel: 0244 329671
Happiness Islands	Tel: 0423 526887
Harlequin Holidays	Tel: 0742 422222
Hayes and Jarvis	Tel: 081 748 0088
Intasun	Tel: 081 290 0511
Interline	Tel: 0707 372886
Jetset Tours	Tel: 071 631 3426
Kuoni	Tel: 0306 740500
New Beginnings	Tel: 0992 447244
Select Holidays	Tel: 0992 554144
Silk Cut Travel	Tel: 0730 68511
Sovereign	Tel: 0293 560777
Speedbird	Tel: 0293 611611
Thomas Cook Faraway	Tel: 0733 330336
Thomson Holidays	Tel: 071 387 1900
Tradewinds	Tel: 071 731 8000
Unijet	Tel: 0444 458611
Virgin Holidays	Tel: 0293 775511

UK villa operators with Jamaican destinations include:

A Place in the Sun	Tel: 071 221 6969
Caribbean Villas	Tel: 0432 263333
Continental Villas	Tel: 071 371 1313
Halsey Villas	Tel: 071 724 1303
JAVA	Tel: 071 486 3560
Meon Villas	Tel: 0730 68411
Palmer & Parker Villas	Tel: 071 493 5725.

When to Go The winter months of December to April are the peak holiday months, and prices tend to go up in mid-December and then drop in May. The winter is cooler but the annual average temperature is 27°C(80°F). For every 300m(1,000ft.) in altitude the temperature drops by 2°C(3.5°F),

147

so that on the peak of the Blue Mountain the average temperature is 19°C(56°F). The annual average rainfall is 200cm(78in.) but distribution varies enormously from the west mountain areas, which get up to 760cm(300in.) a year, and the drier plains on the south coast, which get about 76cm(30in.).

Summer clothing is needed all year round, with a light sweater for cooler winter evenings or for a journey into the mountains. Informal clothes are accepted in most places but some hotels like guests to dress up slightly for the evening and most will only allow guests in bathing costumes around the pool or on the beach. Some beaches have nudist areas and these are always clearly marked.

Passports No visa is required for British Passport holders, but they must travel with a valid passport and return ticket.

Visitors are not allowed to take certain items into the country. These include flowers, plants, honey, fruit, meat and vegetables, black coral and tortoiseshell products. It is also illegal to import or export drugs into the country. The Jamaicans are very strict on this and sniffer dogs check all luggage at the airports. Heavy prison sentences are imposed on those caught.

When you arrive in the country you will be given a customs declaration form and currency form. These must be returned as you leave the country and keep all receipts for foreign exchange as customs might ask to inspect them on departure. Your hotel may ask to keep the forms while you are resident. A departure tax of J$80.00 must be paid in cash as you leave.

Health No vaccinations are required for entry to Jamaica. The water is safe to drink straight from the taps anywhere on the island.

Getting About

Car Rental is generally more expensive than the States and it is a good idea to give the cars a thorough inspection for dents and bumps before taking them out. Most of the international companies, such as Avis, Budget and Hertz, are represented and can be booked in advance. Offices can be found at most airports and in most major towns. There are also plenty of local firms offering slightly cheaper deals. Some companies have a minimum age requirement of 25 when paying by cash, or 21 if paying by credit. A security deposit of J$13,750 can be covered by a credit card imprint. Bills will include a government tax of 10 per cent, while health and accident insurance is optional but advisable.

British driving licences are acceptable as long as the driver is over 21 years old. Driving is on the left.

Driving is on the left and, in the country areas, a good map is a must. Watch out for road signs as they are sometimes turned around and you could find yourself heading into the mountains instead of to the beach. Driving in certain areas of the major cities can be risky. It is best to ask advice at your hotel or in the local Tourist Office rather than rely on people on the street for directions. You may find yourself up a blind alley. But, when in the rural areas, people are very friendly and more than willing to put you on the right road.

Most of the roads are in good condition, but on the smaller road, watch out for pot-holes and approaching vehicles on the wrong side of the road. Travelling does take longer than you would expect and it is better to stick to the main road, particularly over the mountains. Speed limits are 48kph(30mph) in towns and 80kph(50mph) on highways. Some petrol stations are closed on Sundays. Garage opening hours tend to be from 7 a.m. to about 7 p.m.

Bikes and scooters are available for hire in most of the major towns.

Taxis Official taxis always display a red PP number plate and you should not get into any taxi without that red plate. It is a good idea to negotiate the taxi fare before starting the journey. There are set fares between certain points, although haggling may cut the cost. Minibuses double up as buses and as taxis. The minibuses have a set route but can be flagged down at any point along the route. They tend to be overcrowded, the driving can sometimes be dangerous and the street traders (or higglers) tend to be waiting to meet you as you step off the bus. They can sometimes be a nuisance.

Trains These are completely different. A cheap method of travelling across the island, they are recommended as the way to see some of the spectacular scenery without the headache of driving yourself. The journey between Montego Bay and Kingston on 'The Diesel' takes just over six hours and trains leave each end twice daily. Jamaicans will tell you that the journey takes you through some of the best scenery and then, it arrives in Kingston through some of the most interesting parts of

149

Couples Hotel, Jamaica

Trenchtown, home to many Rastafarians. The train also stops at towns *en route*, including Mandeville.

Internal Flights also operate daily between all the country's airports. Trans Jamaican Airways (Tel: 952 5401) fly light aircraft into the small airports at Negril, Ocho Rios, Port Antonio, and Tinson Pen, near Kingston city centre, while the airline also operates flights between the international airports of Donald Sangster Airport in Montego Bay and Norman Manley Airport in Kingston.

Accommodation There is a huge range of accommodation across the island. British operators offer beds in hotels from luxury all-inclusive to simpler packages. Jamaica has a large selection of self-catering accommodation, which is an option many people take when they want to hide away in a secluded spot. Villas, cottages and apartments make up about 40 per cent of the island's tourist facilities; it is one of the best islands in the Caribbean for self-catering.

To help tourists discover exactly what villa accommodation is available, the owers formed an organization known as JAVA, which is recognized by the Government. JAVA has offices in Ocho Rios, Miami and London (Tel: 071 486 3560 or 071 935 8200).

While JAVA offers a wide range of accommodation, the Government has also approved the Inns of Jamaica network. This group of small, mostly owner-managed, hotels are designed to give visitors a real insight to Jamaican life. Residents are treated to home cooking Jamaican style in a hotel with less than 50 rooms, often tucked away in the more secluded parts of the country. Many of the Inns are featured in tour operators' brochures.

All-inclusive resorts are springing up around the country. Many people prefer to stay in one, for security, comfortable accommodation and for value for money. But visitors can miss out on local experiences. There are plenty of excellent restaurants in every resort area. The all-inclusive resorts also provide very good food, plenty of entertainment for their guests, both in the day and in the evening, as well as well-laid-out hotel accommodation.

All accommodation is subject to a Government tax which ranges from US$2 to US$12 daily, according to the type of room and season.

The electricity supply is 110 volts, 50 cycles but some hotels use 220 volts. Most hotels will have adaptors for guests' use upon request.

Money The official currency is the Jamaican dollar. It is illegal to change your money anywhere other than at commercial banks, official bureaux de changes, or at major hotels. Make sure you get a receipt, you will need it to change any money back at the end of your stay and customs might ask for it as you leave. It is also illegal to take any Jamaican dollars in or out of the country.

Some shops show prices in US dollars, so make sure you know which currency you are dealing in before purchasing any goods.

Banks There are nine commercial banks operating, with branches across the island. Opening times are generally 9 a.m. to 2 p.m., Monday to Thursday, and on Fridays from 9 a.m. to 12 p.m. and 2.30 p.m. to 5 p.m.

Major credit cards and travellers cheques are widely accepted. Any credit card transactions will be converted to US dollars and will show up in US dollars on your statement.

151

Tipping is usually between 10 and 15 per cent. Most hotels will add a 12.5 per cent service charge to your bill. No tipping is allowed at all-inclusive resorts. Taxi drivers and tour-bus drivers will be quite open in asking for a tip – something Americans are more used to than the British.

Safety Be careful carrying large sums around with you. If you are walking in downtown areas, a moneybelt is a good idea and do not wear flashy jewellery. Muggers and purse snatchers are dealt with harshly in Jamaican courts but are still on the streets and, like many large cities around the world, it is wiser not to travel in downtown areas on foot after dark. Most hotels have safety deposit boxes, which are free to guests. It is a good idea to use them. There are not too many cases of hotel theft nowadays, perhaps because of the widespread introduction of the boxes.

Walking around the resort areas, you will get approached by higglers trying to sell you everything from ganja to paintings or just asking for money. The Government has introduced a tourism-awareness campaign that starts in junior schools. The idea is to teach young Jamaicans that trying to threaten tourists to force them into buying things will eventually result in no tourists – and no more money. But the process is slow and the easiest thing is to say 'No', keep on walking and act confidently. Jamaica did have a very bad reputation for safety in the 1970s. This has greatly improved and, as long as you are sensible, you are not under any threat at all.

Some of the favourite arguments from higglers include things like claiming to work in your hotel and wanting a bus fare back or pretending they met you yesterday and that you promised to visit their craft stall. Another tack is to accuse you of racism in not stopping to talk to them because they are black or taking advantage of their country and climate and not spending any money there.

This may sound worrying but do not panic. It is easy to walk away, saying 'No' and, as long as you are prepared, will not spoil your holiday in any way. And you may well find that there are people who approach you who are genuine, and meeting them will enhance your holiday. The Government runs a Meet the People programme for just that purpose. People from a similar profession or background are introduced to visitors and then they take them to their homes and show them the local area.

Most restaurants in the Montego Bay area will provide you with a free taxi service to and from your hotel. Book the taxi when you book your table. The only disadvantage of this system is that it discourages people from ambling around the town selecting a restaurant. It is better to do that during the day. Taxi fares around the town can be quite expensive if your hotel or villa is off the beaten track, so the restaurant service can be a benefit.

Food and Wine Some of the more unusual foods that you might come across include.

Ackee and saltfish. Ackee looks a bit like scrambled egg and is often served with fish as a breakfast dish. Ackee is poisonous eaten raw.

Curried goat. Usually served with rice, this strong-tasting meat is often highly spiced.

Jerk Pork. This method of cooking originated on the east of the island and is a cross between smoking and barbecuing. The meat is highly spiced and cooked on pimento wood. Chicken and fish are also cooked in this way. It is sold in many roadside stalls and usually by weight.

Jerk chicken being prepared at Pete's on the beach at Negril

153

Fruit and Vegetables. Plenty of exotic varieties are served in season, including pawpaw (pronounced pa-pie-a), mango, banana, pineapple, melon, sweetsop, soursop, sapodilla, sweet potatoes and yams. Callaloo is the Jamaican version of spinach.

Patties. Again, these are sold in roadside stalls or as a light snack. Spicy meat or fish fills a flaky pastry case and should be tried.

Rice and peas. The peas are actually red beans and are usually served mixed with boiled rice. This is a staple diet for many Jamaicans and is often served in restaurants with meat dishes and a side salad.

Soups are usually thick broths, full of meats and vegetables. Among the traditional Jamaican dishes are pepperpot soup, made mostly of callaloo and very highly spiced, pumpkin soup or red bean soup.

There are numerous restaurants in all resort areas as well as some wonderful places tucked away. Most tastes are catered for, from marvellous international feasts, local Jamaican cuisine to

The rum industry is one of the major exports for many Caribbean islands

American hamburger chains. You do not have to go indoors to find good food as the roadside stalls selling jerk chicken, pork or fish have some mouth-watering morsels. The jerk-cooked food is a cross between barbecued and smoked meat. And, unlike so many places, it is quite safe to eat from these food stalls. The food is fresh, clean and well cooked. Jamaican patties are also a good buy for a snack between meals.

Lobster and steak are the highlights on many of the menus. The local steak can be a bit stringy but you will pay a premium price for American steak. There are no such problems with the lobster and other locally caught fish. It will be fresh, cooked in a variety of ways and much cheaper than in Britain. Local specialities include jerk chicken, pork and fish as well as curried goat, all served up with the traditional rice and peas. Soups are to be recommended, including pepperpot, pumpkin or fish.

Imported wines are expensive but some of the local wine is very reasonable, both in taste and price. Home to dark rum manufacturers, Jamaica has a wide range of rum cocktails, from a

Sunset at Rick's Café. Negril is a must for those staying in western Jamaica

straightforward rum punch to exotic mixes such as Pirates Revenge, Sun Stroke or Blue Mountains Delight, different in every bar. Red Stripe is the local lager and Tia Maria the local coffee liqueur.

Some of the better known restaurants include *Rick's Café* , in Negril (Tel: 957 4335). Open from 12 p.m. to 10 p.m., it is slightly above average in price but is worth it just for the view. People gather regularly at sunset to eat, drink or just to admire the amazing sight as the sun sets over the westerly point of the island. In Montego Bay there are numerous excellent restaurants. *Gloucester House* (Tel: 952 6500) has a balcony restaurant which serves a mix of Jamaican and international foods with excellent seafood. *Julia's*, which is perched on the hills just outside town, offers guests magnificent views of the whole Montego Bay area.

In the quiet resort of Runaway Bay, the choice is more limited, but a good place to try is *Bird-Wind Restaurant* at the Tamarind Tree Resort Hotel which has a wide selection of fish dishes. At Ocho Rios, the *Almond Tree* (Tel: 974 2813) has some of the best food, served in a romantic setting by the sea, but you need to book. *Ruins Restaurant* (Tel: 974 2442) also has a romantic atmosphere, with a waterfall setting. It offers Chinese and international cuisine.

Getting to restaurants in Port Antonio can be half the fun. You need to catch a boat to reach the *Admiralty Club* on Navy Island for breakfast, lunch or dinner. Seafood is the speciality here. Just outside town you can mix with the stars at *Blue Lagoon* at San San. While face-spotting, you can also admire the natural scenery. The reputedly bottomless lagoon is floodlit at night, providing a spectacular backdrop to your meal.

Mandeville may be hidden away in the mountains but it still has some good restaurants to lure you away from the beach. *Pot Pourri* at the Manchester Club provides local Jamaican cuisine served in a style reminiscent of colonial times. Or climb 180m(600ft.) above the town to *Bill Laurie's Steak House* to get a good view and, of course, a good steak. Kingston has plenty of places to try, including *The Lychee Garden* (Tel: 98619), a Chinese restaurant in the New Kingston Shopping Centre, or the *Grog Shoppe* (Tel: 97027), offering Jamaican fare at Devon House.

Shopping With so many self-catering apartments and villas on the island, the local markets and shops are geared to help the tourist out. Market stalls will have a wide range of familiar – and not so familiar – fruit and vegetables. Seasonal fruits include pineapple, bananas, guavas and mangoes, as well as ortanique, which is a cross between an orange and a tangerine. Vegetables include green bananas, plantains, bread-fruit and yams. Ackee is one of the most popular local dishes. This vegetable looks a bit like scrambled eggs once cooked and is usually served with codfish.

As well as a good network of local markets, the towns all have good supermarkets. In Negril, the *Cash and Carry* on Negril Square is open Monday to Saturday, 9 a.m. to 8 p.m., while the *Save-A-Dollar* on Negril Plaza is open Monday to Thursday, 8.30 a.m. to 5.30 p.m., and Friday to Saturday 8.30 a.m. to 6.30 p.m. In Montego Bay, *Parkway Supermarkets* near to the Holiday Inn is open seven days a week, Monday to Saturday from 8.30 a.m. to 8 p.m. and on Sundays from 9 a.m. to 5 p.m. *The Shopper's Fair* in Westgate Plaza is open Monday to Saturday from 9 a.m. to 6 p.m. and has a good selection of vegetables and baked products.

Ocho Rios also has a supermarket open seven days a week. The *Rexo Supermarket* in the New Ocho Rios Plaza, Main Street, is open 9 a.m. to 7 p.m. Monday to Thursday, 9 a.m. to 8 p.m. Friday and Saturday and from 9 a.m. to 1 p.m. on Sundays. *Willy's Variety Supermarket*, also on Main Street, is open from 9 a.m. to 8 p.m., Monday to Saturday.

In keeping with the atmosphere of Port Antonio, shopping is a laid-back experience at *Sang Hing* on West Street. It is open from 9 a.m. to 6 p.m., Monday to Thursday, and on Friday and Saturday from 9 a.m. to 7 p.m. and stocks a variety of fresh meats and fish. *Cheapside* at 44 William Street is open from 9 a.m. to 4 p.m. Monday to Wednesday, closing at 9 p.m. on Thursday and open from 9 a.m. to 6 p.m. on Friday and Saturday.

Both supermarkets in Runaway Bay are open seven days a week. *A & B Valumart* next to the Club Caribbean is open from 8.30 a.m. to 7.30 p.m., selling a range of international foods, while *Taylor's Supermarket* in the square is open from 8.30 a.m. to 6.30 p.m.

Jamaica has many good shopping centres as well as plenty of local craft markets and small shops where one craftsman or artist sells his wares.

Most of the resorts have large duty-free shopping centres, selling items from crystal, lace and cigars to T-shirts. Places like the straw market in Montego Bay and the craft market in Ocho Rios are ideal for finding cheap cheerful presents but to find the more unusal crafts, good paintings or wooden carvings, you are better stopping off at the small stalls along the road or going to up-market art and craft shops. There you will not have the fun of haggling over the price but at least your purchases will be of good quality.

Items to look out for include wood, straw, beads and embroidery in the markets, or gold, silver, china, crystal, watches, cameras and electrical goods in the duty-free centres. Other good buys are blue mountain coffee, Jamaican rum, liqueurs, perfumes and cigars.

Business hours are generally 9 a.m. to 5 p.m., Monday to Friday. Shops will also open on Saturday but some areas have half-day closing on either Wednesday or Thursday. Kingston's half day is Wednesday, Montego Bay's Thursday and Ocho Rio's Friday.

Most of the hotels sell stamps but, be warned, cards take a long time to get home and it may take you a week to find a hotel that actually has any stamps to sell. Airmail postacards cost J\$.70 and letters cost J\$.70.

Jamaica has two morning newspapers. *The Daily Gleaner* and the *Jamaica Record*. It also has an evening paper, *The Star*, which appears Monday to Saturday, and in Montego Bay there is also *The Western Mirror* that is published twice weekly. There is one television channel, JBC/TV, two AM radio stations, JBC and RJR, and four FM stations including JBC and FAME.

Most hotels will have telephones in every room but ask for the tariff; it can be expensive and varies at every hotel. Some hotels insist that you pay for a call before it is made, either with cash or by leaving a credit card imprint at reception. Many hotels will also have cable, telex and tax facilities but, again, it is best to check costs before making any calls. Also bear in mind that international calls will not necessarily go straight through so be prepared to spend some time making each call. Also, after heavy rain, one of the first things to break down is the telephone system. It is usually quickly repaired but can be inconvenient.

Fishing is an important part of the Jamaican economy

Local Colour

The People Jamaica has more than two million residents from a wide variety of cultures, although over 90 per cent are of African descent. The population of Kingston is about 700,000, though six out of every ten Jamaicans live in rural areas. A youthful country, 66 per cent of the population is under 29 years old. The country's motto is 'Out of Many One People' and it is true of their attitudes. Rastafarians live alongside former colonialists quite happily, while people from across the world are welcome to move into the country. The official language is English but it is usually spoken with the local Patios dialect.

Jamaica is famous for its reggae music, a music that has developed out of the Rastafarian culture. Cult followers are easily identified by their dreadlock hairstyles. Many of them are vegetarians and none eat pork. Rastafarians worship the late Emperor of Ethiopia, Haile Selassie, whose call for the end of one race's superiority over another forms part of their reliigion. Their god, Jah, will lead blacks out of oppression back to Ethiopia. One of Jamaica's national heroes is Marcus Garvey. He founded the idea of black nationalism and is considered by Rastafarians to be a prophet in the return of blacks to Africa.

While the Rastafarians might be considered the largest sect in Jamaica, they are in fact a minority. The majority of Jamaicans are Protestant or Roman Catholic. There are also Methodist and Baptist chapels, and Judaism, Moslem and Hindu religions are all practised on the island. Churches and chapels are found in most areas but the only Jewish synagogue is in Kingston.

To learn more about the culture of Jamaicans, the easiest place to go is Kingston. It is the cultural centre of the country and is home to The African Caribbean Institute, The Institute of Jamaica, The National Gallery of Jamaica and the National Library. The National Archives, containing all the country's public records, are in Spanish Town.

The Country Jamaica is the largest English–speaking island in the Caribbean and is the third largest island in the region. It measures 7,058 sq.km.(4,411 sq.ml.) and lies 1,120km(700ml.) south of Miami and 800km(500ml.) north of the Panama Canal.

Europeans first arrived in 1494 with Christopher Columbus, who found Arawak Indians already living there. These Indians

had originally come from the Orinoco region of Venezuela in South America and had been on the island for the previous 500 years. Columbus's followers established a Spanish settlement, Sevilla Nueva, near St Ann's Bay on the north coast. Columbus himself was stranded in Jamaica for nearly one year on his fourth voyage when his ships were in such poor state of repair that he had to put into shore for safety and then had to wait for rescue.

The Arawak Indians died out very quickly once the Europeans arrived and put them to work, so the Spanish started to import African slaves to carry on the work for them. The Spanish abandoned the settlement at Sevilla Nueva in 1538 and founded Spanish Town on the south coast, close to Kingston. Spanish Town was first called St Jago de la Nueva before being renamed by the British.

The British arrived in 1655, led by Admiral Penn and General Venables, and captured the island. Under the Treaty of Madrid, signed in 1670. Britain gained Jamaica and the Cayman Islands from the Spanish. Jamaica remained a British colony until 1962

Cigar-making is done throughout the Caribbean and forms an important part of some economies

161

when it gained independence. The Cayman Islands were a dependence of Jamaica until 1961 when they chose to remain a British colony and to move completely away from political ties with Jamaica. But people still travel freely between the islands, and many Jamaicans travel to the Caymans looking for work in the tax-free colony.

Although the British settled on Jamaica after beating the Spanish, the first years of their reign were dominated by the pirates, like Henry Morgan, who were based in Port Royal but roamed the Caribbean plundering Spanish treasure ships as they left the Americas and headed for Europe. The earthquake of 1692 destroyed much of Port Royal; it killed about 2000 people and tamed the pirates.

The British then turned to farming and milked Jamaica for all it was worth, using every bit of available soil for sugar-cane plantations. The British had to import huge numbers of African slaves to work on the plantations. A few of them escaped and joined the few remaining Spanish settlements in the mountains.

The old way of extracting juice from sugar-cane

These people became known as the Maroons and their descendants still live in an area known as Cockpit Country. The Maroons were very successful in fighting the British and eventually won the rights to their mountain homes in an agreement signed in 1739. Maroons are found all over the Caribbean and South America but one of the largest populations is on Jamaica.

Discontent grew among the slaves, and Jamaica was a hotbed of rebellion until Sam Sharpe's rebellion of 1831. This was the catalyst for slavery being abolished in 1838 and the former slaves became the core of the existing population. After losing their African slaves, the British turned to Indians and Chinese to provide labour. Small Jewish settlements have been in existence since the Spanish first arrived. Now all the cultures and races have been through generations of intermarriages to provide a truly multiracial society.

Politics has always been a stormy affair in Jamaica and the Morant Bay Rebellion of 1865 provoked the House of Assembly to voting to become a Crown Colony under full British rule. Jamaica still retains many British traditions. It is a member of the Commonwealth and its parliamentary system is based on Westminster. The Queen is still titular head of state and is represented on the island by a Governor-General. There are two tiers of Government: the house of Representatives is the lower house and is voted in by general elections every five years; the upper house or The Senate is made up of members selected by the Governor-General, the Prime Minister and the leader of the opposition.

Jamaica's Independence movement really got started in 1944 and politicians such as Sir Alexander Bustamante and Norman Manley helped achieve that independence in August 1962. There are three political parties, although since the first general election in 1944 only two have ever led the Government. The two main parties are The Jamaica Labour Party and the People's National Party. The third party is The Worker's Party of Jamaica. Although elections have to be held every five years, the Prime Minister can call one earlier if he chooses. The minimum voting age is 18. The current Prime Minister is Michael Manley, leader of the People's National Party, who was voted into power in 1989. He replaced

**Columbus Park holds many
artefacts from his early
voyages and of the first
settlers in Jamaica**

Edward Seaga's Jamaica Labour Party which had been in power for the previous eight years.

Jamaica has been hit by recession since the early 1970s. It used to be one of the most prosperous countries in the Caribbean but decline in its traditional markets has created internal problems. Sugar-cane and bauxite were its biggest exports but now tourism has developed to become the country's largest foreign currency earner. Jamaica is still the world's third largest producer of bauxite which it still exports for other countries to use in aluminium smelting, but a fall in demand has hit the Jamaican industry hard.

Tourism is the fastest-growing industry in the country and in 1987 the number of visitors passed the one million mark for the first time. With a population of just 2.3 million, this large number of visitors had had a big impact on the country and led to some of the problems with high crime figures in the 1970s. The Government recognizes the importance of tourism and its unpredictable nature. It has worked hard to eradicate the violence and to counter the bad press the country received abroad.

But it has had natural disasters to contend with, too. Hurricane Gilbert in 1988 devastated much of the island and hit tourism hard. The Government instantly reserved money to cover the costs of restoring the industry to normal and spent much of its annual budget in advertising once Jamaica had recovered. The Government supported the view that by restoring tourism it would help support hundreds of thousands of families and keep the economy buoyant. Poorer housing and remote villages that were destroyed had to wait their turn for help after the hurricane.

The Labour Government nationalized the tourist industry in the 1970s and took control of all the large hotels but it has slowly been selling them back to the private sector to encourage more foreign investment in the country. This programme has been going well, with several hotels a year returning into private hands and providing the government with a useful source of revenue.

Geographically, Jamaica is dominated by its mountains and rivers. Almost half the island, which measures 232km (145ml.) long and 82km(51ml.) wide, is above 305m(1,000ft.), and its highest peak, Blue Mountain, stands at 2,258m (7,402ft.). There are 120 rivers crossing the country, most flowing out of the mountains down to the coast. Jamaica also has plenty of mineral springs and three are developed for the public at Sans Souci, St Thomas and Clarendon. More than 1.5 million acres are farmed or are commercial forests. South-east of Montego Bay there is an area of limestone depressions and sinkholes known as Cockpit Country.

Calendar Events Jamaica has nine public holidays annually. These are:

New Year's Day, 1 January

Ash Wednesday, February

Good Friday

Easter Monday

Labour Day, May

Independence Day, first Monday in August

National Heroes Day, third Monday in October

Christmas Day

Boxing Day

There are plenty of annual events, from sports to the arts, and the Jamaica Tourist Board produces a six-monthly calendar listing events and contacts to get more details. Some of the most notable include:

The Accompong Maroon Festival, which dates back to the nineteenth-century. Held in Accompong, St Elizabeth, Western Jamaica, in January, the festival includes traditional dancing, singing, Maroon feasts and ceremonies.

The annual *Miami/Montego Bay Yacht Race* starts on the first Friday in February in Miami, finishing a few days and 1,298km(811ml.) later in Montego Bay. It attracts some of the world's top sailors and finishes with a post-race party of four days of rum and sun.

The Sugarcane Ball is held annually in Round Hill. A formal event, it is held in the elegant setting of Round Hill Hotel.

The Hague Agricultural Show is held at the showground, May Pen, every February. It has the usual selection of agricultural displays and competitions along with the crowning of the agricultural queen and traditional dancing. Contact the Jamaica Agricultural Society. Tel: 922 0610.

The *Port Antonio International Spring Fishing Tournament* is held in March from the town's marina (Tel: 923 8724) and there are competitions for all categories of fish.

An annual *Song Competition* is held in Montego Bay in March, from reggae to ballads, at Cornwall Beach.

Jamaica's annual *Orchid Society Show* is held in Kingston during March. Contact Ancille Gordon on 927 2171.

Montego Bay's Yacht Club has an *Easter Regatta* which attracts international entries. Tel: 952 6101.

There is also a *Tennis Tournament* every Easter in Montego Bay. Tel: 953 2732.

The *St Ann's Bay Singers* also have an Easter event and they hold a concert every Good Friday.

St James Agricultural Show is held at Easter in Montpelier, near Montego Bay. Tel: 922 0610.

St Elizabeth Horticultural Society's *Annual Show* is held on Easter Monday at the showground, Black River. Tel: 965 2203.

Carnival in Jamaica. Held annually in April, there are two main events. The Orange Carnival lasts four days and is concentrated around Kingston and Port Royal. The Jamaica Carnival lasts about a week and is in Kingston, Montego Bay and Ocho Rios. Contact Jamaica Tourist Board offices for details of the street parties, parades, tours and musical events.

At the end of April Jamaica boasts the largest *Flower Show* in the Caribbean. Held in the National Arena, Kingston, it is organized by the Jamaica Horticultural Society Show.

Montego Bay's latest annual attraction is the *International Hot Air Balloon Festival* which attracts balloonists from the UK, Canada and the USA. The festival is held on Jamaica's Labour Day weekend towards the end of May. It was first held in 1988 but is already a firm fixture. For two days, balloonists compete from 7.30 a.m. to 10 a.m. and then the day's entertainment for the crowd switches to parachuting and kite flying with concerts, stalls and bars on the ground.

St James Horticultural Society Show is held at Montego Bay High School. Tel: 952 3504.

The *Manchester Horticultural Society* has been in existence for over 125 years and holds its annual show in May at the showground in Mandeville.

The *Negril Carnival* is held in May. Tel: 957 4437 for details.

Ikebana International Show is held in Kingston in June.

Manchester Golf Week is held at the Manchester Club, Mandeville in July. It has been going for over 55 years and attracts a mix of local and international players.

All-Jamaica Open Tennis Championship is held at the NCB Sports Club, Kingston in July.

Hi-Pro Family Polo Tournament is at Chukka Cove, near Ocho Rios, in July.

The NDTC Season of Dance is held in Kingston in July.

Reggae Sunsplash. This reggae festival has been internationally famous and attracts thousands of fans to the Bob Marley Centre in Montego Bay during July.

The Royal Jamaica Yacht Club in Kingston holds its annual *Independence Regatta* during the first week in August.

The *Denbeigh Agricultural Show* at the showground, May Pen, is held at the beginning of August.

Jamaica Independence Day Festival Street Parade and Grand Gala is held on the first Monday in August. The parade travels through Kingston along a publicized route to the National Stadium.

Great Bay Carnival is a relatively new event but has quickly become a firm fixture in the calendar for August and is held at Treasure Beach.

In Monteego Bay, the annual *Marlin Fishing Tournament* is held in September.

Another *Marlin Tournament* held in October is the Ocho Rios tournament which also includes a canoe fisherman's tournament.

The most famous competition is the *Port Antonio International Marlin Tournament* which is held in October and is reputed to be one of the Caribbean's oldest and best fishing tournaments.

Jamaica's Orchid Society's Fall Show is held in Kingston in October and is a colourful international event.

Woman '91. A trade fair and exhibition, with relevance to women, is held in Kingston during October.

Oktoberfest is an annual celebration of German and Jamaican foods and beers, held at the Jamaica–German Society Headquarters, Kingston.

Harmony Hall's Anniversary Show is usually in November and features works by Jamaica's leading artists.

The Liguanea Open Tennis Tournament is held at the Liguanea Club, Kingston in November.

ICWI Women's International Polo Tournament is held in December at Kingston Polo Club, Caymanas. Local women players compete and international players provide an exhibition match.

Appleton International 10K and Marathon Races are held in Ocho Rios in December.

Kingston is Jamaica's capital. It is also the business and cultural centre of the country and is where the Government is based. It has a large international airport and extensive port facilities.

The Norman Manley International Airport is on the road to Port Royal in an area known as the Palisadoes. There are regular buses and taxi services out to the airport but no rail links. The railway station is in the downtown area close to the waterfront on Barry Street. A regular service runs into the interior of the island with daily services to Montego Bay.

Kingston has been Jamaica's capital since 1872 and the city is built around the world's seventh largest natural harbour. The city was first developed by pirates, who used the harbour as their base for roaming the Caribbean and plundering British and Spanish treasure ships. Port Royal was said to be the most notorious port in the 1600s when British pirates preyed on Spanish ships. Port Royal was built at the entrance to Kingston Harbour and was home to one of the most famous pirates of all, Henry Morgan, who was eventually knighted and became Lieutenant Governor of the island.

A day in Port Royal is well worth the trip but Kingston itself also has plenty to offer the tourist. Many people staying in any of Jamaica's north-coast resort areas do not bother to visit the south coast and Kingston but by not going there they miss out on much of the best of Jamaica.

The port area has been rebuilt and can accommodate large cruise ships, while for the land-based tourist there are plenty of splendid buildings in the port area, including the Bank of Jamaica building which houses the *Coin Museum. The National Gallery*, in the Kingston Mall, has a permanent display of some of Jamaica's best art works. It costs J$1 for entry into the National Gallery and it is open from 9.30 a.m. to 4.30 p.m., Monday, Tuesday, Thursday and Friday. The *Jamaica Conference Centre* is open for tours. The *Institute of Jamaica* on East Street is just behind the waterfront and houses the

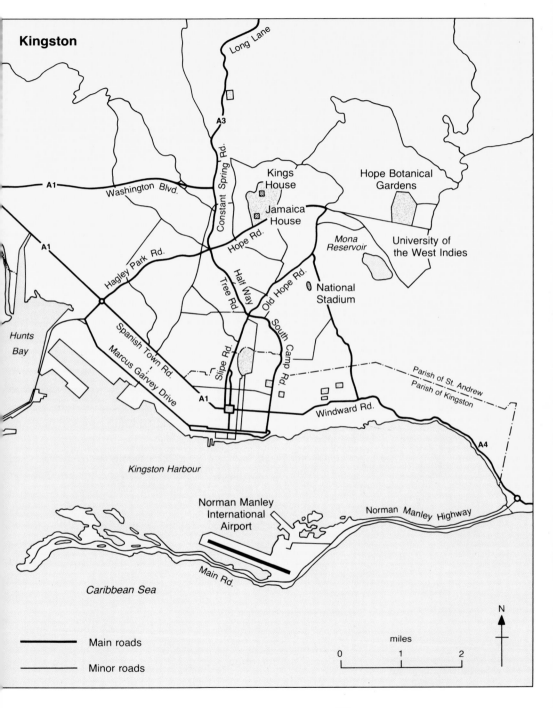

Kingston

Long Lane

A3

A1 Washington Blvd.

A1

Constant Spring Rd.

Kings House

Jamaica House

Hope Rd.

Hope Botanical Gardens

Mona Reservoir

University of the West Indies

Hagley Park Rd.

Half Way Tree Rd.

Old Hope Rd.

National Stadium

Hunts Bay

Spanish Town Rd.

Marcus Garvey Drive

Slipe Rd.

South Camp Rd.

A1

Parish of St. Andrew

Parish of Kingston

Windward Rd.

A4

Kingston Harbour

Norman Manley International Airport

Norman Manley Highway

Main Rd.

Caribbean Sea

N

Main roads

Minor roads

miles

0   1   2

Museum of Natural History, *History Gallery* and *Reference Library* and is reputed to have the finest collection of West Indian history in the world. Entry to the Institute is free and it is open from 8.30 a.m. to 4 p.m. Monday to Saturday.

The downtown area is home to the *Victoria Crafts Market* and at Kingston Shopping Mall. Two city-centre parks include St William Grant Park and the National Heroes Park, which holds the tombs of national heroes as well as those of former prime ministers. There is an eighteenth-century church south of the Parade, where Admiral Benbow is buried. Coke Chapel was built in 1840 on the site of the first Methodist Chapel in Jamaica. *Gordon House*, on Beeston Street, houses Parliament. Visitors can sit in the Strangers Gallery but men must be wearing jackets and women need to be wearing dresses to gain entry. Opposite Gordon House stands Headquarters House, built in the 1750s for a wager. One of the oldest theatres in the Americas, *Ward Theatre*, is also in the downtown area on South Parade and has a regular programme of concerts and plays.

Port Royal Victoria Pier, close to the craft market, is the stepping-stone to Port Royal. Ferries leave every two hours throughout the day for the small town. The journey takes 20 minutes and costs under a dollar. Once there, visitors should see *Fort Charles*, which was built in 1656. Inside the old officers' quarters is the *Port Royal Museum* and a plaque commemorates the fact that Lord Nelson once served there. The *Archaeological Museum* is also worth a visit to see some of the treasures recovered from the sea after the earthquake of 1692. The earthquake and following tidal wave had pushed almost two-thirds of the town into the sea and the sunken city is still lying in shallow waters just off the coast.

In *St Peter's Church* there are other amazing stories from the 1600s. There is the tomb of Louis Glady who was swallowed up by the earth during the earthquake but was later thrown up again, still alive. The church also has a communion plate donated by pirate Henry Morgan and the eighteenth-century organ loft and chandelier are worth seeing.

Back in the main city of Kingston there is plenty to see in the uptown areas. Half-way between the waterfront and the hills there used to be an old cotton tree. This major road junction

Opposite above
Kingston Yacht harbour

Opposite below
Kingston has a large number of old colonial buildings as well as its modern centre

Port Royal used to be the home to famous pirates before an earthquake struck

became known as Half Way Tree. The parish church dates back to 1699, record on some of the tombstones in the graveyard. Half Way Tree is still the capital of the parish of St Andrew.

To the east of Half Way Tree is New Kingston, an area of new and old. A great house, *Devon House*, has been restored beautifully to accommodate a museum, restaurant and shops. The house was built in the 1880s for George Steibel, a black Jamaican who made millions in South America. Devon House is on Hope Road, and tours costs J$11. It is open from 9 a.m. to 4 p.m. daily. Devon House is not far from Jamaica House, the prime minister's residence, and Kings House, which is the official residence of the Governor-General.

Further down Hope Road is the *Bob Marley Museum*, dedicated to reggae singer Bob Marley. Arguments over tax and who owns his former studio and rights to his songs have raged since his death and so the Museum is not always open. The official hours are Monday, Tuesday, Thursday and Friday from 9.30 a.m. to 4.30 p.m., and on Saturday, Wednesday and public holidays 12.30 p.m. to 5.30 p.m. It costs around J$10 per person (Tel: 92 79152).

Devon House in Kingston, Jamaica

Hope Road eventually leads to the *Hope Botanical Gardens* where bands play on Sunday afternoons in the largest gardens in the Caribbean. The Orchid Garden is spectacular and there are hundreds of different tropical species here. The Gardens also have a children's zoo and entry is free. The Gardens are open daily from 8.30 a.m. to 6.30 p.m.

Close to the Gardens is the *University of the West Indies*. Its chapel was built with stones taken from an old sugar warehouse in Trelawny. The other side of the Mona Reservoir from the University is the *National Stadium and Arena*. The Stadium is close to New Kingston, which has the older buildings along Hope Road but is also an area of banks, shopping centres, several embassies, including the British High Commission, and the headquarters of the Jamaica Tourist Board on Dominica Drive. The New Kingston Shopping Centre houses a mix of shops and restaurants.

Travelling out of the city westwards takes you through *Trenchtown*, the place where reggae music was developed and still home to many Rastafarians. It is better not to go into this area on foot after dark unless with Jamaican friends who know the area well.

Further out of town is *Caymanas Park*, where many sporting events take place. Horse-racing takes place every Wednesday (half-day closing in Kingston) and Saturday as well as on Public Holidays. The Park is open from 12.30 p.m. to 6 p.m. Entry is roughly J$25 per person. Polo is played on grounds close to the race-track.

Hotels As with most capital cities, there is a wide range of accommodation available. Most of the international hotels are either in the downtown or uptown city areas, close to the business areas and also to the main tourist attractions. Some cheaper hotels and guest houses are located further out of town and are best for those with their own transport.

One of the best of these is the *Kingston Ivor Guest House and Restaurant*. The villa has four bedrooms with bathrooms, it is about 20 minutes from the city and costs up to US$64 for a double room per night, including breakfast and transport to Kingston (Tel: 927 1460).

On the waterfront at Kingston the *Oceana Hotel* is on King Street, next to the Conference Centre. Prices vary at around US$100 per room per night (Tel: 922 0920/9).

At Port Royal, *Morgan's Harbour Hotel* costs between US$45 and US$120 per night (Tel: 924 8464/5).

The majority of city-centre hotels are in New Kingston. Among the best are the reasonably priced *The Courtleigh*, on Trafalgar Road, which has both a hotel and self-catering apartments. Prices vary from US$48.50 to US$145 (Tel: 926 8174 or 929 5320). Cheaper hotels include the *Indies Hotel* on Holborn Road with prices up to US$43 (Tel: 926 2952/0989).

Both The Courtleigh and Morgan's Harbour are Inns of Jamaica. The association has several other properties in Kingston. *Medallion Hall*, on Hope Road costs up to US$50 per night (Tel: 927 5721/5866); while the *Mayfair*, just round the corner on West King's House Close, is close to King's House. It costs up to US$60 per night (Tel: 926 1610). *Hotel Four Seasons* on Ruthven Road is in a converted Edwardian house and costs up to US$55 per night (Tel: 929 7655/7).

Two of Kingston's top hotels are the *Wyndham* and the *Jamaica Pegasus*. Both hotels are on Knutsford Boulevard in New Kingston. The Wyndham costs around US$130 per room (Tel: 926 5430/9) and can also be booked in London (Tel: 071 367 5175). Jamaica Pegasus is a Trusthouse Forte Hotel and costs around US$145 (Tel: 926 3691/9 or in London: 071 567 3444).

The city can be divided into two areas for touring. The uptown area is much larger and you need transport, while the downtown area can be covered on foot. A drive along Hope Road takes in most of the sights of uptown Kingston from the Hope Botanical Gardens in the east, past King's House, Jamaica House and Devon House. Continuing westwards past Half Way Tree junction into Hagley Park Road. St Andrew's Parish Church is on the right. Turning left at Half Way Tree down Half Way Tree Road takes you into downtown Kingston.

As the road merges with Old Hope Road, it becomes Slipe Road and you pass the Carib Theatre as you travel towards the waterfront. Eventually you arrive at St William Grant Park, surrounded by the North and South Parade. Ward Theatre is on North Parade while Queens Street runs to the east and west of the

Modern Kingston is a far cry from the deserted south-coast beaches a few kilometres away

A sculpture found in Kingston

Park. Travelling along East Queens Street is Coke Church. Continuing past the police headquarters, turn left up Duke Street to get to Gordon House, where Parliament sits, and to Headquarters House opposite. Further along the road is the Jewish Synagogue, while turning right along North Street will take you to the Roman Catholic Cathedral, which is close to Kingston College.

Continuing south from St William Grant Park takes you down to the waterfront past the parish church and then the main Post Office with public buildings opposite. Turn right into Port Royal Street to find the Victoria Crafts Market on your left. Turn left down Ocean Boulevard to go along the waterfront past the cruise-ship piers.

To the left will be the Kingston Mall housing the National Gallery, the conference centres and then many of the major banks. Turning left up Duke Street and then right down Tower Street takes you to the Institute of Jamaica.

Shopping in Kingston, is also mainly in the downtown area, with the crafts market and many smaller craft shops along Port Royal Street. The *Kingston Mall* and the *New Kingston Mall* on Dominica Drive both have a good variety of shops. There are plenty of supermarkets and off-licences around town and the main banks are off Ocean Boulevard. Devon House also has some nice shops and a good restaurant, *The Grog Shoppe*, for having a quick lunch while sightseeing.

Restaurants Other good places to eat are numerous. All the big hotels have a selection of restaurants, such as the *Court of Arms* and the *Pool Bar* at the Courtleigh Hotel in Trafalgar Road. At the Jamaica Pegasus try *Le Pavillon* gourmet restaurant or the casual *Country Kitchen*; at the Oceana you will find the *Fort Charles Restaurant* for Jamaican or international cuisine. *The Lychee Garden* in the New Kingston Shopping Centre is very good and also does take-aways. Another Chinese restaurant is the *Jade Garden Restaurant* on the first floor of the Village Plaza, Constant Spring Road (Tel: 929 2232), while for excellent food try *Norma* on Belmont Road, which is open Monday to Friday for lunch, or for dinner on Thursday and Friday (Tel: 929 4966).

Spanish Town Leaving Kingston behind you for a day, it is worth a trip out to Spanish Town. It was the capital of Jamaica for over 300 years and dates back to 1534. About 21km(13ml.) west of Kingston, the journey takes you past the *White Marl Arawak Museum*, which is worth a stop.

Once in Spanish Town, head for the old town square, which has a very Spanish feel to it, having been laid out like a Spanish medieval square. Much of the old town, first called St Jago de la Neuva by the Spanish, was destroyed by the British when they gained control of the island in 1655.

Among the buildings erected since then is the *Cathedral Church of St James* which dates back to 1714. On the north side of the square is a monument to Admiral George Rodney. It was designed by the eminent British artist John Bacon in the late eighteenth century. On the north-eastern corner is the Records Office, which houses all Jamaica's national records, while the office containing the Colonial Archives is on the north-western corner. Fire destroyed the former governor's residence, King's House, in 1925. It stood on the west side of the square but now the Jamaicans have rebuilt the façade of the house and installed the *Museum of Craft and Technology*. Opposite stands the old red brick former House of Assembly, which is now local government offices. On the south side of the square is the Court House.

Just off the north side of the square along Adelaide Street is the town's main *Post Office*, while to the south on the corner of Constitution Street and Barrett Street is the *Cathedral*.

Going south out of Spanish Town, skirting around Portmore, takes you to one of the best beaches in the Kingston area. Hellshire Beach is popular with the locals, but you do need a car to get there. The beaches around Kingston, particularly on the Palisadoes between Kingston and Port Royal, are dirty.

Going north out of Kingston takes you into some of Jamaica's most spectacular scenery. The best way to see the area is to hire a car for the day and take your time, travelling through the mountain roads. Alternatively, you can stay at Stony Hill, getting good views of both Kingston and the mountains. The *Stony Hill Hotel* costs up to about US$50 per night per room (Tel: 942 2357). An excellent place to stop for lunch on your way out of Kingston is the *Blue Mountain Inn* which is well known for its good food (Tel: 927 1700/2606).

The roads up in the mountains are narrow and winding. Lorries do use them frequently so watch out on the corners. But the hard

Spanish Town was where the Spanish founded the first capital

driving is worth it for the scenery, with steep-sided hills and smallholdings perched at what seem impossible angles. Rivers cascade down the mountain sides and there are plenty of small villages to stop in, buy fruit, have a drink or just take pictures. There is a botanical garden at Castleton, on the road to Annotto Bay on the north coast. It would be easy to get there and back in a day.

The Blue Mountains and East Coast

The Blue Mountains Travelling slightly north-east from Kingston takes you towards the Blue Mountain, Jamaica's highest peak, which stands at over 2,257m(7,400ft.). Travelling in the area is best done in four-wheel-drive vehicles, although you can get to some of the small towns in the mountains in normal cars. To explore the area properly, it is best to stay overnight at one of the small hotels in the area. *Pine Grove Mountain Chalets* cost about US$45 a night and there you can get expert advice on where to go and how to get there. You can also hire four-wheel-drive vehicles there, or get a lift to Cinchona where there is a botanical garden, or to the start of the Blue Mountain Trail (Tel: 922 8705).

180

If you are fit and energetic, you can climb the Blue Mountain itself. The climb takes about four hours and another three to come down. Raincoats are a good idea as it is very wet up there, and you will need your own packed lunches.

There are masses of trails through the region from both Pine Grove and from the Cinchona area. Many are easy walking and keen bird-watchers will find hundreds of different species, some unique to Jamaica. Botanists, too, will enjoy walking through these hills.

The mountain roads are difficult to drive across but there is a good road around the east coast linking Kingston to Port Antonio. This area is not frequented much by tourists but still has some worthwhile sights. The drive will take most of the day and there are not many places to stay along the route. People tend to stop off while travelling from one resort area to another, rather than basing a holiday there.

Morant Bay The road takes you past some good beaches but, if you go swimming, watch out for the undertows. A short diversion at Golden Grove will take you to the cliffs at Morant Point Lighthouse, a scenic spot. Holland Bay is a remote beach leading to the lighthouse which is Jamaica's most easterly point. The lighthouse was built in London in 1841 from a 30.5m(100ft.) cast-iron tube. Morant Bay is also the site of a rebellion in 1865 and a statue honours the hero, Bogle. The beach at nearby Pera is spectacular but difficult to get to.

Reach Falls Another diversion at Muirton will take you to Reach Falls at the foot of the John Crow Mountains. These falls are reputed to be the most spectacular in Jamaica but they are difficult to get to and you need to have a car. The Falls are about 5km(3ml.) inland from the main road and are sited in an area of natural basins and caves. You will sometimes see divers plunging into the cave pools. The Falls can be visited daily from 9 a.m. to 4 p.m.

Bath The inalnd town of Bath is a good place to base walks into the Mountains but there is only one small hotel, the *Bath Fountain*, which has natural hot-water spring baths. The baths are open to the public and are believed to provide relief for people suffering from rheumatism. The mineral spa is in botanical gardens, which contains rare trees up to 200 years old. The gardens are reputed to be amongst the oldest in the Americas.

Port Antonio This part of Jamaica has long been the haunt of the rich and famous. It is still an exclusive area, not served by an international airport and it is a couple of hours' drive from Kingston and nearer four hours to Montego Bay, keeping it isolated from the mass tourism further along the north coast. There used to be a railway link to Kingston but the line was damaged in a hurricane several years ago and there are no plans to repair it.

Port Antonio used to be a thriving port acting as a centre for the export of bananas. It was also the first place that tourists visited. But now, areas such as Ocho Rios and Montego Bay attract the cruise ships and the package-holiday visitor, leaving the north-eastern coast frozen in time. With an air of a town from another age, the splendid Victorian houses and hotels are beautifully maintained, and luxurious villas nestle in the wooded hillsides.

Errol Flynn used to own Navy Island, a small island in the harbour, and it was he who first started the popular raft rides down the Rio Grande. He used to travel down the river on the rafts used daily for taking bananas to the port and the idea soon caught on and is now one of the things visitors should do while in Jamaica. The raft ride takes a couple of hours and is a tranquil way to pass a morning, drifting slowly downstream through leafy hills.

Flynn once lived in the *Admiralty Club*, which was formerly a naval station. The Club is now a restaurant open from 8 a.m. to 12 a.m., serving breakfast, lunch and dinner. As you would expect with a restaurant nestled in the middle of a harbour, most of the menu is seafood and a meal costs around J$200 for two. The ferry crossing costs about J$10 and there is a regular service across the bay from the West Harbour. Errol Flynn had wanted to be buried on the island and it was one of his favourite places. Navy Island has two beaches and one of them is clearly marked as a nudist beach.

Other famous stars from the 1920s and 1930s who visited Port Antonio include Bette Davis, Ginger Rogers, William Randolph Hearst, Clara Bow and J.P. Morgan. They all stayed in an area known as Titchfield. This was the original name of the town. It was named after the estate of Lord Portland, which is the name of the surrounding parish. Titchfield School is in *Fort George* and was founded in 1785. Cannons can still be seen amongst the remains

**Opposite
The De Montevin Lodge in
Port Antonio**

183

of the Fort which is on the most northerly tip of the point between the twin harbours on which Port Antonio is built. The ferry to Navy Island leaves from the west side of the point.

The point also houses the *De Montevin Lodge* which has an old-world atmosphere resembling an old New England mansion, and costs around US$450 for a double room (Tel: 993 2604). Further south along Fort George Street is the *Capitol Cinema* and the Court House. Fort George Street turns into West Street, which runs along the edge of West Harbour. Follow this to find the market. The *Sang Hing* supermarket is on West Street and *Cheapside* is on William Street, opposite the market.

Go the other way from Fort George Street into Harbour Street along the East Harbour and you will pass the *Jamaica Tourist Board* offices (Tel: 993 3051). Turn right off Harbour Street into West Palm Avenue and then left into Bridge Street to find the parish church, *Christ Church*. It is an Anglican church and was built in 1840. Follow Harbour Street until it becomes Allan Avenue to find *Olivier Park*, *Carder Park* and then *Eveleigh Park*.

If you follow the road out of town, take the first turning to the left and follow the coast out to *Folly Point Lighthouse*. On

Rafting on the Rio Grande was started by Errol Flynn

your way to the Point turn right up to the Folly. Built at the turn of the century by American millionaire, Dan Mitchell, for his wife, it crumbled because salt water had been used to mix the cement and his wife did not like the house so left it unrepaired. The legend is that the house fell down when the millionaire was jilted by his lover.

A good time to visit Port Antonio is in October during the annual marlin fishing tournament. It is one of the oldest and most prestigious contests in the Caribbean and fishermen travel long distances to take part. The day's fishing is supported by plenty of parties and evening events. If you are after a quiet break, it may be the week to avoid but it is one time in the year when the town is really buzzing. The tournament is one of four sport-fishing tournaments held in Jamaica.

Hotels Staying in Port Antonio gives you plenty of choice. As well as the *De Montevin Lodge* and *Dragon Bay*, there is *Bonnie View* on Richmond Hill which costs up to about US$66 (Tel: 993 2752/2862). Just outside the town is the *Trident Villas & Hotel* which costs from US$165 to US$700 (Tel: 993 2602). The hotel annexe is another of Port Antonio's follies. Built in the style of a

The Folly near Port Antonio is now just a crumbling ruin

Rhine castle, it is guarded by two stone alligators, and peacocks roam around the estate. The expense keeps it exclusive and often royalty are on the guest list.

There is also the *Jamaica Palace Hotel* (Tel: 993 2020) which costs between US$95 and US$165 per night and is on the road to the Blue Lagoon. The hotel has an excellent restaurant with live music every night. Just down the road is *Frenchman's Cove*. Access to the beach, which is one of the best in the area, costs

Frenchman's Cove, Jamaica

about J$5 for non-residents. And at the *Blue Lagoon*, the Villas at San San provide luxurious, expensive accommodation. Villas all along this coast have a reputation for having the best facilities of anywhere in Jamaica and are in beautiful locations. They all have cooks who serve some of the best local food, and the beaches nearby are secluded.

Restaurants The town has a good variety of restaurants as well. *The Garden Kitchen* restaurant on Somers Town Road is open from 7 a.m. to 10 p.m. A favourite among local people, it serves excellent Jamaican food at very reasonable prices. *Centre Point* also produces local cuisine and is owned by a Jamaican couple who have returned to Port Antonio from London. Reggae music adds to the lively late-night atmosphere and it is open seven days a week.

Boston Bay Travelling by road from Kingston, around the coast, the first part of the Port Antonio area that you reach is Boston Bay. Well known for the jerk-pork stops on the beach, it is said to be where jerk cooking was developed. The method of cooking is a cross between barbecuing and smoking and until recently this was the only place on the island to get the spicy meat.

Boston Bay has a nice beach and there are also plenty of watersports on offer. It is open to the public from 9 a.m. to 5 p.m. daily, free of charge. Boston Bay is within easy reach of Port Antonio for a day out. Driving along the coast road takes you past the northern end of the Blue Mountains but there are few roads into the mountains and those that exist are not that good. If you want to stay near Boston Bay, the 54-acre property at *Dragon Bay* provides good-quality villas on a private beach. It also has tennis courts and swimming-pools. (Tel: 993 3281).

Nonsuch Caves The next major landmark along the road from Boston Bay is the Nonsuch Caves. Turning left off the main road at Fairy Hill takes you through Sherwood Forest to the Caves, (the road then turns back to the coast and to Port Antonio). The caves are over a million years old and the largest is now open to the public. Eight chambers are floodlit and the caves contain evidence of the Arawak Indians as well as some fossils. Be warned: there are also plenty of bats flying around. The caves are set in a botanical garden, *The Athenry Gardens*. It costs J$27.50 for a guided tour of the caves, which are open from 9 a.m. to 5 p.m. every day except Saturday.

The Blue Lagoon If you return to the main coast road, the next stop along is the Blue Lagoon next to San San Beach. One of the most romantic places on the island the 'bottomless' bay is a deep sapphire blue. It is also known as the Blue Hole. The bay is not, of course, bottomless but there are freshwater springs bubbling up at the bottom, about 198m(650ft.) below the surface. It is a favourite haunt for divers and swimmers and also has a beautiful restaurant, the *Blue Lagoon*. Again the haunt of the rich and famous, it is still possible to spot the stars as you sample some excellent seafood. The lagoon is floodlit at night, providing a spectacular backdrop to a romantic dinner. Although film stars frequent the restaurant, it is not over-pricey. Meals for two can cost in the region of $200.00; this is quite expensive for Jamaica but not compared to London prices, and the restaurant is open seven days a week.

Just along from San San is Monkey Island. It was once the gift of Baron von Thyssen to his bride, Princess Nina Khan.

Continuing along the coast road to the west of Port Antonio takes you to two of the town's most popular sights, Somerset Falls at Hope Bay and the Rio Grande river rafting.

Rio Grande This river is the largest in Jamaica and the trips takes about two and a half hours on two-seater bamboo rafts. Rafting trips cost JS$245 and rafts travel down the river from 8.30 a.m. to 4.30 p.m. daily. The trips start at Berridale and finish at Rafters' Rest in St Margaret's Bay. Made famous by Errol Flynn this trip is well worth doing but take some suncream, it is easy to get very sunburnt on the water.

Somerset Falls Also out of town to the west is Somerset Falls. A nature reserve for birds and animals, it is a pleasant place to take a picnic or go for a walk. The Falls are open from 10 a.m. to 5 p.m. daily and entry costs J$20. The Falls are part of Daniel River and are a series of cascades, pools and waterfalls. There is a restaurant and toilets in the park.

Moore Town Leaving town to the south takes you up into the mountains and to Moore Town. This is the home of the Maroons and there is the *Sam Streete Maroon Museum* in the town. The Maroons were an isloated group of people, descended from runaway slaves and Spaniards who moved inland when the British conquered the island. Nanny Town, between Moore Town and the Blue Mountain peak was sacked by the British in 1734 and only rediscovered about 30 years ago. It was the original home of the Maroons. These people were fierce fighters and were never completely defeated by the British, who finally settled peacefully with them by granting them land concessions. The majority of the Maroons still live in Cockpit County, south-east of Montego Bay, but it well worth a visit to Moore Town where there is a small community of Maroons.

Crystal Springs Still in the parish of Portland but back on the coast, a new development is underway at Crystal Springs. Close to the small town of Bluff Bay, Crystal Springs has a bird sanctuary and a wonderful collection of orchids. Some cottages are being built in the area. Crystal Springs is open daily from 9 a.m. to 6 p.m. and has a small restaurant. To get there from Port Antonio, turn left off the coast road on to the road to Skibo just after crossing Spanish River Bridge and you will find the park a couple of miles along the road. If you have a car, it is worth diverting off the main coast road into the mountains just to take in the views and to see some of the small mountain communities.

The resort town of Ocho Rios is a two hour's drive from Port Antonio and makes a pleasant day trip. There are plenty of sights along the way, from Noel Coward's house at Port Maria and Ian Fleming's house nearby at Oracabessa to great houses such as Harmony Hall.

Ochos Rios The small fishing village of Ocho Rios has been transformed in the past twenty years. Cruise ships now regularly moor at the town's port. Although it has become a bustling resort town, it has a pleasant atmosphere and it is easy to escape the crowds. It has a resident population of about 6,600 and is really still like a small market town. It was originally named by the Spanish after they discovered eight rivers around the town.

Some people regard the beach in the town as one of the best in Jamaican resort towns, but there are nicer places just along the coast and it does have some disadvantages. The cruise-ship pier is alongside the beach and the ships tower over the west side of the beach. The beach itself is not that big and can be a little crowded.

But that is the worst of this delightful town, which has such eccentrics as the Tree Man wandering around town quite undisturbed. Covered from head to foot in green branches, he ambles around the town centre and does not mind tourists taking

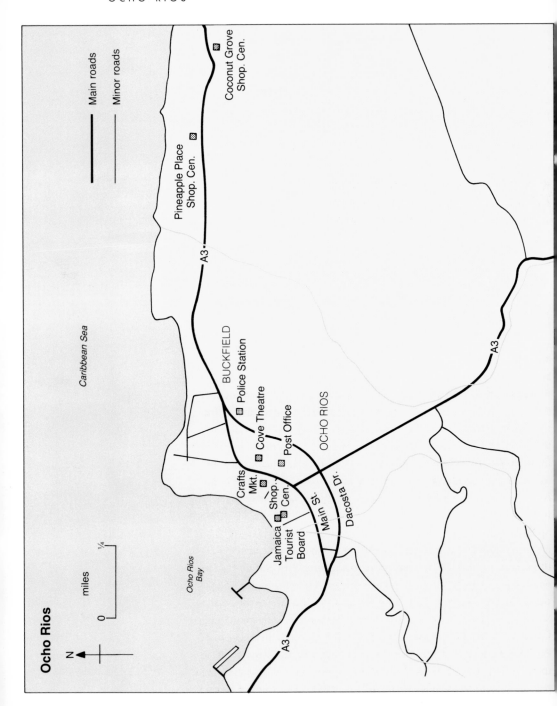

Ocho Rios

Caribbean Sea

Main roads
Minor roads

Pineapple Place
Shop. Cen.

Coconut Grove
Shop. Cen.

A3

A3

BUCKFIELD

Police Station

Cove Theatre

Post Office

OCHO RIOS

Crafts
Mkt.

Shop.
Cen.

Jamaica
Tourist
Board

Main St.

Dacosta Dr.

Ocho Rios
Bay

A3

N

miles

0   ¼

his picture. He is most frequently stopped on the days when cruise ships are in town and when he can be found wandering around the craft market area.

This craft market has a wide range of souvenirs from wood carvings and paintings to tacky T-shirts and plastic toys. But it does have a good atmosphere and haggling for gifts is fun. The vendors try hard to sell their wares but do not give you any hassle, unlike in the more commercial Montego Bay. A good guide for bargain hunting is that the price usually starts around double what the vendor expects to get but, once you have hit their true price, they will rarely budge a cent below it. The market is really designed to cater for the cruise-ship passengers as are the growing number of duty-free shopping centres around the town. These sell a wide selection of crystal, lace, jewellery and duty-free drinks. Most of the goods are bargains for the Americans rather than British visitors. In the low, summer season, these shopping arcades sometimes have a rather neglected air and many half-price sales. If you are looking for a souvenir that is really Jamaican, you are better off going to the numerous galleries and smaller shops dotted around the country, often owned and run by the artists themselves.

Ocho Rios is a good place to base a holiday. Many people travel out from Montego Bay, about two hours' drive away, but there is so much to do in the area it is worth staying in one of the town's many hotels. The town itself is only about 1.5km (1ml.) long, built around two roads. Main Street and Dacosta Drive, which is more like a by-pass and on some maps is actually called Main Road. Driving down Main Street can be hazardous, with locals and tourists wandering into the road.

Approaching the town from Port Antonio, you pass most of the hotels and all-inclusive resorts. Opposite Sandy Beach Bay there is the Coconut Grove Shopping Centre. The complex houses *Le-Gournand*, a French restaurant that is a good place for a special night out. Most guests dress up for an evening at this friendly restaurant.

Slightly closer to the town is the Pineapple Place Shopping Centre. As well as the usual selection of duty-free shops, Pineapple Place has a small bistro and wine bar. *Neille's* is open from 10 a.m. to 12 midnight and sells a selection of snacks, from pasta and pâté to salt fish and smoked marlin. Pineapple Place is

Ocho Rios Beach

also the headquarters for the Jamaica Association of Villas and Apartments (Tel: 974-2508), which will supply you with information about any of the villas owned by members across the island. The properties range from the luxurious to small family-run guest houses. *Willy's Variety Supermarket* is on Main Street near to Pineapple Place.

Another place to stop and eat between shopping while touring Ocho Rios is at the Little Pub Complex on Main Street. This centre has about twenty shops along with the *Little Pub Inn* and the *Frame Centre Art Gallery*, which has a good display of Jamaican art. It also has some accommodation but it can be noisy. A calypso

band plays every lunchtime and the resident band plays each evening. It is a popular place with the tourists and is usually very busy (Tel: 974-2324/5826).

As you enter the main town from Port Antonio, the road divides into Main Street and Dacosta Drive. The police station is on the left of Dacosta Drive, while most other offices and shops are on Main Street. One of the first sights on Main Street is the *Geddes Memorial Church* on the right. *The Cove Theatre* is just before the main Post Office, which is almost another duty-free shopping centre, Ocean Village and the *craft market*. Further down Main Street is the *Rexo Supermarket* in the new Ocho Rios Plaza.

Take a small right turning off Main Street past the Ocean Village Centre to find the Jamaican Tourist Board offices (Tel: 974-2570/2582).

The office has plenty of information about tours to the local places of interest as well as details of places to stay. The road also takes you down to the town's beach, *Turtle Beach* where you will find plenty of watersports available. Boats and guides are also on hire for both fresh-water and deep-sea fishing. Sailing boats and windsurfing boards are also on the beach and you can go water-skiing or snorkelling from there. There are three main dive operators in town. These are *Fantasea* (Tel: 974-2353), *Sea and Dive Jamaica* (Tel: 972-2162) and *Sun Divers Watersport* (Tel: 973-3509). If you have the energy to run in the Jamaican sunshine, then the annual Appleton/Ting marathon might appeal. The event is split into two races, a full marathon and a 10km (6ml.) run. Held on the second weekend in December, which usually heralds the start of the high season, the race starts near Discovery Bay and the course goes along the coastline into Ocho Rios to finish at the Mallards Beach Hotel in the centre of town. The race attracts international runners from all over the world as well as some of Jamaica's athletic stars.

Hotels actually in town include the Turtle Beach Towers and Apartments (Tel: 974-2801/5), a complex of apartments where guests have the services of a hotel, costing between US$70 and US$150. The hotel is pleasant enough but, while it has a good view of the beach to the east it also has a good view of the cruise-ship terminal and a little further away, Reynolds Pier and the cargo ships. *The Inn on the Beach* (Tel: 974-2782/4) is cheap and cheerful at about US$55 per night and is just behind the craft market. It is one of the Inns of Jamaica, a group of hotels known for their basic but cheerful style, offering true Jamaican hospitality and cooking. The nearby *Hibiscus Lodge Hotel* is also an Inn of Jamaica and costs about US$44 per room per night (Tel: 974-2678). With its air of time gone by, it is an extremely popular hotel, not least for its restaurant, *The Almond Tree*, which serves some of the best food in town. You need to book to guarantee a table in its romantic seaside setting (Tel: 974-2813). This hotel is just out to the east of the town centre on the edge of Mallards Bay beach.

Sans Souci Hotel, Jamaica

The Mallards Beach Hotel is actually on The Point between Mallards Bay and Turtle Beach and costs up to US$100 per night (Tel: 974-2201/9). It is one of the town's leading conference and incentive hotels so you could find large business groups sharing the hotel with you. It is worth a visit to its *Vivaldi* restaurant which has live music to accompany your Italian food. *Pineapple Penthouse* is just behind the Pineapple Place shopping centre and costs about US$50 per night (Tel: 974-2727). If you prefer to stay slightly out of town, there is a wide range of good hotels, including the two Elegant Resorts of Jamaica properties, *Sans Souci* and *Plantation Inn* at Boscobel Beach, all-inclusive hotels that welcome children. The Elegant Resorts of Jamaica is a group of six hotels that have joined together to market their properties. They are all of a very high standard and tend to be decorated and run in a style more reminiscent of days gone by. Sans Souci has one of Jamaica's three natural spas to add to its charms. It is an expensive place to stay but its pastel pink and white buildings nestle on the hillside to make it a wonderfully romantic destination (Tel: 974-2353/4 or 974/2535). It also has an excellent restaurant, *Casanova*, with Italian-trained chefs to guarantee a superb meal. The Plantation Inn is on Sandy Beach Bay and costs up to US$195 per night. It is close to town but has a nice, quiet beach (Tel: 974-5601).

Jamaica Inn (Tel: 974-2514/6) used to be a member of Elegant Resorts but now does its own marketing. One of Jamaica's most famous hotels, its old-world charm has attracted guests to return for year after year, including Sir Winston Churchill, who used to stay at the hotel to paint his watercolours. Most guests dress up for dinner on Saturday night. It costs between US$135 and US$205 and is situated between the two Elegant Resorts next to the Shaw Park Hotel.

On the beach at Cutlass Bay, *Shaw Park* is a lovely hotel and a firm favourite among the British. It has a spacious, elegant air while providing all the modern-day amenities you would expect. Slightly cheaper than the Elegant Resorts hotels, it costs up to about US$162 per night. The old Shaw Park Hotel used to be in the mountains overlooking the town and its gardens have now been opened as a public park.

The number of all-inclusive hotels is increasing in Jamaica and there are three in the Ocho Rios area. A number of them are linked to Superclubs and more details of them can be got by telephoning 0992-447420 in the UK. The Superclubs in Ocho Rios are *Couples* and *Boscobel Beach*. Most of the all-inclusives cater for single people or couples but Boscobel Beach, which is close to Oracabessa, will also take children. The hotel has plenty of nannies to look after the children and give parents a break and it costs in the region of US$1,100 for seven nights. Couples is close to Ocho Rios but, as the name suggests, will only take couples. It costs around US$2920 for seven nights. Eden II, which is on the west of town, costs in the region of US$1,100 for seven nights. Again, the hotel only accepts couples. The room rate includes green fees and transfers at the nearby 18-hole golf-course and the hotel has complimentary trips to Dunn's River Falls and into Ocho Rios.

Sandals have two properties in Ocho Rios. Sandals Dunn's River opened in 1990 with 256 rooms. Guests at any of Sandals' Jamaican properties can take advantage of their 'stay at one: enjoy all five' policy which allows you to take day trips to the other resorts at no extra charge. *Sandals Ocho Rios* (Cibony) houses some paintings by local artists, including four by Seya Parboosingh. A famous Jamaican artist, she left the country after the death of her husband, Karl, in 1975. He had been a well-known painter before even meeting Seya and bringing her to Jamaica. She returned thirteen years later and has started work again at her home in St Andrews.

Restaurants Many of the hotels have excellent restaurants that attract non-residents as well as residents, but there are also plenty of other restaurants in town. The *Carib Inn Restaurant* (Tel: 974-2445) is in the middle of town and specializes in seafood. Close by is the *Palm Beach Restaurant* in the Ocean Village Shopping Centre (Tel: 974-5007) which has a garden terrace overlooking Ocho Rios Bay. Rivers and waterfalls dominate much of the tourist activity in Ocho Rios, and *Ruins Restaurant* reflects that watery atmosphere. Built around a waterfall on the Turtle River, it can be found on Dacosta Drive (Tel: 974-2442/2789) and is open for lunch and dinner from Monday to Saturday and for dinner only on Sunday.

On Main Street, *Tradewinds* restaurant can be recommended for its pleasant setting in a courtyard garden; it is open from 7.30 a.m. to 10.30 p.m. (Tel: 974-2433). Slightly further out of town is the fairly new *Nuccio Italian Restaurant* on Eden Bower Road, opposite the Carinosa Gardens. This is the 'in place' to go in Ocho Rios and is slightly over-priced but is in a good setting overlooking the town, and the food is good, too. Still further out of town towards Port Antonio is *Harmony Hall*. This restaurant was once a Great House and is worth stopping at while visiting the art gallery. Open for both lunch and dinner, it has a good selection of light meals (Tel: 974-4222).

Gardens Ocho Rios is a paradise for botanists. The parish of St Ann's is known for its spectacular gardens and many of those are found within easy reach of the town. The *Cariñosa Gardens* are set in 20-acres of waterfalls and rain forest. Only recently opened it costs J$55 to enter and opening hours are from 9 a.m. to 5 p.m. daily. The gardens are also home to a wide selection of exotic birds – over 200 birds are housed in a walk-through aviary. Cariñosa Gardens are perched in the hills overlooking the town,

**Dunn's River Falls are climbed
daily by hundreds of tourists**

much like neighbouring *Shaw Park Gardens* where the entrance fee is much lower. Open daily from 9 a.m. to 5 p.m., it costs just J$12 and it is easy to spend a day wandering through the trees and plants, catching glimpses of tropical birds and rare orchids.

Continuing out of town on the road to Moneague, is the spectacular *Fern Gully*. Jamaicans claim that the Gully has the widest variety of ferns anywhere in the world. Over 500 different species are found along the 5km (3ml.) of old river bed. Although you need a car to get there, it is easy to stop and spend a couple of hours under the cool green canopies away from the heat of the beach and bustle of town.

All the botanical gardens in the area feature waterfalls. But at *Dunn's River Falls*, the water dominates the gardens. The Falls cascade over 200m (650ft) down to the beach. Open from 8 a.m. to 5 p.m. daily, it cost J$4 to get into the gardens and a total of J$21 to hire a guide to help you climb the Falls. Although it looks a dangerous and difficult climb, it is quite easy and it has been done both by pensioners and by a one-legged man. Holding your guide's hand, he will lead you up the Falls, stopping to take your picture to prove you did it. If you prefer not to get wet, there are steps alongside the Falls, from which you get a bird's eye view of everyone scrambling up through the water. You may well recognize the Falls. They have been the setting for many films and adverts.

Yet another watery experience in the Ocho Rios area, and another tourist trap, is *Jamaica Night* on the White River. On Tuesday and Sunday evenings, you can be taken on a short boat ride to a barbecue and folk show. It costs J$212 and lasts four hours, from 7 p.m. to 11 p.m.

The Jamaica Tourist Board organizes tours to most of these places (Tel: 974-2582) and most of the hotels also have details of local tours.

Harmony Hall There are plenty of day trips in the Ocho Rios area. Going along the coast road towards Port Antonio, one of the first stops is just over the White River. Harmony Hall is about 6km (4ml.) out of town. The house was built in 1886 and was originally a Methodist Manse. In 1980, a group of enthusiasts bought the property and started restoration work. A year later it was officially opened by the Rt Hon. Edward Seaga who was then Prime Minister. In its centenary year, Harmony Hall received an award from Berger Paint's as part of its Heritage in Architecture scheme. It is now home to an art gallery, shops and a restaurant. The gallery specializes in Jamaican art and has regular exhibitions and craft shows. The shops sell a variety of art, antiques, books and ceramics. Both the gallery and shops are open daily from 10 a.m. to 6 p.m. (Tel: 974-4222). The pub and restaurant are open from 11 a.m. to 12 a.m. (Tel: 974-4233) and is styled on an English pub with typical pub food. A shuttle runs from Ocho Rios to Harmony Hall, picking up passengers from

Staff at Circle B Plantation are happy to cut up fruits for visitors to sample

the Inn on the Beach, Little Pub, Plantation Inn, Jamaica Inn, Shaw Park and Sans Souci. Ask for Watson's Shopping Shuttle.

Prospect Plantation If you turn right in Frankfort, just before reaching Harmony Hall, the road takes you up to one of the working plantations that surround Ocho Rios. Prospect Plantation is a working estate and visitors are shown the banana, cocoa, pimento, sugar-cane, coconut and bread-fruit crops. An unusual feature of the farm is that trees have been planted by many famous names to commemorate their visits to Prospect. Trees have been planted by Jamaica's first native-born Governor-General, Sir Clifford Campbell, Prince Philip, Sir Winston Churchill, Lord Hailes, the Governor of the West Indies Federation, Edward Heath, Henry Kissinger, Pierre Trudeau, Noel Coward and Charlie Chaplin.

The Plantation surrounds the White River Gorge where Jamaica's first hydro-electric power station was built by Sir Harold Mitchell. The guides are full of interesting information and happy to answer all your questions. Tours operate from 10.30am to 3.30pm daily and cost J$52. There are also four horseback trails across the farm, open from Mondays to Saturdays (Tel: 974-2058) and bookings must be made in advance. The farm also contains a 18-hole miniature golf-course which is open seven days a week from 9 a.m. to 5 p.m. (Tel: 974-2058). The plantation also has an undenominational chapel which has regular services.

Brimmer Hall Further down the coast road to Port Maria is another plantation, Brimmer Hall. Take the road out of Oracabessa towards Free Hill and then head for Bailey's Vale. Brimmer Hall lies between the two villages. Entrance costs J$60 and the farm is open from 9 a.m. to 5 p.m. It was originally a Great House and is still owner-occupied. The Great Houses were built across Jamaica by plantation owners and are monuments to the wealth and grandeur of the sugar-cane farmers. The tour gives visitors a chance to see the old farming methods in action.

Between the two plantations is the Rio Nuevo. It is the site of the last battle between the Spanish and English and is preserved by the Jamaica National Heritage Trust. The *Boscabel Beach Hotel* is close to Oracabessa where you will also find plenty of holiday cottages, such as *Marven Beach Cottage* owned by Maurice and Pat

Noel Coward's house is open to the public

Sale. The cottage costs about us$1000 'per week and sleeps four (Tel: 925-8783). This section of the coastline has long been a hideaway for the rich and famous.

Goldeneye, just outside Port Maria, was once owned by Ian Fleming, the creator of James Bond. Fleming used to shut himself away in the house to write. Since his death, the house has been rented out, and one of its most famous visitors was Noel Coward. After one visit in the 1950s he was so impressed with the estate that he built the nearby Firefly, where he lived until his death. Goldeneye is still occasionally rented out but you can make a reservation to tour around. Even without a special appointment, you can get into the seven-acre gardens leading to a private beach without anyone objecting. Noel Coward's house Firefly is far more interesting. The entrance fee is J$5 and it is open Monday to Saturday from 9 a.m. to 4 p.m. Everything is left exactly as it was the day he died, with songsheets still on the piano and books left open. He is buried in the garden overlooking Blue

Harbour, his first home on the island, where he used to entertain his many friends. Both these houses are also easily reached from Port Antonio.

Port Maria itself is a sleepy little coastal town. If you want to stay at a hotel in the area, try the *Casa Maria* which costs from US$55 to US$116 per night (Tel: 994-2323). Villa accommodation is plentiful around Ocho Rios. To the east of town there is *Rock Edge Bay Villas* at Oracabessa (Tel: 974-3232), *Sea Chalet Villas* (Tel: 974-3265) and *The Margarita House* (Tel: 974-3230) at Boscobel. To the west of town is *Sunny Sands* (Tel: 972-2323) and *The Laurentia Villa* (Tel: 972-2552) at Mammee Bay.

Ocho Rios is linked to the capital, Kingston, by two main roads. One is via the Fern Gully and Moneague. The road takes you past the scenic *Upton Country Club* and its golf-course. The Club is close to *Friendship Farm*, which is another of the area's working plantations. In *Walkers Wood*, the 583-acre farm also offers visitors horse-riding, swimming and fishing. It also has a picnic area and a small restaurant. The village also has a woodworking shop, which is one of the best places on the island to buy carvings. The other road to Kingston is via Port Maria. Turn right just before Annotto Bay and head towards Castleton. You can stop off at the Botanical Gardens in this mountain town before descending out of the mountains down to Kingston.

Travelling west out of Ocho Rios is just as interesting as the eastward road. Only 11km (7ml.) along the coast road is St Ann's Bay where Christopher Columbus was stranded for a year after his ships fell apart. His statue commemorates the event. The town's other large statue is of national hero Marcus Garvey who was born here. He played a major role in leading the Black Consciousness movement. Before reaching St Ann's from Ocho Rios, is *Drax Hall* where polo is played on Saturday afternoons. Drax Hall is close to the Eden II resort and Arawak Inn both on Mammee Bay Beach, which is one of the best in the Ocho Rios area.

St Ann's to Falmouth The whole stretch of coastline between St Ann's and Falmouth is easily accessible for day trips from both Ocho Rios and Montego Bay. There are plenty of tour operators who will take you around, either in groups or as one party. Local buses and taxis also travel up and down this road

Runaway Caves, Jamaica

regularly. Just to the west of St Ann's is *Sevilla Nueva* which was Jamaica's first Spanish settlement. Founded in 1509 by Christopher Columbus's son, Diego, the remains of the old fort can still be found.

Continuing west, turn left down the road to Bamboo to get to the *Circle B Plantation*, which is well signposted. This farm is open daily from 10 a.m. to 5 p.m., costing J$62, and visitors can enjoy a traditional Jamaican feast after a tour of the working farm.

Back on the coast road, the next stop is Chukka Cove, which has taken over from Drax Hall as the international polo ground. The resort (Tel: 974-2593/2239) offers riding tuition, treks and international competitions. Guest have the use of the show-jumping, dressage, cross-country and polo facilities. Two- and three-day trips can be organized to the nearby seventeenth-century Great House, *Lilyfields*, which has recently been restored by former cultural minister Arnold Bertram. *The Chukka Cave Cliffs* have been used as film sets for *Papillon* and *Return to Treasure Island*.

Runaway Bay The quiet resort of Runaway Bay has plenty of accommodation although most of it is all-inclusive and there are few restaurants in the area. But there is plenty to do. It is one of the most historic areas of Jamaica. It was in this area that Columbus first landed, that the Spanish tried to settle, that the British chased them off and where Arawak Indian caves abound.

Runaway Bay was named after the Spaniards escaped from here to Cuba after being routed by the British in 1658. They were led by ex-governor Ysasi and escaped through the Runaway Caves which had been home to Arawak Indians centuries before. The 16km (10ml.) cave system was also a haven for pirates and smugglers but now 11km (7ml.) of caves are open to the public. The highlight of the tour is a boat ride 37m (120ft) below ground across the Green Grotto. The Grotto is linked to a large lagoon, and thirsty tourists get a chance to stop off at Black Beard's saloon to quench their thirst.

Runaway Bay is also a mecca for keen golfers. The club used to be part of the Jamaica Jamaica complex and the hotel's room rate still includes green fees. The golf-course was designed by British naval commander James Harris and is the site of the annual Jamaica Pro-Am tournament in November. This is Jamaica's oldest golf tournament, established in 1953. For more details, contact the club on 973-2561.

Hotels Among the hotels at Runaway Bay is the *Runaway Bay* HEART *Country Club*. Slightly inland but with good views of the ocean, the hotel costs about US$50 per night. It has a restaurant, *Cardiff Hall*, open to non-residents and is a hotel training centre (Tel: 973-2671/4). Surrounding Cardiff Hall Beach is the American *Jack Tar Beach*, Jamaica Jamaica, Silver Spray and Club Caribbean. *Jamaica Jamaica* (Tel: 973-2436/8) costs in the region of US$284 per night, while *Silver Spray* (Tel: 973-3413/2006) costs up to about US$60 per night. *Jamaica Jamaica* is a member of Superclubs and can be booked in the UK on 0992-447420.

The *Club Caribbean* was badly hit by Hurricane Gilbert in 1988 and took almost a year to recover but the extensive refurbishment does mean that the hotel has every up-to-date facility. It costs between US$88 and US$150 per night (Tel: 973-3507/8). The *Caribbean Isle* to the west of the town is more modest in price, costing about US$57 per night (Tel: 973-2364). This is one of the Inns of Jamaica, known for its good Jamaican cooking and welcoming atmosphere.

There are also plenty of villas in Runaway Bay, such as *Pimento Villa* overlooking the golf-course (Tel: 952-6115), *Ponciana Place Villa* with its private swimming-pool (Tel: 926-9284) or *Rambling Rose Villa* with its own private beach (Tel: 973-2447). The villas are nearly all fully staffed but often guests are asked to do their own shopping before the cook takes over. The town has two supermarkets, the *A & B Valumart* next to the Club Caribbean, and *Taylor's Supermarket* which is in the square.

Restaurants Eating out in the town is limited. Most of the hotels have very good restaurants but there is little else. For a local experience, try *Aunt May's Bird Restaurant and Lounge*, which is near Ambiance Hotel. Cheap and cheerful, it is busy, noisy and open seven days a week.

Discovery Bay A short drive out of Runaway Bay is Discovery Bay. This was where Columbus was first thought to have landed. Now the archaeologists believe he actually landed a little further to the west of Rio Bueno. Now the town is dominated by the bauxite loading port just to the west of the town. Bauxite is used in aluminium smelting and was once one of Jamaica's most important exports. Jamaica is still the third largest producer of bauxite in the world but demand has fallen. The port activities create a fine red dust over everything but the real problem is the traffic. Lorries hurtle along the road through the town, making it difficult to cross the road. The noise of the traffic can also be a nuisance, particularly at night.

But despite the lorries and busy port, this is a delightfully quiet little town from where it is easy to see much of the north-coast region and inland to the mountains.

Hotels If you want to stay in Discovery Bay, try *Portside Villas*, which are across the Bay from the bauxite port. There are villas on the beach and also slightly up the hill where it is quieter.

The *Accommodationer* is a pleasant guest house which costs about US$40 per night (Tel: 973-2559).

Columbus Park Between Discovery Bay and Rio Bueno is Columbus Park, an open-air museum containing many artefacts from the first days of European settlement in Jamaica. The park is well laid out with good information boards. Entry is free and there is a small snack and soft drink stall. If you are driving from Montego Bay to Ocho Rios, it is a nice place to stop and take in the spectacular sea views. This whole area is likely to undergo a transformation in the next couple of years, building up to the Columbus celebrations in 1992. He first discovered the Caribbean five hundred years before and the entire region is planning special celebrations. Jamaica is also likely to continue those celebrations into 1994, five hundred years after Columbus first landed in Jamaica.

Arawak Caves Just beyond the Rio Bueno and the site of Columbus's landing is a cave system known as Arawak Caves. These Indians had originally come from South America but are believed to have colonized the island hundreds of years before the first Europeans arrived. The caves provided shelter for the Indians.

In more recent times, the caves have been the haunt of smugglers. Pirates roamed the coastline a few hundred years ago but today the modern-day smugglers are more interested in drugs than hidden treasure.

Duncans The road from Discovery Bay to Duncans and on to Falmouth is very straight and up to a few years ago was used by drug smugglers to land their small aeroplanes. As you travel along the road you will see many telegraph poles scattered around the road but no wires. These poles were deliberately planted to stop the planes from landing and you will also see the remains of some of the planes that did not make it.

Villas There are no hotels in Duncans but there is villa accommodation. Visitors to this area are attracted by the peace and quiet and beautiful beaches. Although this coastline was hit hard by the hurricane in 1988, it is difficult to tell. With the warm, wet climate, the vegetation quickly recovered and any damage to holiday villas and hotels was quickly repaired. Many of the villas were given a refurbishment and many hoteliers and villa owners joke that the best time to stay is after a hurricane because all the properties get redecorated.

It is about a 30-minute drive to Montego Bay from Duncans and you will probably find it easier if you have your own vehicle. Some villa owners do provide transport with the accommodation but often the drivers will really only take you to the nearest beach or shops. Among the villas to choose from are *Blue Vista, Casuarina, Ebb Tide, Je Suis Content, Kamarr Villa, Lucknow, Oh Boy* or *Pineapple Villa*. All the villas in this area can be booked on Tel: 954-2001 or in the UK, Tel: 071-486 1301/2.

Closer to Falmouth is the all-inclusive resort, *Trelawny Beach Hotel*. Set around a beautiful private beach, the hotel has an excellent programme of watersports. It also has some good restaurants and shops, and offers guests trips to the nearby sights, including a free shuttle service to Montego Bay. Rates vary between about US$100 and US$180 (Tel: 954-2450/8) and can be booked in the UK through Lawson International on 081-541 1199.

Heading towards Falmouth, only a five-minute drive away, takes you past the unusual luminous lagoon. Moonlight sets off the tiny phosphorescent creatures, allowing you to see right down in to the water. The Martha Brae River reaches the sea at this point between Trelawny Beach and Falmouth. Rafting was made popular by Errol Flynn in Port Antonio but the sport has spread across the island. Guides will pole you slowly down the river for about an hour, on a trip costing about J$205. The tour operates from 9 a.m. to 4 p.m., call 952-0889 for details. It starts from Rafters' Rest about 5km (3ml.) south of Falmouth where there are some souvenir shops selling T-shirts and similar items, picnic grounds, a swimming-pool and a small restaurant. At the mouth of the river is some of the best fishing in the area. Tarpon and kingfish are among the easiest catches.

Also on the east side of Falmouth is the batik gallery displaying the work of Muriel Chandler. *Caribatik Gallery* is open mid-November to mid-May from 10 a.m. to 3 p.m., Tuesday to Saturday and admission is free. Groups or visits at other times can be arranged on Tel: 954-3314. The open-air studio is set among tropical trees and flowers at Rock Wharf. Muriel and her husband, Keith, moved to Jamaica in 1970 and she has used the country as her inspiration for fabric designs that have been snapped up by world-famous fashion designers such as Calvin Klein, Anna Klein, Oscar de la Renta and Bill Blass. Muriel's

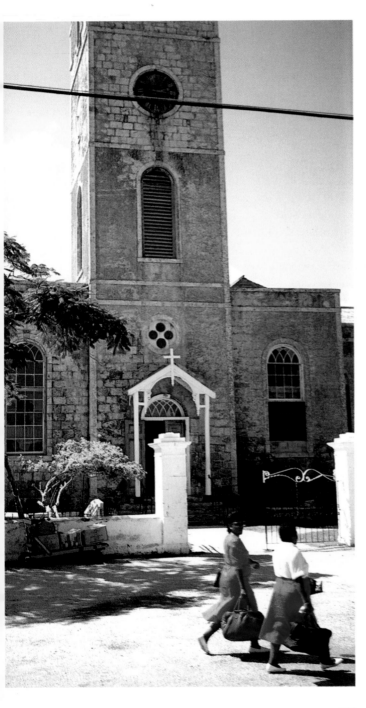

**Falmouth, Jamaica is famous
for its old church and
Georgian buildings**

paintings are hung in many private villas across the country as well as in some of the international hotels. Close to the studio, she also has an art gallery devoted to her paintings.

Falmouth As you enter Falmouth from the east you pass one of its best restaurants, *Glistening Waters*. The town itself is full of Georgian buildings, some of which have been carefully restored. As you enter town from the east, turn left by a strange-shaped building that looks like a Kent oast house to get into the bustling market. This market is for local people rather than tourists and is a good place to find exotic fruit and vegetables. The market is close to the town's bus station so there are always plenty of people milling around.

Among the Georgian buildings that have been restored is a colonial court house and some houses. There is a fine parish church on the eastern side of town. It is still in regular use every Sunday with choir practice during the week. The Church of St Paul has a fine Victorian portico. The William Knibb Memorial Church on the corner of George Street and King Street is dedicated to one of the abolitionists of the early 1800s. These missionaries came from London after appeals for help from ministers already working in Jamaica.

A good local restaurant is the *Seventh Heaven Lobster Pot* on the west side of Falmouth. Known throughout the area for its excellent seafood, diners travel out from Montego Bay to this restaurant.

Just to the west of Falmouth is the *Jamaica Safari Village*. Once the set for the James Bond film *Live and Let Die*, the farm still has plenty of crocodiles and brave visitors get the chance to pick up some of the snakes bred at the Village. The Village is open daily from 8.30 a.m. to 6 p.m. and entrance is J$50. There is a small bar and snack stall at the farm.

Travelling south out of town towards the Cockpit Country on the road to Good Hope will take you to the Good Hope Plantation. Unlike the other Great Houses scattered around the country, Good Hope, is still lived in and is not a museum. Coconuts and coffee are among the crops grown on the estate. One of the highlights of a visit to the plantation is the horse-riding through spectacular scenery and past Georgian relics. The house does take in guests at US$160 per night and has a private beach on the coast 16km (10ml.) away. Staying at the Good Hope Plantation, you may well be among cultural experts, from historians to naturalists, who flock to this living monument to the plantation days (Tel: 954-3289).

The Cockpit Country This a wild and weird area of the island, full of intrigue and mystery of days gone by. The Maroons used its wildness to full effect in keeping the English at bay and managed to survive despite the remoteness of the area. Even now the descendants of the Maroons still live in these mountains leading their own particular way of life. The Maroons were a group of runaway slaves, first from the Spanish and then from the British. To add to their numbers, the Maroons sometimes raided farms and stole the slaves. The British never managed to conquer these people and in the end were forced to give them rights to the Cockpit Country. Maroons are found on several of the other Caribbean islands and on the South American mainland.

Geographically, this is an area of pitted limestone. It is mountainous and covered with dense foliage. Most visitors to Jamaica miss out completely on this area. There are organized tours which give you a glimpse of the country, but the best way to see it is to go on your own, stopping where you want and

Inland, away from the hustle and bustle of the resorts, everything is peaceful

211

getting to meet the local people. The main places to visit in Cockpit Country are Maroon Town, Accompong, Seaford Town and the Windsor caves. These sites surround an area of mountain that is virtually inaccessible. To explore further you need a good, local guide and will probably have to walk most of the way because the roads are impassable.

If you continue up the road from Falmouth, past the Good Hope Plantation, the road will eventually come to a T-junction. Turn left and take the first right to head out to the *Windsor Caves* and the start of the Martha Brae River. The caves are full of bats which all surge out of the caves at sunset. The caves contain underground rivers and springs but none has been opened up for the public. Pot-holers are the only people who venture down into the system.

Bunker's Hill Returning back down the road, turn left at the T-junction and carry on past the turning to Falmouth and you will come to the tiny community of Bunker's Hill. Despite this being a remote village, its carvings have been exported world-wide. A dozen carvers work in *Obed Palmer's* tiny workshop, crafting Jamaican cedar into a wide selection of animals, which are then brightly painted and shipped off to *Liz DeLisser's Gallery* in Church Street, Montego Bay. The animals have also been shipped to New York, Japan and the Cayman Islands. Most carvers in Jamaica use cedar because it carves well and does not crack easily, and Palmer's work is in such demand that he goes through at least a tree a week. There are plenty of carvers around the whole island but these brightly painted animals and birds have become particularly well known.

Continuing along the road from Bunker's Hill takes you to Maroon Town, the capital of Cockpit Country. Tours operate on a daily basis from Montego Bay to the heart of Maroon country. The tours often take in Catadupa where you can order a garment from the local tailors and collect it as you travel home later in the day. Catadupa is close to the *Croydon Estates*, which is a coffee, pineapple and citrus plantation. Tours operate from Montego Bay (Tel: 952-4137) and include lunch with Blue Mountain coffee. While at the farm, visitors get a chance to see the coffee being processed as well as sample the fruits in season. The *Governor's Coach Tour* is run by Jamaica Tours and takes in the *cloth market* at Catadupa, *Ipswich Caves* and on to the *Appleton Rum Distillery*.

The day-long trip by train costs about J$220 and operates from Tuesday to Friday (Tel: 952-2887/1398).

Seaford Town Catadupa is close to the unusual German settlement of Seaford Town. Germans first arrived in Jamaica in the late 1830s but Seaford is really the only complete community. It was founded in 1835 and a museum by the Sacred Heart Mission tells the tale of the settlement. Residents are poor and inbreeding has produced some strange characters because they refused to integrate with the Jamaican community. About 200 survive in the mile-long town, eking out an existence from poor-quality farming land.

Accompong Further into Cockpit Country is the other major Maroon town of Accompong. This is where the Maroons hold their annual festival in January. Dating back to the nineteenth century, the festival is still full of traditional singing, dancing, feasting and ceremonies. The traditional music includes blowing the Abeng and playing maroon drums. The Abeng cow horn was used as a signal in the days when the Maroons fought their guerilla war with the British soldiers. They also used to blow the conch shell. The Maroons from across Cockpit Country gather for this lively event.

Appleton Rum Estate Tours to the Appleton Rum Estate leave Montego Bay on a regular basis. The two main tours are either the Governor's Coach Tour or the Appleton Express. Like Governor's Coach Tour, the *Appleton Express* (Tel: 952-3692) takes you on a train journey from Montego Bay to Ipswich Caves and on to the rum distillery, where you sample the estate's produce. The train was stopped for several months while they straightened out and repaired the track, which winds through the mountains, so the journey should be easier and quicker in the future. You can also visit the Appleton Distillery from Mandeville or Kingston.

Mandeville Mandeville is perhaps the most British of the Jamaican towns and cities. Nestling high in the mountains, it has retained a colonial feel. The air is cooler, the pace slower and the residents are welcoming. The tourist industry has not hit Mandeville with its full force, unlike Montego Bay, and people often go to Mandeville to get away from the hustle and bustle of the seaside resorts.

The Manchester Club, Mandeville, Jamaica offers guests good food in a colonial atmosphere

It is perhaps a quiet town but there is still plenty to do and places to visit in the surrounding countryside. The most dramatic way to arrive in Mandeville is along the road from Kingston which takes you through a large gorge, appearing like a gate to the town.

The town, founded in 1816, was originally named after Viscount Mandeville, the eldest son of the Duke of Manchester who was Governor of Jamaica. The surrounding parish was created in 1814 and named after the Duke, who served as Governor for nineteen years.

There are no slums in the town, which owes its prosperity first to farming and then, in the 1950s, to the bauxite. The bauxite is used in aluminium smelting. Mining is still intensive in the area, with a huge Alcan plant just a few miles out of town, but it does not impinge on the serenity of the area. Visits to the plant can be

214

arranged but usually require a day's notice. The town has several shopping centres with a range of small shops and supermarkets. To find out what is going on in the town, it is worth just stopping and having a chat to people in the stores. They are all friendly and eager to point you in the right direction to find a restaurant or to find a place to visit.

Hotels With relatively few tourists, restaurants and hotels are fairly limited but those that are there offer good food and service at a good price. A visit to the *Astra Hotel* (Tel: 962-3265) on the outskirts of town is well worth it. It is another of the Inns of Jamaica, so you are guaranteed a high standard of service. Staying at the hotel costs up to US$100 per night but it is also the local information centre. Trips into the countryside can be arranged and accommodation for other places around the island can be booked.

The other main hotel in the town is the *Mandeville Hotel* right in the town centre which can cost up to US$110 (Tel: 962-2138). This hotel was built in 1875 as the officers' quarters and mess for one of four British regiments stationed in Jamaica at the time. It is now owned by Mark and Ceciline McIntyre, parents of Diana McIntyre-Pike who owns the *Astra Hotel* with her husband Carey. Both hotels have restaurants.

Restaurants The Pot Pourri, is a somewhat rickety building, but it houses one of the best places for value for money on the island. The meal of excellent Jamaican-style cooking was served by waiters and waitresses in starched white uniforms. The Manchester Club, which is the oldest club in the Caribbean, founded in 1868, has a 9-hole golf-course and tennis courts but to play you must be introduced by a member. The club also has a small crafts shop attached. It sits on top of a small hill in the centre of town and gives you a good view of Mandeville.

Another excellent restaurant is *Bill Laurie's Steak House*, which is in the old Bloomfield Hotel on the edge of town, perched on the mountainside for panoramic views. Closed on Sundays, this restaurant is a mecca for car enthusiasts who visit the restaurant to get a look at Bill Laurie's vintage car collection and other antiques. And if you are looking for something different, try the *International Chinese Restaurant* on Newport Road.

While staying in Mandeville, take a walk around the old town centre. The Mandeville Hotel on Hotel Street is just down the road from the local police station, which is close to the village green known as Cecil Charlton Park. It is named after a former town mayor who used to live at Huntingdon Summit. Visits to his house can be arranged for any day except Wednesday or Saturday. Entry is free but donations to a local charity are welcomed. The court house is also on the green along with St Marks parish church, built in 1820. This area was developed when the town was first founded and was built to resemble a New England town.

The town's Post Office is just to the north of the park and the Manchester Club is to the west. A market is held daily by the parish church but the best days to visit it are on Mondays, Wednesdays and Fridays. North of the park, just off Hargreaves Avenue, is the Hargreaves Memorial Hospital, reputed to be one of the best outside Kingston, and the town library. The Jamaica Tourist Board has offices on Ward Avenue (Tel: 962-1072).

Slightly further out of town is the SWA Craft Centre, off North Racecourse. The craft centre is sponsored by the Soroptimists and the Women's Auxiliary of the Parish Church to provide work for unemployed girls. Work at the centre includes embroidery, crochet, toys and cooking. South of the town centre is another charity workshop, the *Paul Cross Nursery*. On Manchester Road, the St Paul of the Cross Church has created a self-help project to get people back to the soil and farming. The idea is to grow more locally and so cut dependence on foreign aid. The nursery has a wide range of tropical flowers and trees as well as a wide selection of citrus fruits and a small coffee grove. Visitors pay a J$10 donation.

Just south of the Astra Hotel on the west of town is the *bammy factory*. This is a Jamaican delicacy made from the cassava root, originally eaten by the Arawak Indians. Clem Bloomfield gives demonstrations of how to cook the root every Tuesday and Wednesday. If you are feeling peckish, a place to make your mouth water is the *Pioneer Chocolate Factory*, which is close to the *High Mountain Coffee Factory* on the north of town.

On your way north to the chocolate factory you can work up an appetite by walking around *Mrs Stephenson's Garden*. She will act as a guide around the garden filled with orchids, anthuria and ortaniques. Many of her plants and flowers have won prizes at the

Annual Manchester Horticultural Show held in Mandeville at the end of May. Entrance to the garden costs J$10.

Another place for nature lovers to visit is *Marshall's Pen*. The Great House itself is over 200 years old but it is now better known for its nature reserve. It is still privately owned and the owners themselves will take you on a tour of the grounds. Robert Sutton, whose ancestors were among the first British settlers in Jamaica, is one of the country's leading ornithologists and while at Marshall's Pen will point out many of the 89 species spotted there. Twenty-three of those are endemic in Jamaica, and endemic reptiles, amphibians, insects and plants can also be found. The best time to visit is between 6 a.m.–9 a.m. and 4 p.m.–6 p.m. and you need an appointment (Tel: 962-2260). A donation of J$30 per person covers the cost of a tour.

One of the best ways to see the surrounding countryside is by horseback. A one-hour ride costs around J$50. *John Nightingale* organizes a morning ride at 9.30 a.m. and an afternoon ride at 3.30 p.m. He needs a day's notice to organize your trip. All these trips can be booked for you by either the Astra or Mandeville Hotel.

Slightly further afield is *Bamboo Avenue*, a 5km (3ml.) stretch of bamboo lining the A2. It was badly hit by Hurricane Gilbert but is growing back and still makes a pleasant place to stop as you travel from Mandeville towards Middle Quarters. This town is known for its shrimps. Women will sell you tiny bags of the highly spiced shrimps, ideal for a snack as you see the sights.

Travelling slightly south-east about 35km (22 ml.) to the coast from Mandeville takes you to *Milk River Spa*. The Spa is open from 7 a.m. to 7 p.m. and is said to have some of the best therapeutic waters anywhere in the world, rivaling some of the great European spas. Scientists who have analysed the water say it has fifty times more radioactivity than places like Baden-Baden.

This section of coastline is unlike any other in Jamaica and is still unspoilt. If you travel along the coastline westwards you will pass through *Alligator Pond* and then on to *Lovers' Leap*. It is a spectacular point along the coast where the cliffs rise vertically by about 215m (700ft). Legend has it that a runaway slave and his lover, who was his owner's daughter, leapt to their deaths from this point, hence the name.

Just along the coast to the west is *Treasure Beach*, one of the nicest beaches in the area. The best stretch is between Great Pedro Buff and Great Pedro Pond. The *Treasure Beach Hotel* was done up a few years ago and offers reasonable accommodation up to about US$86 per night (Tel: 965-2305).

Continuing west along the coast brings you to one of Jamaica's oldest settlements, *Black River*. The Black River meets the sea at this point, having travelled south from the Black River Swamp that surrounds Middle Quarters. South Coast Safaris (Tel: 962-0220) will organize a trip for you up the river at a cost of about US$12 per person. Charles Swaby will take you on a two-hour tour through the bull-rushes where you can glimpse the occasional alligator or the exotic birdlife, such as jacanas, white egrets and ospreys. Fishermen can sit in wait for tarpon or snook. Mr Swaby will tell you the history of the area and the town which used to be the centre for import and exports from the island. He will also take you to one of the lesser known, but most spectacular, of the island's waterfalls, YS, which are close to Middle Quarters.

If you want to stay in Black River try the Hotel Pontio (Tel: 965-2255) which offers cheap accommodation up to about US$40 per night. There are a couple of guest houses at Whitehouse. *Natania's* has an excellent seafood restaurant and costs about US$40 per night (Tel: 965-2536) or try *South Sea View* for about the same price.

For higher-quality accommodation in this area, it is worth going west to Bluefields to stay at the *Wilton on the Sea* guesthouse which cost nearer US$60 per night (Tel: 955-2852). Bluefields has played an important part in Jamaica's history. It was from here that Henry Morgan set sail in 1670 for Panama. He fought his way through the jungle to capture Panama City and returned to Port Royal laden with treasure. Bluefields and Black River both have some of the most secluded and beautiful of the JAVA properties. Details of these villas are available from JAVA in London on 01-486 3560.

Negril Negril is one of the most laid-back towns you will find. It makes the unhurried pace of Mandeville seem positively metropolitan. Nothing can be hurried in a town where time seems irrelevant, with only the sunsets taking on any significance. Negril is on the most westerly point of the island and people gather every evening at the most westerly point of the town,

An aerial shot of Negril Beach

Rick's Café, to see the sun disappear over the horizon and catch the occasional glimpse of the green flashes that sometimes accompany the sunset. The resort has only developed in the past twenty years since it was discovered by American visitors, first by the hippies and then by the jet-set who really started the development of many of the high-quality hotels and resorts. Although development slowed in the 1970s, it has burgeoned in the 1980s, resulting in many new hotels. It is definitely for the young, or young-at-heart, with little to do except lie on the 11km (7ml.) of white sand or try a few of the many watersports on offer.

Historically, there is little of interest in the town. Bloody Bay, which is just to the north of Negril Beach, was the scene of the capture of famous pirate Jack Rackham. He had plagued the north coast of Jamaica for several years before being caught on the beach having a rum punch party. He was tried and executed for his crimes. He was nicknamed Calico Jack because he preferred to wear underwear made from calico and, when he was caught, his surprised captors discovered two of his crew were pregnant women. Bloody Bay was not actually named after the pirate and his raids but after the stories of whales being killed in the bay.

Negril was an important place in the days of sailing ships but never developed into a port because of the Great Morass swamp that runs for two miles behind the town. It now has a drainage system allowing development. Negril is only a couple of hours' drive from Montego Bay and its international airport but there is now a small airport in Negril itself for internal flights. The town itself is a long line of hotels and shops between the beach and the Great Morass. There is no large town centre but most of the activity does centre around the market-place where the major roads from north, east and west all meet.

Norman Manley Boulevard runs into the town from Montego Bay, taking you past many of the smarter hotels and all-inclusive resorts along the 11km of Negril Beach. The airport is on the left of the road as you enter town. Further along the road is the town's Roman Catholic Church. There is also a bank, car rental shops and yoga centre.

As you reach the main road junction you will see the *craft market* on your right between the road and the sea. It is not particularly exciting, with mostly T-shirt stalls, although there are some nice carvings. There are other craft stalls along West End Road, but, be warned, these are excellent hagglers and it is very difficult to negotiate a bargain. But, if you want a particular carving, they will sit down, find a suitable piece of wood and do the work for you. Do make sure you both know what the carving will cost.

Norman Manley Boulevard ends in a roundabout. The road off to the east goes to Sheffield, and on to Mandeville, while the road to the west is West End Road and travels along Negril's cliffs to Negril Lighthouse.

The *Jamaica Tourist Board Office* (Tel: 957-4243) is close to the roundabout in Negril Plaza. The Plaza also contains the doctor's surgery, open from 11 a.m. to 4 p.m. (Tel: 957-4443), two banks, *Vernon's Car Rentals, Joy's Boutique*, a duty-free shop and the *Save A Dollar* supermarket. Next door is the town's taxi stand. Turn on to West End Road to find the town's *Post Office*, the *Negril Yacht Club* and the *K. West Pharmacy*, which is open daily from 9 a.m. to 7 p.m. on Sundays from 11 a.m. to 5 p.m. There is also a resident doctor at Llantrissant opposite the St Mary's Anglican Church on Lighthouse Road (Tel: 957-4259).

The narrow road continues past many guest houses, hotels and restaurants until it ends at the end of Long Bay and at the lighthouse, which is 100 years old and 100 feet high. Just before the lighthouse you pass two of the most popular cafés, *Kaisers* and *Rick's*. Rick's is the traditional place to watch the sunset, sipping a daiquiri, munching lobster and marvelling at the divers who launch themselves off the cliffs into the dazzling blue sea below. The cliffs with their arches and inlets make a good place for snorkelling, and scuba-diving lessons are available from here. Rick's is a bit pricy compared to the rest of Negril so many young people are moving along the cliff top to Kaisers. The Café has live music at least once a week. The West End is also home to artist Geraldine Robins who has a studio there.

Turn left at the roundabout down the road to Savanna-La-Mar, to find a petrol station, the fire and police station as well as the health clinic. There are no hospitals in Negril but there are two about 32km (20ml.) away, one in Savannah-La-Mar and one in Lucea (pronounced Lucy).

Hotels There are plenty of places to stay in the town, both on the beach and on top of the cliffs. There are two SuperClub all-inclusive resorts in the town. The latest is the *Grand Lido Resort* and the other is *Hedonism II,* which costs in the region of US$1000 for a week's stay. Both can be booked in advance in the UK on 0992-447420. *Foote Prints in the Sand* can also be booked in the UK (Tel: 0798-32197). It has 30 bedrooms spread out along the beach and costs in the region of US$50 per night. Another beach property is the *Charela Inn* which was developed in the days of the jet-set visitors. Costing up to US$105 per night, it can be booked on 01-948 7488 or on 957-4277 in Negril. Both the Charela Inn and Foote Prints in the Sand Hotel are Inns of Jamaica, specializing in Jamaican cooking and owned by Jamaicans.

If you prefer to stay on the cliff tops, the *Mariner's Inn* is excellent value for money and has an outdoor restaurant offering some of the best Jamaican food, particularly seafood. The small cottages are well spaced out and all have lovely views of the cliffs and sea. It costs about US$75 per night for a room or US$90 for an apartment (Tel: 957-4348). *Hotel SamSara* underwent major renovations in 1989 and is well situated above the cliffs (Tel: 957-4395). *The Ocean Edge Resort Hotel* also has spectacular views across the cliffs, with a sundeck built into the cliffs (Tel: 957-4362/4278) and costs around US$30 a night.

Thrills Hotel is set back from the cliffs on the other side of Lighthouse Road and costs around US$50 a night. It offers a peaceful, shady location with a friendly staff always ready to help (Tel: 957-4390). If you prefer to take your tent, there are camping facilities at the Lighthouse Park (Tel: 957-4346), just beyond the lighthouse. The Park has cabins at US$20 or tent spaces at US$10.

Restaurants Eating out in Negril is easy; choosing the restaurant is more difficult because there is such a choice. Nearly all the hotels, big and small, have good restaurants. *Ricks's Café* and *Kaiser's Café* have their own appeal. And then there is a wide choice of Jamaican restaurants.

Try eating at one of the jerk-pork stops on the beach. Ideal for a cheap and cheerful meal and a cool Red Stripe beer. The only problem with eating at one of the Jamaican stalls is that you will get approached by the higglers and women offering to massage you with aloe creams. They will charge you a small fortune, making London clubs look cheap. If you do start to get any problems, the restaurant owner will usually chase them out for you. Staying on the beach in front of any of the major hotels is no problem as the higglers know they are not allowed there.

Other places to try are the *Sundowner* (Tel: 957-4225) for a West Indian buffet, *Cosmo's Seafood Restaurant* on Norman Manley Boulevard (Tel: 957-4330) for a cheap, casual meal. The Negril Yacht Club has a restaurant specializing in Chinese cuisine and, for French cuisine, try *Café au Lait* at Mirage Cottages (Tel: 957-4471) or 957-4277).

Watersports Once you have had enough of lying on the beach, there are plenty of watersports to try. Scuba-diving courses are available at many of the hotels. *Pringle Water Sports* on Negril Beach offers parasailing, water-skiing, snorkelling, deep-sea fishing, windsurfing and sunset cruises. *Fantasy* sight-seeing cruise lasts from 4 p.m. to 7 p.m. on the yacht *Fantasy* (Tel: 957-4218). *Ray's Parasailing* is based on the beach near Hedonism II (Tel: 957-4349) and offers island picnics and cruises as well as beach-

Wakefield, Jamaica seems a million miles from Wakefield, England from where it took its name

There's good fishing in the Caribbean Sea, which is calmer than the proverbial millpond

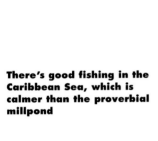

based sports. *Aqua Nova Water Sports* offers the same sort of trips on its 14m (45ft) Trimaran yacht (Tel: 957-4323) and is based at the Negril Beach Club. It also organizes trips to Booby Cay. This is a small island just off the north end of Long Bay and is a nude bathing site. Topless sunbathing is also common in Negril. Booby Cay was used in the filming of Walt Disney's *Twenty Thousand Leagues Under the Sea*.

Horse-Riding To see more of the surrounding countryside, the easiest way is on horseback. Several stables are based around Negril offering two or three-hour rides into the countryside. *Horseman Riding Stables*, Whitehill Estate, offers a trip to the ruins of a 300-year old Great House with views across the Morass and beach (Tel: 957-4472). Other stables in town are *Babo's* on Red Ground Road and the *Country and Western* stables. Most two-hour rides cost around us$25 per person.

Tours to Mandeville and the south coast, Montego Bay and to Ocho Rios are available from Negril. Call Holiday Services for details on 957-4348.

224

Heading out of Negril towards Savanna-La-Mar takes you through fields and fields of sugar-cane before you reach this small coastal town. There is no big beach in the town but just to the east is Wakefield. Nothing like its English namesake, Wakefield is a tiny, sleepy village with a strangely, beautiful coastline. The water is calm and shallow with fish jumping and fishermen chasing them in their dugout canoes. Stakes mark out fishing nets and the whole scene could be centuries old.

Savanna-La-Mar has had a disrupted history. The town was destroyed by a hurricane and tidal wave in 1780. It was the home of one of the few whites to fight against slavery in Jamaica. Henry Clarke started out as an Anglican priest and was later instrumental in founding one of Jamaica's biggest building societies, the National Building Society. Savanna also has one of Jamaica's oldest schools, Manning's which was founded in 1738 with money left by Westmoreland planter Thomas Manning.

Lucea If you travel north from Negril towards Montego Bay, you will come to the capital of Hanover parish, Lucea

The court-house in Lucea stands in this tiny northern town

(pronounced Lucy). This quaint town has a large, modern courthouse on the left-hand side of the road as you enter town. It contrasts completely with the somewhat neglected air of the rest of town. Its other incongruous building is the clock tower in the town centre. It was a gift from the German Kaiser to the island of St Lucia but a muddle-up over names resulted in the tower being left in Lucea, Jamaica. Lucea has the deepest natural harbour around the island which is why the British built *Fort Charlotte* three hundred years ago. It is one of the best-preserved forts on the north coast. French refugee Martin Ruseau was so grateful for finding a new life in Lucea that he gave money for a school to be built. Ruseau's is now in the old barracks.

Montego Bay Mo' Bay is probably the best-known town in the Caribbean. The name conjures up images of sun, sea and sand. It has a large international airport and is the place where most visitors to Jamaica arrive for the first time. Tourists have been coming to Mo' Bay since the turn of the century wanting to try the waters at Doctor's Cave Beach which are meant to have healing powers.

226

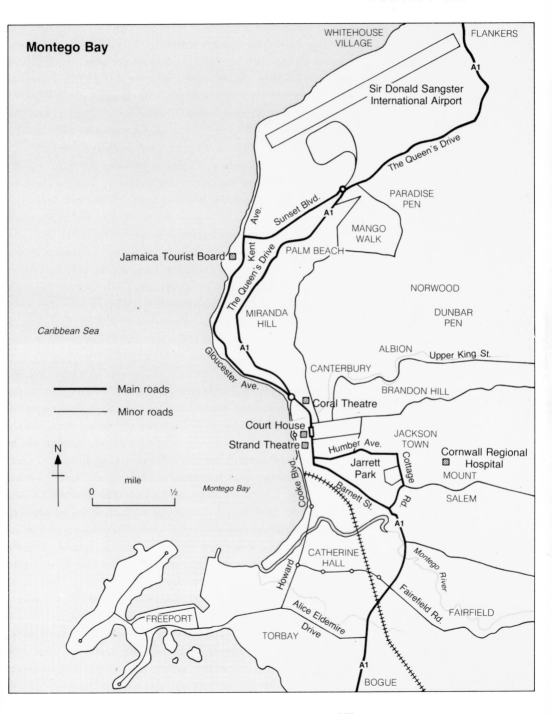

The name Montego came from the Spanish word *manteca*, meaning 'lard'. The Spanish settlers used to kill wild pigs in the mountains and then brought the lard to the port to sell to the ships that called in. At one stage, the town was actually known as Lard Bay before the Spanish word was re-adopted and changed to the present-day Montego Bay. Christopher Columbus was the first European to discover the bay on his voyage in 1494 and he named it the Bay of Good Weather, *Golfo de Buen Tiempo*.

The town is squeezed in a long arc between the coast and the hills behind. Many of the nicer town houses are built on the hills, with commanding views of both the town and the bay. Several of the top restaurants are on top of the town, too, and make good places to sit and sip sundowners The hub of the town is in the centre of the bay, with the majority of hotels and resorts to the north. To the south of Montego Bay there are the exclusive resort areas of Roundhill and the Tyrall Country Club.

The Sir Donald Sangster International Airport is to the north of the town. There are plenty of taxis available there. Check their fares before you get in, and make sure you know whether they are quoting US or Jamaican dollars. The airport itself is a wonderful introduction to Jamaica. As you approach immigration, a group of singers welcomes you and glasses of rum punch are pressed into your hand. Immediately you go through immigration there is a bureau de change and it is worth cashing some money there as the rate is as good as anywhere on the island. Most of the major car-rental agencies have an office at the airport.

The downtown area is centred on *Sam Sharpe Square*, named after the man behind the slave rebellion of 1831. It is also known as the Parade. Sam Sharpe was hanged for leading the rebellion in which all the slaves simply stopped work. They destroyed a lot of property but did not deliberately harm anyone. Hundreds of slaves were killed after the rebellion ended and the event has become known as the Baptist War. *The Cage* is on the north of the square. It was built in 1806 to imprison runaway slaves and the drunken sailors. It now contains a small museum and art gallery.

The ruins of the Courthouse are on the west of the square, close to the *Strand Theatre* on Strand Street and the large *craft market*. The market sells a large variety of T-shirts and other cheap souvenirs. If you visit it you will get a lot of hassle from the vendors and other higglers. There are other craft stalls around the town and plenty of galleries which may mean you lose out on the fun of bargaining for the goods, but they are easier to leave behind, too. This is not a good area to walk around after dark, but in the daytime, there are no problems as long as you do not carry large sums of money or jewellery. If you catch a taxi from this area, make sure it has a red number-plate signifying that it is an official carrier. If you want to visit an authentic Jamaican fruit and vegetable market, go out to the *Charles Gordon Market* on Fustic Street where the colourful array of food will amaze you. Much of it is the exotic produce of the island but it looks like a little piece of Africa.

Other historic sights in Montego Bay include the few remains of the old *Fort*. It was built in a time when every coastal town needed defence but it was rarely used and little remains. Higglers will follow you around in this area, too. The parish church of *St James* was built in 1778 in the shape of a Greek cross but was almost completely destroyed by an earthquake in 1957. The church was restored brick by brick and it is worth a visit. The sculptor John Bacon, who designed the Rodney monument in Spanish Town, built two of the monuments in the 1700s. The church is on Payne Street, not far from Sam Sharpe Square. Every Sunday many of the local residents will dress up in their Sunday Best, complete with colourful ribbons for the weekly service.

Just to the north of the Anglican church is the *Burchell Memorial Church* on the corner of Market Street and King Street. It was built in 1824 by Baptist missionary and abolitionist the Rev. Thomas Burchell. Sam Sharpe was a deacon in the church and many of its first congregations were slaves. Opposite the church and next door to the Georgian House restaurant is the *Gallery of West Indian Art*.

The Dome tower was built in 1837 to protect a spring of fresh water, and the keeper of the Creek had a store there. The Spring supplied the town with water until the end of the last century.

There are still some Georgian townhouses left in the downtown area. The English red bricks were brought from England as ballast, with the sugar-cane crops filling the holds for the return journeys. Two of the town's best restaurants occupy the sites now. *Town House* was built in 1765 by a prosperous merchant David Morgan, ten years before the Parish Church was built opposite. After the death of Mr Morgan it was used as the church manse for several years before the mistress of one of the islands governors took it over. Queen Victoria stayed in the house on her way to the estate of Count Diacre-de-Liancourt at Mosquito Cove, where his descendants still live. Since then the house has been used as a masonic lodge and as a synagogue as well as a private house for Lady Sarah Churchill before becoming a hotel. It is now split into offices, with the restaurant in the converted cellars. It specializes in steaks and seafood (Tel: 952-2660). The *Georgian House* on Orange Street has also been restored and converted into a restaurant, including a garden courtyard area (Tel: 952-0632).

Shopping If you prefer to go shopping than to visit the old buildings, there are plenty of new shopping centres, duty-free areas and more traditional craft and art galleries. Montego Bay has a freeport area on the south of town out towards the Seawinds Hotel. This area was originally a group of cays which were reclaimed and now form the piers for the cruise ships, which call daily in Montego Bay. It is also the home of the Montego Bay Yacht Club and the dock for the boats in the annual Miami to Montego Bay Yacht Race. The freeport has a large number of shops selling glass, jewellery, drinks and tobacco as well as the usual selection of T-shirts and souvenirs. Women will approach you to plait your hair, a process that can take several hours and cost around J$200.

More duty-free shops can be found in the centre of town to the north of Sam Sharpe Square. In the hotel area to the north of the town centre, there are even more shopping centres. St James' Place has some more upmarket shops and also contains *Raines*, a definite must for coffee lovers and those who need a break from sightseeing. This small café has a whole range of coffees as well as cocktails and sometimes a mixture of both. It is open daily from 8.30 a.m. to 11 p.m.

For crafts, go to *Liz Delisser's Gallery of West Indian Art* on Orange Street and see her brightly painted wooden animals and birds carved in cedar wood brought down from the Cockpit Country. Other craft shops line Gloucester Avenue and there is a crafts complex next to Cornwall Beach, along with the Jamaica Tourist Board Offices (Tel: 952-4425).

Beaches There are three public beaches in Montego Bay and there is an admission charge of between J$2-J$4 to the beaches. The most well known is Doctor's Cave Beach; this became famous in the 1920s after Englishman Sir Herbert Barker wrote a paper on the healing powers of the water which is believed to be fed by a mineral-water spring. There are underwater coral gardens just off Doctor's Cave Beach which are easily seen from glass-bottomed boats or by snorkelling. The *Walter Fletcher Beach* is supposed to be the safest for families with young children. The entrance fees to the beach pay for lifeguards and keeping the areas clean but there have been some reports of sewage in the water off Walter Fletcher Beach. There are plenty of watersports available on the beaches with water-skiing available off *Cornwall Beach*. The beach is also the scene for many evening beach parties, complete with barbecues and calypso and reggae bands. Fire-eaters and limbo dancers are all part of the evening's entertainment. Held every Friday and Saturday evenings, the entrance fee covers the food and an open bar. Evening cruises can be booked through *Rhapsody Cruises* (Tel: 952-1760) for trips on the Montrose II. The boat sails from Pier 1 at 5 p.m. and also takes people on day trips to a private beach.

Sailing has always been important to Montego Bay. First to develop the town itself, then as a recreational sport for tourists and residents alike. The annual yacht race from Miami to Montego Bay has become one of the highlights of the year. The race covers 811 nautical miles and lasts five days, but for landlubbers the party afterwards is the real highlight. It lasts for four days and spreads from the Yacht Club to events all over town, ending with the presentation of the Pineapple Trophy. The event takes place in February and is co-hosted by the Montego Bay Club (Tel: 952-3028) and by the Storm Trysail Club in Florida.

Hot Air Ballooning Another new, and very different event, is the annual Hot Air Balloon Festival. Held on Labour Day Weekend at the end of May, ballooners from around the world gather in town to compete and display their craft. Other aerial activities keep the crowd entertained between racing and there is always plenty of music, food and drink available. The event was set up by Norma Stanley, the organizer of the *Hilton*

231

High Day Tour. This tour takes you to the family's private estate in the hills. A hot air balloon trip, walks and a visit to the German settlement at Seaford Town are all options. The tour operates from 8 a.m. to 3.30 p.m., Tuesday to Friday and on Sundays. It costs approximately J$210 (Tel: 952-3343 or 952-5642).

Reggae Sunsplash Another of Montego Bay's annual events that attracts worldwide attention is the Reggae Sunsplash. It turns the town into one huge reggae carnival. Red, green and gold colours adorn everything for the week in August as thousands of reggae fans pour in from all over the world. Extra flights are laid on and Rastafarians from across the island add to the numbers. The actual event takes place in Jarrett Park off Cottage Road and has been running for the past twelve years. Stars such as the late Bob Marley, Ziggy Marley, Chalice, Black Uhura and Jimmy Cliff have all appeared here. The organizers usually line up about forty bands for each festival. Special trips are organized from London through the Music Travel Centre (Tel: 01-383 7518).

Hotels As Jamaica's largest tourist resort, Montego Bay has plenty of hotels and restaurants to offer visitors. With the advent of charter flights into the airport, the town lost its appeal to the jet-set who moved on elsewhere, but there are still plenty of top-quality places to stay. There are thirteen Inns of Jamaica in the town. These are mostly owner-managed, offering good Jamaican cooking and an insight into Jamaican life. Those in Montego Bay are the *Beach & City Hotel, Blue Harbour, Cariblue Beach, Chalet Caribe, Chatwick Gardens, Coral Cliff Hotel, Montego Bay, La Mirage, Richmond Hill, Royal Court, Toby Inn, Waxford Court* and *Winged Victory.* Prices at these hotels vary from about US$40 to US$80. Richmond Hill and Wexford Court can both be booked in the UK through Hotels of Distinction on 071-387 1555.

Doctor's Cave Beach can also be booked through Hotels of Distinction in London. As the name suggests, it is opposite the Doctor's Cave Beach. It is a pleasant, quiet hotel with friendly staff and good service. On Gloucester Avenue, it costs in the region of US$80 per night (Tel: 952-4355/9). *The Casa Blanca Beach Club* offers the same sort of service in a hotel built in a Spanish style. It is also on Gloucester Avenue but on the beach side of the road. It offers a quiet haven from the hustle and bustle on Gloucester Avenue for about US$80 per night (Tel: 952-0720).

If you prefer to stay at an all-inclusive resort there are several in the Montego Bay area. The closest to the town centre is *Carlyle on the Bay* which costs in the region of US$1500 for a week. It is restricted to couples only (Tel: 952-4140/2). This is a Sandals resort and there are two other resorts close to the town. *Sandals Montego Bay* is just to the north of the airport runway and *Sandals Royal Caribbean* is further along the coast towards Falmouth. All the Sandals hotels in Jamaica can be booked in advance in London on 071-581 9895.

Slightly further afield is the *Half-Moon Club* (Tel: 953-2211) which is rated among the best 300 hotels in the world. It is the largest of Jamaica's Elegant Resorts. This is a group of six independently owned hotels who have got together to market their product internationally. To keep it among the top hotels, it has recently added eighteen Royal suites, fit for a king, as well as more tennis courts and improved the 18-hole Robert Trent Jones designed golf-course. The hotel can be booked in the UK through Windotel (Tel: 071-730 7144). Windotel also takes bookings for two other top hotels in the Montego Bay area. *Round Hill* is one of the most exclusive areas around Montego Bay and this hotel reflects the general wealth of visitors and has a wealth of sports to offer guests, all in a 98-acre secluded garden.

A little further out of town is the *Tyrall Golf, Tennis and Beach Club*, centred around a Great House built in 1834, which has been declared a national monument by the Jamaica National Trust. There are 44 rooms in the Great House or, for further privacy, guests can stay in a villa in the grounds, each complete with its own pool and sea view. Tyrall has the only LPGA championship golf-course in Jamaica and it is the site for at least one major LPGA tournament each year.

Another great golfing hotel is back on the other side of Montego Bay, close to the Half-Moon Club. *Wyndham Rose Hall Beach and Country Club* (Tel: 953-2650) has a 18-hole course that is said to offer quite a challenge to all but the most expert golfers. The hotel can also be booked from the UK through Morris Kevan Associates (Tel: 071-367 5175).

Restaurants Staying outside Montego Bay does isolate you from the hustle and bustle of the town but does not mean cutting you off from its good restaurants. Most will give customers lifts to and from their restaurants within about a 24km (15ml.) radius. Just make sure you book a lift when you make a reservation. The choice is good, as these are restaurants catering for the rich as well as for those on a tight budget. Jamaican, Chinese and international cuisine is available. For a snack, try *Raine's Café* in St James Place or the *Greenhouse*. Opposite the entrance to Doctor's Cave Beach on Gloucester Avenue. Open from 7 a.m. to 11 p.m., it offers burgers and chillis, or snacks like omelettes, quiches and sandwiches.

For local food try the *Pork Pit*, also on Gloucester Road. Here they price the food according to weight and you just pick your meat, or even better the whole fish that are steamed with herbs and spices. Open between 10 a.m. and 11.30 p.m., you sit at trestle tables and eat with your fingers. Unlike the downtown area, Gloucester Avenue is safe to walk along at night and, if you are staying close by, it is easy to amble along the road and take your pick from the many good places. Another casual place, and the only one actually on the waterfront, is *Marguerite's Beer Garden*, which has a big satellite TV showing sports, and serves snacks. For a formal dinner try *Marguerite's Restaurant*, open from 6 to 11 p.m. It is slightly more expensive than many of the neighbouring places on Gloucester Avenue but it is worth it for the romantic atmosphere (Tel: 952-4777).

Gloucester House (Tel: 952-6500) also has two sections. *The Tavern*, styled like an English pub, is a great place to sit and chat with local businessmen, while having a snack or choosing from the menus in the more formal dining-rooms. There is also a patio to eat under the stars and sample the wide range of excellent seafoods. The imported wines tend to be expensive for what they are, but it is worth trying the local wine, some of which is quite good. Other places to try along Gloucester Avenue include the *Pelican Restaurant* which is good value for families, and inside *Cascades*, with its waterfall backdrop to the dining-room. (Tel: 952-3171), or *Le Chalet* for cheap local food or Chinese cooking.

To get good views of the town as you eat, try *Julia's* which nestles in the hills to the south of the town. But it is expensive for what you get; you are definitely paying for the view. The other places with good views across the bay are the *Gold Unicorn* restaurant on Queens Drive (Tel: 952-7136) and the *Richmond Hill Inn* (Tel: 952-3859). Also up in the hills is *Siam Restaurant and Jazz Club* (Tel: 952-5727).

One of the island's best restaurants can be found at the *Sugar Mill Restaurant*, the Half-Moon Club. It offers free transportation, so there is no excuse not to try it out. With one of the best cellars on the island, the food is a blend of Jamaican and *nouvelle cuisine*. Reservations are essential but worth the effort (Tel: 953-2314).

Night-Clubs If you are looking for more entertainment after dinner, there are plenty of discos in and around Montego Bay. *Sir Winston's Reggae Night Club* is open seven nights a week, *The Cave* at Seawinds Hotel is also very popular and on Friday nights the place to go is the *Pier One Restaurant*. Avoid eating at the restaurant on Fridays if you are planning a quiet evening out, but otherwise it is a good place to go for a meal before dancing the night away under the stars on the pier (Tel: 952-2452).

Outside the town, there are several good day trips. Montego Bay is the centre for many tours, rail trips into the interior of Cockpit Country and the Appleton Rum Distillery, trips to Ocho Rios and Dunn's River Falls, or to the 11km (7ml.) beach of Negril. But there are also many places to visit much closer to the town.

Rio Grande Leaving the town to the west, the road takes you through Roundhills and on to Tyrall. Just before reaching Roundhill the road crosses the great river. Day and night trips down the river feature in many tours around the area. For the day trip, travel into the mountains and then find a boatman waiting to gently steer your bamboo raft down river (Tel: 952-0527). At night the trip livens up, with calypso bands and rum punches. You are taken on a boat ride up river with flaming torches lighting the banks to a dinner with an open bar, dancing and singing (Tel: 952-5047). The trip costs around J$220 and operates on Tuesdays, Thursdays and Sundays from 7 p.m. to 11 p.m. A day's rafting down the Martha Brae River between Ocho Rios and Montego Bay can also be organized from Mo' Bay. Those trips go daily at a cost of J$170.

Roundhill There is not much of Roundhill visible from the road. Wealthy visitors pay for their seclusion and want to remain hidden away. It used to be the haunt of famous names such as

Roundhill, Jamaica is home to many famous names

Noel Coward and Jack Kennedy, while now it is frequented by people like Paul McCartney and Ralph Lauren. George Bush stayed here, too, before becoming US president. The Roundhill juts out into the sea and is an easy landmark to spot as your plane arrives or leaves from Montego Bay.

Tyrall Country Club A little further down the road to Negril, you come to the Tyrall Country Club. The Great House stands back on the left hand side of a hill with good views out to sea. But before you cross the golf-course, it is worth stopping of at the old water wheel which is over 200 years old but is still working. It used to power the sugar works and was turned by water brought down by a system of aqueducts. As with Montego Bay, every tourist attraction has its own group of salesman selling crafts or soft drinks. Tryall water wheel is no different, but in the country, there is less aggression and much more friendliness.

Bamboo Bay For water-lovers, a day trip not to be missed is the Miskito Cove Beach Picnic, which actually takes you to Bamboo Bay, just outside Lucea. The tour moved to Bamboo Bay

after Hurricane Gilbert washed away the beach at Miskito Cove. Watersports are included within the price as is a barbecue and open bar. On the edge of Bamboo Bay there is the ruins of a cannon port, giving protection to the harbour at Lucea. Tour guide Carolyn will also take you on a nature walk through the farm and coastline of an old Jamaican estate. She can point out several herbs as well as plants that were used for their healing powers. Jamaican-born Carolyn can remember being sent out as a child to search for herbs to help her mother. The day out costs around US$40 (Tel: 952-5164).

The guides in Jamaica are generally well-informed, not just about the dates in history but also about the environment around them. Most can name a surprising number of trees and plants and tell you what they are used for.

Rocklands Bird Sanctuary Travelling south out of Montego Bay, turn left in Reading and take the B8 towards Anchovy and the Rocklands Bird Sanctuary. A turning off to the right, shortly after leaving Reading takes you to Lethe and the

start of the day's rafting down the Great River. Continue toward
Anchovy to find the bird sanctuary which is run by Lisa Salmon
and opens from 3.30 p.m. when it is feeding time. If you belong
to any ornithologist's club you can visit any time. Over 250 bird
species have been seen in the gardens, including 24 species
endemic to Jamaica. Even if you are not a keen bird-watcher, it is
worth a trip to enjoy the peace and calm that Lisa has created in
her gardens. Walks can be arranged to give you a tour of the
gardens and its birds. Entrance is about US$28 and the sanctuary is
open every day. If travelling independently, it is also worth
stopping off in Anchovy at the *Budhai's Art Gallery*.

The trains to the Appleton Rum Distillery and on to Mandeville
and Kingston run through Anchovy. They leave from Montego
Bay station daily. Tours into the interior by train are organized by
governor's Coach Tours (Tel: 952-2887/1398) or by the Appleton
Express (Tel: 953-2297). To go to Kingston, catch 'The Diesel' and
have a pleasant six-hour journey through the mountains.

Further down the B8, the road divides at Cambridge. Take the
right fork to *Hilton House*, where a day's tour includes an optional

Right
**The Tyrall Water Wheel still
stands at the old plantation**

Below
**Bamboo Beach, close to Lucea,
Jamaica**

The staff of Rose Hall Great House, Jamaica

balloon trip or take the left fork down the B6 for the *Croydon Plantation Tour.* You can also take a tour called *Accompong Maroon Tour.* It takes you to the Maroon town Cockpit Country and through the District of Look Behind. Leaving on a Thursday, the tour costs about J$193 and takes from 8 a.m. to 4 p.m.

Travelling east from Montego Bay you can do a *Great House Tour,* stopping at two of Jamaica's most famous houses. *Rose Hall* is just beyond the Half-Moon Golf Club. It has a fascinating history and is rumoured to be haunted by the White Witch of Rose Hall. The house was built in about 1770 by John Palmer who lived there with his wife Rose. When she died he commissioned Bacon to carve her profile in St James Church. The estate passed from John to his great-nephew John Rose Palmer, who brought his young bride Anne to the house. Rumours of great cruelty soon spread and Anne was believed to be a witch, ensnaring many men who fell in love with her. Once she was tired of them, she was rumoured to kill them until one terrified slave, believing he was to be her next victim stabbed her. The story goes that none of her slaves would touch the body and, in the end, neighbouring planters forced their own slaves to remove the body. Now guides dress up in the fashion of the early 1800s to show you the building. The nearby Wyndham Hall Beach Club has its golf club surrounding the house. It is open daily from 9 a.m. to 6 p.m. and cost J$46 (Tel: 953-2323).

240

Greenwood Great House is a little further along the coast road to Falmouth. It was built by the Barrett family, better known as the Barretts of Wimpole Street, who had come to Jamaica in the 1660s and made a fortune with sugar-cane plantations. The Great House was built in 1790 as a place for the family to do their entertaining and it still contains many of its original features. It has been opened to the public as a museum and on show are the original Barrett family library containing books dating back to 1697, oil paintings of the family, Wedgwood china made specially for the family and a collection of musical instruments.

The house was restored by its present owners Bob and Ann Betton, who also live in the house. The china and books were donated by the last surviving member of the Jamaican Barretts. Included in the collection is a rare set of maps of Jamaica. Only one other set, dating from 1804, survives and it is in the British Museum of London. Bottles and coins found on the estate during its restoration are on display and the Bettons have added a collection of coaches which are housed in the stables. Greenwood Great House is open daily from 9 a.m. to 6 p.m. and the entrance is J$33.

If you want a tour combining both houses take the *Queen's Valley Great Houses Tour* which takes you along the coast road through an area known as the Queen of Spain Valley and into both Great Houses. Contact the Jamaica Tourist Board for details (Tel: 952-4425).

Further Information

Sports Jamaica offers visitors a wide range of sports, from cricket and polo to football. Water-lovers can choose from the full range of water-sports at just about every resort. Fishermen will find plenty of good rivers or can go off-shore. Tennis courts and golf-courses abound, horse-riding is available widely, and for hikers there are good trails through the Blue Mountains.

Ballooning Balloonists can contact the organizers of the *Hilton High Day Tour* on 952-3343. A hot-air balloon ride is part of the tour and they also help to organize Montego Bay's annual ballooning festival.

Cricket is played throughout the island. The international matches are played in Kingston.

Golf Golfers have a choice of nine courses around the island, the majority on the north coast. Four of them are in the Montego

Bay area. *The Half-Moon Club* (Tel: 953-2211) has 18 holes on a par 72 course of 7,130 yards. Green fees rise to about J$71.50 in winter, caddy fees are about J$39, cart rental is J$140 and club rental J$35. The *Ironshore Golf Club* (Tel: 953-2381) also has 18 holes and a par of 72 over 6,633 yards. Green fees rise to about J$61 in winter, caddy fees are about J$33, cart rental J$94 in winter and club rental J$28. *Wyndham Rose Hill Golf Club* (Tel: 953-2650/2655 has 18 holes with a par of 72 over 6,598 yards. Green fees rise to about J$110, caddy fees J$38.50, cart rental J$110 and club rental J$33. The fourth course around Montego Bay is to the west of town and is the island's only LPGA course. *Tyrall Golf, Tennis and Beach Club* (Tel: 952-5110) has 18 holes with a par of 71 over 6,680 yards.

There are two courses near Ocho Rios. *The Upton Golf and Country Club* (Tel: 974 2528) has 18 holes with a par of 71 over 6,600 yards. Green fees are around J$83, caddy fees J$39, cart rental J$88 and club rental J$17. *The Runaway Bay Golf and Country Club* (Tel: 973-2561) has 18 holes with a par of 72 over 6,884 yards. Green fees are about J$66, caddy fees are J$28, cart rental J$77, club rental J$28.

Mandeville has the island's only 9-hole course. *The Manchester Club* (Tel: 962-2403) has a par of 35 over 2,865 yards. Green fees are around J$32, caddy fees J$17, club rental is also about J$17.

Kingston has two courses. *The Caymanas Golf and Country Club* (Tel: 923-7538) has 18 holes with a par of 72 over 6,844 yards. Green fees are about J$39, caddy fees are about J$22, cart rental J$110 and club rental J$51. *The Constant Spring Golf Club* (Tel: 924-1610) has 218 holes with a par of 70 over 6,196 yards. Green fees are about J$48, caddy fees are J$20 and club rental about J$20.

For the not so serious golfers there is a mini-golf course just outside Ocho Rios. The 18-hole course is at the *Prospect Plantation* (Tel: 974-2058). It is open daily from 9 a.m. to 5 p.m. and all ages, including children, are welcome.

Hiking trails through the Blue Mountains vary from easy to for the fit only. Contact the *Maya Hiking Centre*, Jacks Hill, Kingston (Tel: 927-0357).

Horse-Racing is available every Wednesday and Saturday at *Caymanas Park*, near Kingston.

Horse-Riding is available in most resorts. *Chukka Cove*, near Ocho Rios (Tel: 972-2506) specializes in horse-riding holidays from show jumping and dressage to cross-country and trekking. *Prospect Plantation*, near Ocho Rios (Tel: 974-2058) has four horse trails on its estate. In Negril there are three stables: *Babo's*, *Country Western* and *Horseman Riding Stables* (Tel: 957-4474).

Polo is played at both *Chukka Cove* and at *Drax Hall*, near Ocho Rios. Most international players now go to Chukka Cove, but the Drax Hall matches are played every Saturday afternoon and entrance is free.

Running Runners can take part in the annual marathon from Discovery Bay to Ocho Rios. There is also a 10km (6ml.) race. The race, held in December, is sponsored by the Jamaican Tourist Board; contact their local office for more details.

Tennis is available at most large hotels. The courts tend to be free for hotel guests, with a fee of around J$35 for non-residents.

Watersports are also available at every resort. Scuba-diving operators can be found in three centres. In the Montego Bay area, try *Montego Bay Divers* on 952-4874, *Poseidon Nemrod Club* on 952-3624, or *Seaworld* on 953-2180. In Ocho Rios, try *Fantasea* on 974-2353, *Sea and Dive Jamaica* on 972-2162, or *Sun Divers Watersport* on 973-3509.

Negril has several operators. Contact *Blue Whale Divers* on 957-4438, *Hedonism II Dive Shop* on 957-4200, *Mariners Inn* on 957-4348, the *Negril Scuba Centre* on 957-4425, or *Ray's Parasailing* on 957-4349.

Many hotels offer free watersports to their guests but for non-residents and at beach operations, the prices are approx. as follows: deep-sea fishing, J$1650 for up to four people for four hours, glass-bottom boat ride, J$55 for one hour; parasailing J$138; sail boating, J$55 for one hour; scuba diving, J$192; snorkelling, J$55 for one hour; water skiing, J$83 for 20 minutes, and windsurfing, J$55 for one hour.

Children Most of the main resort hotels have nursemaid services for children. The all-inclusive hotels that will accept children and not just couples, also tend to have special children's games during the day, with constant supervision, and then offer baby-sitting services in the evening.

243

If the children get bored of the beach and water-sports, there is the mini-golf at Prospect Plantation, Ocho Rios (Tel: 974-2058).

There is a small children's zoo called *Coconut Park* in the Hope Botanical Gardens on the outskirts of Kingston. The zoo has lions, tigers, monkeys and crocodiles and there is a short maze in the gardens.

The Rocklands Feeding Station is open to the over-fives, and children can help owner Lisa Salmon feed the birds that flock to her station, near Anchovy, just to the south of Montego Bay.

Flora and Fauna Jamaica may be first thought of for its beaches but it has an abundance of exotic birds and plants. Over 250 species of birds have been spotted on Jamaica, including 25 species endemic to the island. The national bird is one of these. The Streamer-tailed Humming-Bird, or Doctor Bird, is one of four humming-birds found in Jamaica and was probably named because of its black 'hat' and its divided tail which could look like a doctor's stethoscope (doctors used to wear black top-hats in the old days). The Doctor Bird is on the Jamaican dollar note.

Other birds frequently seen are the black John Crow, with its bald red-head; egrets; jacanas are common along the Black River banks, along with green and white herons, orioles and gallinules. Another of Jamaica's endemic bird species is the Jamaican tody, which makes its nest in the ground. It is sometimes called robin redbreast but is not the same as the British robin.

There are no snakes on the island due to the introduction of the mongoose. These were brought from India to kill the snakes in the canefields but they killed all the snakes across the island and are now considered pests. There are a very few iguanas and plenty of harmless lizards.

Another import to the island was bread-fruit. It was this plant that Captain Bligh was trying to bring to the island on his ship the *Bounty* when his crew mutinied. He had set sail from Tahiti in 1793 and the crew mutinied because Bligh was said to be such a hard task master and was giving more water to the plants than to the men. The next attempt was more successful and bread-fruit is now grown all over the island. Many of Jamaica's crops were introduced from elsewhere. Yams, ackee, okra and coffee came from Africa, tobacco and maize came from South America and mangoes came from Mauritius.

Native plant life is also plentiful and exotic. The national tree is the blue mahoe, but the mahogany, satin wood, cotton wood, cedar and Spanish elm are all used in furniture and carvings. The cedar is the carver's favourite because it is strong and does not split easily as it is worked on. Cotton-tree wood is used in fishermen's canoes. The national flower is the Lignum Vitae which was widely used in medicine. The wood from the tree is still sought after by furniture makers.

Bougainvillaea grow wild all across the Caribbean islands

Orchids are now exported from Jamaica. The island has over 220 native species but others have been introduced. Most of the island's botanical gardens have a large number growing naturally in the gardens. Jamaica is thought to have over 3000 species of flowering plants, but many are endangered as more and more of the country is cultivated and as imported plants continue to thrive and take over from the native species. There are over 500 species of ferns, 300 of which can be found in Fern Gully, a stretch of dried-up river bed south of Ocho Rios.

This red flame of flower is also found across the Caribbean

Jamaican periwinkle is found across the island

Jamaica also has about 50 species of coral growing on reefs just off-shore. After bad storms you can pick up some beautiful pieces as you walk along the beaches. Export of coral is illegal and, if you pick live coral you will instrumental in destroying the reefs which help protect the beaches from heavy seas and storms.

Gardens There are plenty of gardens to visit without getting your feet wet. Ocho Rios has the most botanical gardens, including *Shaw Park Gardens, Cariñosa Gardens, Dunn's River Falls* and *Fern Gully*. The *Rocklands Feeding Station* is a bird sanctuary at Anchovy, to the south of Montego Bay, with large gardens. The working plantations give visitors a chance to see both native and imported crops, find out how they are grown, what they are used for and often try a few samples.

The *Somerset Falls* to the west of Port Antonio is a peaceful haven for many species of birds and plants. The *Nonsuch Caves* and *Athenry Gardens* provide a home for some of the island's many thousand bats. In *Mandeville*, Mrs Stephenson opens her gardens to visitors and will give you a guided tour pointing out the many species of orchids she has grown there. Nearby *Marshall's Pen* is a wildlife sanctuary and the Black River is home to many birds and to crocodiles.

247

The *Blue Mountains* are a must for keen bird-watchers. taking a trail from the *Cinchona Gardens* gives you the opportunity to see many native birds and the gardens themselves contain many exotic plant species. There is another botanical gardens in the mountains at *Castleton*. The spa town of *Bath* also has a botanical garden. In the capital Kingston, it is worth visiting the *Hope Botanical Gardens* and, to learn more about the natural history of Jamaica, visit the *Institute of Jamaica*.

Essential Addresses

Medical The hospitals are found in all the major towns, along with doctor's surgeries. The hotels will call out a doctor for you if you are resident there. No vaccinations are required to enter Jamaica and the water is safe to drink from taps across the island.

There are two large specialist hospitals in Kingston, the *Kingston Public Hospital* and the *University of West Indies Hospital*, and one in Montego Bay, the *Cornwall Regional Hospital*. There is a regional hospital in Lucea on the north coast between Montego Bay and Negril, and one in Savanna-la-Mar, south of Negril. Negril itself does not have a hospital but there is a doctor's surgery in the Negril Plaza. Mandeville has the *Hargreaves Memorial Hospital*, off Hargreaves Avenue in the town centre. Spanish Town has a hospital on the outskirts of town on Barrett Street, and Port Antonio has a public hospital on Nuttall Road.

Information

Twenty-seven countries are represented in Jamaica. The *British High Commission* is at 26 Trafalgar Road, Kingston 5. Tel: 926-9050.

The USA also has a representative based at the Blue Harbour Hotel in Montego Bay.

The *Jamaica Tourist Board* has offices in all major resorts and in capital cities around the world.

Head Office: 21 Dominica Drive, Kingston 5, PO Box 360 Tel: 929-9200/19.

Offices at the international airports in both Kingston and Montego Bay.

Montego Bay: Cornwall Beach, PO Box 67, Montego Bay. Tel: 952-4425/8, fax: 952-3587.

Ocho Rios: Ocean Village Shopping Centre, PO Box 240, Ocho Rios. Tel: 974-2570 or 974-2582/3, fax: 974-2559.

Port Antonio, City Centre Plaza, PO Box 151, Port Antonio.
   Tel: 993-3051/2587.

Negril: Shop 20, Plaza de Negril, Negril PO Westmoreland.
   Tel: 957/4243.

Mandeville: 21 Ward Avenue, Mandeville. Tel: 962-1070.

London: 111 Gloucester Place, London W1H 3PH.
   Tel: 071-224 0505, fax: 071-224 0551.

New York: 866 Second Avenue, 10th Floor, New York, NY
   10017. Tel: 688-7650, fax: 759-5012.

For *villa accommodation*, contact JAVA at Pineapple Place, Ocho
   Rios, Box 298, Tel: 974-2508; or at 21 Blandford Street,
   London, NW1 6HZ. Tel: 071-486 3560, fax: 01-486 4108.

Air Jamaica has offices in Kingston (Tel: 992-4661), Montego Bay
   (Tel: 952-4300), Negril (Tel: 957-4210) and Ocho Rios
   (Tel: 974-2566). For internal flights, contact *Trans Jamaican
   Airline* on 952-5401 in Montego Bay.

Car rental offices represented in London are Avis
   (Tel: 071-848 8733) and Hertz (Tel: 071-542 6688). Other
   companies in Jamaica include Anna Car Rentals
   (Tel: 952-3274), Budget Rent-A-Car (Tel: 952-2019), Central
   Rent-A-Car (Tel: 952-3347), Galaxy Car Rentals
   (Tel: 925-4176), Jamaica Car Rentals (Tel: 952-5586),
   National Car Rentals (Tel: 952-2650), Northern Car Rentals
   (Tel: 953-2803) and United Car Rentals (952-3077).

Part Five: **Puerto Rico**

**Sunset over the harbour
in the capital San Juan**

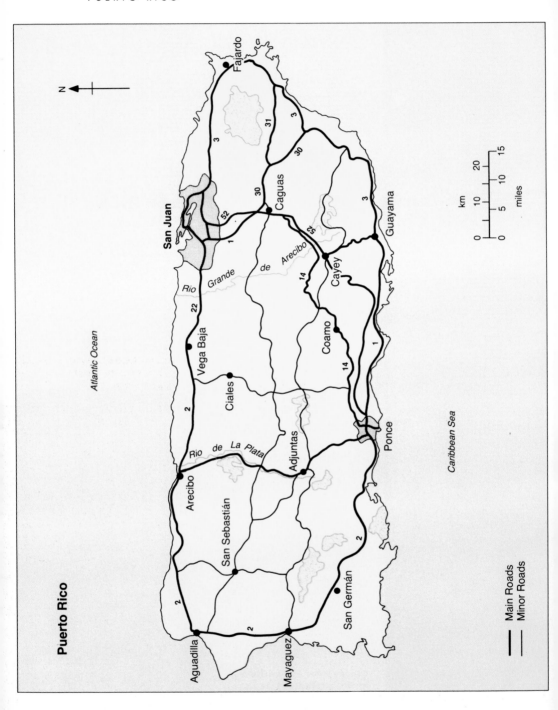

Puerto Rico

Puerto Rico At first glance, Puerto Rico does not appear to belong in the Caribbean. It is so Americanized, things move quickly and efficiently and the laid-back atmosphere of the small islands seems to have disappeared in a cloud of American burger chains and three-lane highways.

But Puerto Rico has much more to offer than that. Many cruise-ship passengers see the island as their embarkation point for their holiday and nothing more. They do not travel beyond the modern capital of San Juan, missing out on going 'Out on the Island', as the locals say.

The island is an American commonwealth; it has many Federal regulations but Spanish is still the official language, first spoken on

The Rio Camuy cave system is vast but visitors enter the system here

the island when Columbus arrived and still very much part of the culture. The American influence has its advantages for the tourists. The island's many attractions are run efficiently and do open when expected. Most people understand English, so communication is quite easy even for those who do not know any Spanish at all.

Having been colonized by Europeans for the past five hundred years, there is plenty of history on the island, but there are also natural wonders, too. The El Yungue forest is the only rain forest in the Caribbean, the mountains are spectacular, there are vast cave systems at Camuy, beautiful lakes and secluded bays covered in white sand.

Puerto Rico is actually made up of one large island and a handful of tiny islands, all but one off its east coast. The largest of these are Culebra and Vieques. These islands, along with the north-east coast of the main island, were hit hard by Hurricane

Old San Juan by night

Hugo in 1989 but, with Federal support, the island recovered quickly. The climate helped, too, vegetation growing back within a few months.

If you are visiting Puerto Rico for several days, you should take the opportunity to leave San Juan and travel around the island. But even if you are just stopping there for a few hours on a cruise-ship transfer, it is still worth taking time to visit Old San Juan and experience a little of what this island has to offer.

Pre-Planning – How to Get There

Flights British Airways flies direct to San Juan twice a week from Gatwick. Air France, Iberia and Lufthansa all have regular flights from Europe. It is easy to connect flights from North America and from other islands in the Caribbean. There are flights from the USA by American Airlines, Delta, Eastern and TWA who all fly from a large number of American cities. American and Eastern have made San Juan their hub to connect all USA flights to other Caribbean Islands. Airlines to and from other Caribbean islands include BIWA, Domincana, Mexicana Aviacion, Antilles Air Boats, Air BVI, Air Jamaica, Air Best, Air Indies, Aero Virgin Islands, Culebra Aviation, Vieques Air Link and Flamenco. Airlines are listed in the Yellow Pages of the phone book under *Lineas Aereas* and many of the international airlines have free phone numbers on mainland USA which you can use from Puerto Rico. A second international airport is planned for the island's second largest city of Ponce.

Tour operators who sell packages to Puerto Rico from the UK include Harlequin Holidays, Kuoni Travel, North America Travel Service, and Peregor Travel.

Ferry Daily ferries shuttle passengers to and from Culebra and Vieques. Car transportation is available on some sailings. There is also a daily catamaran ferry service between Puerto Rico and the US Virgin Islands of St Thomas and St Croix.

Cruise Ships There are currently 18 cruise lines operating from San Juan. A new cruise-ship pier has been opened at the second city of Ponce on the south coast and increasing numbers of ships will be calling there in the future.

When to Go Like the rest of the Caribbean, the winter is the peak season. Prices tend to rise in mid-December and stay high until the end of April. The hurricane season is from August to October but the island has rarely been hit and has a well-planned emergency procedure. As with the other islands, tourist facilities get a high priority if they are hit.

Passports As a US Commonwealth, the visa requirements are the same as in the States. British passport holders no longer need to get a visa in advance but should ask their travel agent for a visa form which should be completed before arriving in the USA. If you arrive in Puerto Rico via the States, you will clear immigration in America and will travel as if you are on an internal flight, so there will be no more immigration to clear in San Juan. If you are travelling through the States, your luggage will have to be checked as you leave San Juan by the US Agriculture Department. Mango, soursop, passion fruit and potted plants are not allowed to be taken into the USA.

The airport departure tax is included in the price of airline tickets.

Health No vaccinations are required for entry into the country and the water is safe to drink. Hospital and emergency services are good, but make sure your travel insurance covers you for the cost of health services in the USA as it is expensive. San Juan alone has fourteen private hospitals. Dengue fever is endemic and bilharzia is present in some rivers.

Getting About

Car Rental There are sixteen agencies across the island. Avis and Hertz have offices at the airport and in town, while Budget has a bus service from its office in town to the airport. They all offer unlimited mileage and are much more reasonable than hiring a car on many of the other Caribbean islands. Car rental agencies are listed in the Yellow Pages of the phone book under Automoviles/Alquiler. Avis, Budget and Hertz all have offices in the UK where bookings for Puerto Rico can be made in advance.

A valid driving licence is required for car rental. A British licence is accepted or use an international licence, but many agencies prefer a national licence.

Petrol is all unleaded and is relatively cheap, about the same price as in the USA. Petrol stations are found in all the major towns and along main roads, but fill up before heading into the mountains.

Driving is in the American style, overtaking on either side of cars on a three-lane highway. Distances are measured in kilometres while speeds are measured in miles per hour. Get a good map, (Esso petrol stations all have maps for about US$2) and then memorize the road numbers and not the town that you are heading for. As you head towards a turning, the first sign will be the road number of the road turning off the one you are on. The second sign will again be the road number but it will be immediately in front of the turning. This can be confusing to start with, especially when there are several turnings close together.

Remember that the speed limits are in miles per hour. Around every school the limit is down to 20mph and it is worth slowing right down as the children are used to the traffic moving slowly and do leap into the roads. The warning sign for a school is *Zona Escolar*. There are on-the-spot speeding fines, which vary according to how fast you were travelling. Speed limit signs are marked *Velocidad Maxima*. There are tolls on the major highways (called *Autopista*) around the island, so have plenty of loose change at the ready. Tolls are marked *Estacion de Peaje*. No Parking signs are marked *No Estacione*.

Driving around San Juan is difficult. The roads are very busy, with plenty of traffic jams at morning and afternoon peak times. Driving around Old San Juan is even more difficult. The roads are very narrow and frequently blocked. It is easier to park and walk around the area during the day. If you are driving yourself back to the airport, give yourself plenty of spare time. Allow extra time for catching taxis or buses to the airport as well.

Taxis There are two types of taxi operating in Puerto Rico. Public cars travel along set routes, usually leaving from a town's main plaza (square), and have set rates. They are identified by a P or PD in their number-plate.

Taxis use meters except for special charter rates. When catching a taxi from the airport, you will be asked by a supervisor at the taxi rank for your destination. He will then put you in a taxi and tell you the fare. In the San Juan area there is a minimum fare of US$3. Fares from the modern area of Condado in San Juan to the Old City are usually around US$7 or US$8. Taxis can be hailed in the street but it is usually easier to find one in the town's main square or around the cruise-ship terminal, bus station or by airports.

Buses There is a good bus system in the San Juan metropolitan area. The buses have exclusive lanes on the highways, travelling in the opposite direction to the traffic, marked by yellow and white lines. Bus stops are marked by yellow posts or metal signs with *Parada* or *Parada de Guaquas*. They are not that frequent and there is a set fare of 25 cents but, be warned, they do not give change. Most buses stop after 10 p.m.

Many tour operators offer sightseeing excursions of the city and of the island. Details are available at most hotel desks within San Juan.

Accommodation San Juan has a wide range of accommodation as you would expect of any modern city. Out on the island the choice is more limited but new resorts and hotels are springing up. There is a major expansion in tourism facilities underway so many of the hotels are new or recently refurbished.

Prices of hotels in San Juan vary tremendously from the all-inclusive and expensive to cheap, family-run hotels. All hotel bills include a 6 per cent government tax. San Juan does have some major conference facilities and accommodation can be more difficult to find if a conference is underway. Most of the large hotels are either in the Condado area or in Isla Verde, overlooking the sea. The cheaper hotels tend to be on the inland side of the Condado Lagoon. The Puerto Rican Tourism Company's monthly magazine *Que Pasa* has full details of hotels around the country.

You can book hotel accommodation for many of the major hotels from London. The booking numbers are: *Hilton International,* 071-631 1767; *Ramada International,* 071-235 5264; *Hyatt Hotels and Resorts,* 071-580 8197; *Howard Johnson's Hotels,* 071-409 0814; *Quality International,* 071-439 2811; *Best Western Hotels,* 071-541 0033; and *Utell,* 071-995 8211.

Outside the city, there is a system of *Paradores Puertorriquenos.* Many of the hotels are close to the most scenic spots on the island. Standards are high and prices relatively cheap. The system is modelled on the Spanish Paradores but these Puerto Rican Paradores are privately owned. For more details and reservations call 721-2884. These Paradors can also be booked in advance; call the *Puerto Rico Tourism Office* for details. From the UK, call the Madrid office on freephone 0800-898920.

Camping is allowed in the forest reserves if you first get a free permit from the visitor centres at the entrance to the reserves.

258

Camping is also permitted on some public beaches, contact the *Recreation and Sports Department* on 721-1551.

Money The currency is the US dollar and credit cards are widely accepted in shops, restaurants and hotels.

Banks There are several Puerto Rican banks and branches of US and foreign banks. Banking hours are from 8.30 a.m. to 2.30 p.m., Monday to Friday, and from 9.45 a.m. to 12 p.m. on Saturdays. Dollar travellers cheques are widely accepted but change sterling into dollars at the banks.

There is no sales tax in Puerto Rico but there is a 6 per cent tax on hotel bills. There is no tax on restaurant or bar bills.

Tipping You are expected to leave a tip of about 15 per cent for waiters and taxi drivers.

Safety On the whole, Puerto Rico is safe. During the day there is no problem wandering around but, like any major city, it is better not to walk around the poorer areas of San Juan flashing money or jewellery around. Women are warned against walking around the Condado area at night on their own. It is safer to get a taxi to travel around at night rather than walk unless you are part of a group.

Out on the island, people are friendly and always keen to help. A little bit of Spanish or an attempt at Spanish is always appreciated but sign language will get you around and you should have no real problems in being understood.

Food Both Spanish and Caribbean flavours influence the food, and seafood is on the menu at most restaurants. Some of the more unusual dishes are:

Asopao. A local stew often with seafood and served with rice.

Camarones Rebosados. A local dish of shrimps cooked in garlic.

Carrucho. Conch.

Empanadilla de Mariscada. A combination of seafood wrapped in pastry, served as a starter.

Enslada de Langosta. Lobster salad.

Flan de Vainilla. A custard similar to a caramel custard in texture but tasting of vanilla, a very popular local dish.

Mavi. A local brew fermented in the bark of a tree.

Papaya con Queso Blanco. Slices of papaya fruit often served with white cheese as a dessert.

Pina Colada. Almost a meal in many bars, with all the pineapple

259

and fruit in this rum cocktail, which the Puerto Ricans claim to have invented.

Pulpo. Octopus.

Yuquiyu. A risotto of sausage, rice, pineapple and peppers.

As you would expect with any major metropolitan centre, there is a huge variety of food. Prices in San Juan are slightly cheaper than in Britain. Eating out on the island, you are more limited, but there is still plenty to choose from in the provincial towns.

Puerto Rican food is a mix of Spanish, Creole and native Indian dishes. In Old San Juan there are plenty of bars and restaurants serving local food. International cuisine can be found on the menus at most of the major hotels in the Condado and in Isla Verde. If you prefer a quick snack, there is a complete range of all the American fast-food outlets behind the hotels on Isla Verde and more on the Condado.

Some of the best restaurants to try include *La Mallorquina* in Old San Juan. This is supposed to be the oldest restaurant in the western hemisphere. It has a good atmosphere and good food, even if the service is a little slow. *Go Bananas* is a good place to stop and have a drink while out sightseeing. It sells clothes as you are served with exotic cocktails. For ice-creams, try the stalls on the Plaza Colon in Old San Juan. If you want a view of the ocean, try *Amanada's* which serves huge portions of nacho chips as you admire the view. The restaurants seem to close early in the evening, with most people going out to eat straight after leaving work rather than waiting until later.

Leaving San Juan behind, there is a system of *mesones gastronomicos.* These restaurants all have a knife and fork symbol displayed outside. They are checked regularly by the Tourism Company to make sure standards are being maintained. At the moment there are twenty-three restaurants which are approved and they are all close to major tourist attractions. Another requirement of belonging to the scheme is that they must specialize in Puerto Rican food, which costs as little as US$7 for a main course.

There are picnic sites all over the island at most of the tourist attractions, on the public beaches and in the forest reserves. But, be warned, in the rain forest it can rain up to fifteen times in one day so be prepared to make a quick dash for cover or to get very wet.

Shopping There are large supermarkets in all the major towns, providing all the supplies you would expect in any American store. There are also markets in the provincial towns for fresh fruit and vegetables, including many exotic crops such as mangoes, coconuts, soursop, pumpkin, pineapple, bananas, pawpaw (pronounced pa-pie-a) and plantains. San Juan has several large shopping centres, including the largest in the Caribbean, the Plaza las Americas. Other good shops can be found in Old San Juan. Outside the city there are large shopping centres in Bayamon, Caquas, Carolina, Mayaquez and Vega Alta.

Pharmacists can be found in every major town in most shopping areas.

Post Offices are also in every major town. The cost of postage is the same as in the States. Many hotels and postcard shops have small stamp machines, but these are designed for the American market so you need lots of small change to get enough stamps for postcards to Britain.

The San Juan area has two telephone books. The commercial volume includes an English language section for tourists. This has a lot of useful emergency numbers and is on all the blue pages. Business listings are on the yellow pages and Government numbers are on the green pages. The white-page section has information about the telephone service, including overseas dialling details.

Most shops are open from 9 a.m. to 6 p.m. but some open for longer in the tourist areas, such as Old San Juan. The shops also stay open until 9 p.m. during the peak Christmas holiday shopping season. Some of the best streets to wander down in Old San Juan are La Forteleza, San Francisco and Cristo.

In San Juan you can buy everything from designer clothes to locally made lace. Goods are imported from all over the world but for local products start with the rum. Puerto Rico is one of the world's leading producers of rum. A rum to suit every taste can be found on the island, both at the distilleries and in the supermarkets or corner shops.

Another locally grown product is tobacco. Cigars are still hand rolled in shops in Old San Juan, but most bought cigars come from other Caribbean islands such as the Dominican Republic.

Other local products include *santos*. These small wooden carvings depict a religious scene or a saint. Each *Santeros* has his

261

own particular style which is passed on to the next generation. So every carving is slightly different and will often have a connection or special significance to the carver who made it. Masks are fashioned out of coconut husks for festivals in Lioza and papier mâché masks appear in Ponce during its carnival.

Mundillo is a form of handmade bobbin lace made into doillies, table-cloths, collars and bands. While for the musical, try your hand at the *guiros*, a gourd with strings, or the *cuatros* which has five double strings. These instruments are hewn from native trees and the method dates back to the days when the Indians lived on the island.

For a more laid-back approach, try a hammock; selecting one to buy is half the fun as the hammock-makers usually have a couple of hooks to hang up their hammocks for you to try their wares.

Puerto Rico is proud of its crafts and has numerous crafts fairs throughout the year. These are spread across the country. July has become the artesan's month when local craftsmen are honoured. For more details, contact the *Formento Crafts Programme* on 758-4747 or the *Tourism Artesan Office* on 721-2400.

Craft shops in San Juan include *Aquadilla en San Juan*, 352 San Francisco, Old San Juan, open Monday to Saturday from 9 a.m. to 6 p.m.; *Galeria Epoca en Turismo*, La Casita Information Center, Old San Juan, open Monday to Wednesday, Saturday and Sunday from 2 p.m. to 11 p.m.; *Kiosko Cultural*, Plaza las Americas, Hato Rey, open Monday to Thursday, and Saturday, from 10 a.m. to 5 p.m. and on Fridays from 10 a.m. to 9 p.m.; *Mercado Artesania Caraball*, Sixto Escobar Park, Puerta de Tierra, open Tuesday to Saturday from 9.30 a.m. to 4.30 p.m.; *Mercado de Artesanias*, Plaza de Hostos, Recinto Sur, Old San Juan, open weekends for afternoon and evening; *Mercado de Artesania Puertorriquena Hermandad de Artesanos*, Muñoz Riviera Park, Puerta de Tierra, open Sunday from 9 a.m. to 5 p.m.; *Plazoleta del Puerto*, Marina, Old San Juan, open daily from 9 a.m. to 6 p.m. and *Puerto Rican Art and Crafts*, Fortaleza, 204 Old San Juan, open Monday to Saturday from 9 a.m. to 6 p.m.

There are also numerous art galleries in San Juan. There are four galleries along Cristo in Old San Juan, three along San José, Old San Juan and numerous others scattered in the tiny streets of the old city.

The daily English language newspaper is the *San Juan Star* and two of the daily Spanish newspapers are *El Mundo* and *El Dia*. A free monthly magazine *Que Pasa* is also published in English and available at all hotels and all Tourism Offices or information centres. There are also two English-speaking radio stations.

San Juan has several good book shops or *Librerias*. *Book Store*, San José, 257, Old San Juan, open daily from 9 a.m. - 7 p.m.; *Book World*, Plaza las Americas, Hato Rey; *Hermes Book and Art Gallery*, Ashford, 1372, Condado; *Thekes Inc*, Plaza las Americas, Hato Rey.

Local Colour

The People The majority of Puerto Ricans are Catholic but other religions are widely accepted and are guaranteed freedom by the Commonwealth Constitution. Catholic services are conducted throughout the island in both English and Spanish. There are English-speaking Protestant services for Baptists,

Loiza mask-makers try out their costumes with local children before the annual Puerto Rican Festival

Episcopalians, Lutherans, Presbyterians, Seventh Day Adventists, and Christian Scientists. There is a Jewish Community Center in Miramar and a Jewish Reform Congregation in Santurce.

The main influence on the country has been the Spanish. The majority of people are descended from the original Spanish settlers and there are currently 3.3 million people in Puerto Rico. As an American Commonwealth, Puerto Ricans carry US passports and have the right to live and work anywhere in mainland America. Many young people do go to New York to find work. Unemployment was very high in Puerto Rico and many people left to find work but have started to return as the economic climate improves. There are about two million Puerto Ricans in New York, almost double the number of Puerto Ricans living in San Juan.

Puerto Ricans have a fairly poor reputation in the States, particularly for crime in the low income areas, and many people still think of the gangs portrayed in *West Side Story*, but on the island, they are a friendly, welcoming people. As in many Catholic countries, you do not see women sitting in parks or shopping centres or even walking around in the streets; that seems to be a strictly male preserve.

Puerto Ricans are always happy to talk to you. They are polite but friendly and you will soon recognize the many Spanish traits, such as their love for family and children, dignity and pride. Like the Spanish, the Puerto Ricans tend to dress up in the evenings. You will need more formal evening wear for a night out in San Juan, evening dresses for the women and jackets for the men. The holiday resort areas are less formal but people will still change for the evening.

There are festivals throughout the year, mostly tied to religious events, when everyone dresses up and celebrates. Every weekend and on holidays, people pour out of the city into the country, and sleepy seaside resorts are transformed. Beach parties and barbecues go on all night.

The people are very proud of their heritage, and historic sites are carefully preserved. A lot of work is being done, ready for the Columbus celebrations in 1992. The city of Ponce is undergoing a huge change as it is restored and developed as a tourist centre.

The Country Puerto Rico is the most easterly and the smallest of the Greater Antilles island chain that forms part of the

Caribbean island group. It is 176km (110ml.) long by 56km (35ml.) in size and is 1,672km 1(1,045 ml.) south of Miami, nestling between Hispaniola to the west and the Virgin Islands to the east. It is surrounded by the Atlantic Ocean to the north and by the Caribbean to the south. Three islands just off the coast are part of Puerto Rico: Mona to the west, and Culebra and Vieques to the east. It is the most industrially developed of the Caribbean islands but also contains the Caribbean's only rain forest.

The island was originally inhabited by the Taino Indians who had moved into the islands from South America. The Taino Indians were descendants of the Arawak Indians who moved into many of the Caribbean islands. The Tainos were a peaceful tribe of farmers. They called the island Borinquen and shared the land with several smaller Indian tribes. Cave drawings indicate that people have been living on the island for the past two thousand years. The more ferocious Carib Indians never moved on to the island but used to raid it from Vieques where they did have a settlement.

The Island was discovered by Christopher Columbus in 1493 while he was on his second voyage in the Caribbean. The island was then named San Juan after John the Baptist. He was accompanied on this voyage by the young Spaniard called Juan Ponce de Leon.

The Taino Indians welcomed the Europeans with nuggets of gold and fuelled the Spaniards with tales of more gold across the

The Caguana Indian Ceremonial Park in Puerto Rico

island. The Indians reached the height of their culture in about AD 1200 and many of their ceremonial areas are still found on the island. They played a ball game in which two teams had to pass a ball across the arena without using their arms, hands or feet and some of these arenas have been left virtually untouched.

Ponce de Léon was attracted by the tales of gold and won permission from Spain to colonize the island. He came back with the first settlers in 1508 when he was appointed Governor. They built a town at Camparra, close to the present city of San Juan. But the first settlement proved unhealthy and in 1521 was moved to the present site of Old San Juan. Ponce de Léon died that year in the attempted capture of Florida. The city was named Puerto Rico, or rich port. The names were switched around many years later.

The tales of gold proved disappointing and supplies soon disappeared. Relationships with the Taino Indians also broke down and by 1550 the numbers of Indians had fallen from many thousands to just sixty. The end of the gold meant that the settlers had to change to farming to survive, and for the next three centuries, the island was dependent on its sugar-cane, tobacco and coffee crops.

Its location in the Caribbean became increasingly important as the crossroads for ships taking gold from the West Indies and bringing goods from Spain. The fort at San Juan was built in about 1540 to protect the port from Sir Francis Drake and the British. The French, the Dutch and pirates were also constantly trying to attack ships as they left or arrived at San Juan.

The British managed to capture the city in 1598, led by the Earl of Cumberland, but he had to withdraw his forces after they succumbed to dysentery. In 1625, the Dutch managed to take over the city but could not capture the El Morro fort and were eventually forced to leave the island.

By 1810, the Puerto Ricans sent their first representative to the Spanish Parliament, the Cortes, and slavery was abolished on the island in 1873. The Spanish-American war in 1898 resulted in the island being handed over to the Americans.

The States gave Puerto Ricans the right to hold American passports in 1917 under the Jones Act. The first elected Governor was Luis Muñoz Marin, who was appointed in 1948, and he guided the country towards its Commonwealth status which the islanders chose in 1952.

The Puerto Ricans still live as a US Commonwealth although there are two movements for change; one is pressing for independence, which is unlikely, and another is pushing for full accession to the states to become the 51st state, which is reported to be more likely.

The current Commonwealth status allows Puerto Ricans to hold US passports and to have a representative in Washington called a Resident Commissioner. Currency, trade and defence regulations are also shared with the States but the island has its own Government and conducts its own internal affairs. Puerto Ricans are not allowed to vote in US elections and do not have to pay Federal taxes, as long as they are resident on the island.

The present Governor is Rafael Hernandez Colon who was elected in 1988. The next elections will be held in 1992. The two main parties are the Popular Democratic Party, of which Colon is a member and which supports the island's existing Commonwealth status, and the New Progressive Party which would prefer full accession to the States.

Income is amongst the highest per capita of anywhere in the Caribbean and unemployment has been cut to about 12 per cent from nearer 25 per cent. Life expectancy is over 73 years old and illiteracy has been reduced to about 10 per cent probably helped by money pumped into the system from gambling. Forty per cent of all profit made by slot machines in the country's eleven casinos is contributed to the school system.

Operation Bootstrap, devised in 1948, helped the country make the leap from an agriculture-based economy to a strong manufacturing system. Supported by both the US and Puerto Rican Governments, US corporations were given tax incentives to set up on the island. Their profits were only taxed if repatriated. This system stopped in 1976 when the plan changed to avoid the low-wage trap, as the corporations had been taking advantage of the low wages in Puerto Rico.

The main industries are clothing, electronics, petrochemicals and textiles. Rum exports have been a major factor in the economy since the nineteenth century and still accounts for about 83 per cent of the rum sold in the United States.

Tourism represents about 65 per cent of the GNP. Some 30 per cent of spending on GNP comes from Washington, which also helps to pay food stamps and benefits for the unemployed. Tourism is a fast growing area for Puerto Rico. The number of tourists is steadily increasing annually and the facilities are constantly being improved to cope with demand. The international airport at San Juan has received a $65 million boost to improve facilities and build a new wing, while there are plans for another international airport at Ponce.

Cruise-ship facilities were opened in 1990 in Ponce and the town's hotels and facilities are all receiving a facelift ready for the 1992 Columbus celebrations that will sweep the Caribbean.

Much of the development is taking place outside San Juan, supported by the Puerto Rico Tourism Company which wants to encourage tourists to visit the whole island and not just San Juan. Most of the development is on the coast and is often a combination of hotel and sports facilities.

The average temperatures are between 25 and 30°C (77 and 86°F) year round. Temperatures drop slightly in the evenings and in the mountainous interior. Easterly trade winds also help to keep the air cool and fresh.

The mountains occupy the majority of the interior, dropping away to flat coastal plains. The highest of the old volcanic mountain range is the Cerro de Punta at 1,339m (4,389ft). In the north-west is karst country, an area of limestone caves, sink-holes and hills.

There are eleven forest reserves. The most interesting are the El Yunque rain forest, managed by the US Forest Service, and the Guajataca Forest, which has 40km (25ml.) of trails through the krast area. El Yunque covers about 28,000 acres but the forest used to cover nearly all of the island.

There are two phosphorescent bays, one on the south-west coast and one on Vieques Island. Another unusual area is Mona Island. This small island to the west of Puerto Rico is now a protected area run by the National Park Service and the Puerto Rican Natural Resources Department. The island has developed its own ecosystem and has both rare and indigenous species.

The north coast is generally wetter and greener than the south west and many rivers flow out of the mountains to the coast.

Events Calendar On public holidays absolutely everything shuts and many local people head out of town the day before.

To encourage tourism, the Tourism Company has developed a

year-round festival known as *LeLoLai*. Based in San Juan, several hotels participate, offering guests the free package. These guests get a week-long insight into the culture of Puerto Rico. Other visitors can purchase the package for $8 for adults, $6 for children. The package gives you cruises around San Juan Bay, historical presentations at San Juan Museum of Art and History, evenings of dance and music, as well as entry into historical homes, sporting events and discounts in shops and restaurants. For more information, the *LeLoLai Festival Office* is in the Puerto Rico Tourism Information Centre at the El Centro Convention Center, Ashford Avenue, Condado (Tel: 723-3135/1513).

Each town honours its own patron saint with an annual festival. These festivals can last up to ten days and include processions, games, eating, dancing and singing. Starting off as Catholic religious festivals, they have changed over the years under the influence of Spain and Africa.

Coffee harvests, flower festivals, musical events and crafts are all excuses for more festivals around the country. For monthly details, check *Que Pasa* or contact the local Tourism Office.

January 6 is *Three King's Day*, a day when people exchange gifts and there are island-wide festivals with music, parades and traditional feasts.

January 11 is *De Hostos Day*. This is a public holiday honouring a Puerto Rican educator, writer and patriot, Eugenio Maria de Hostos.

January 18-21. The *San Sebastián Street Festival* takes over this area of Old San Juan with nightly celebrations and processions.

February 15–18. Arroyo's *Cristobal L. Sanchez Carnival* with a carnival queen and parade, followed by the traditional burying of the sardine. There are both day and evening events.

February 16–19. *Coffee Harvest Festival* in Maricao, a small town in the mountains about an hour from the coastal town of Marguez. There is folk music, a parade, crafts and feasts.

February 22–27. Ponce's *Carnival* is one of the most spectacular carnivals across the island. Masquerades, parades and street parties take over this historic town. The brightly coloured and unusual masks are a particular feature of the festival.

February 22–25. The *Captain Correa Carnival* is held at the Luis Muñoz Rivera Plaza, Arecibo.

Events Calendar

Annual Bank Holidays are on:
New Year's Day
Three King's Day, 6 January
Eugenio Maria de Hostos Day, 11 January
Martin Luther King's Birthday, 15 January
George Washington's Birthday, end of February
Abolition of Slavery, 22 March
Good Friday
Easter Sunday
Memorial Day, 29 May
St John the Baptist Day, 24 June
Independence Day, 4 July
Luis Muñoz Rivera Day, 17 July
Constitution Day, 25 July
José Celso Barbosa's Birthday, July 27
Labor Day, first Monday in September
Columbus Day, at beginning of October
Veteran's Day, 11 November
Discovery Day, 19 November
Thanksgiving, 23 November
Christmas Day

March. A *Fish Festival* is held at Puerto Real, close to Cabo Rojo with crafts and music.

March. *Coffee Festival* in Yauco; music, crafts and coffee preparation demonstration.

March. *Regional Crafts Fair* held in Ponce

March. Annual *Copa Velasco Regatta* attracts about 100 racing and cruising yachts to Palmas del Mar resort in Humacao for the first leg of the prestigious Caribbean Ocean Racing Triangle.

March. *Sugar Cane Festivals* held in Guanica and Vega Alta with arts, crafts, foods and music.

March 22. *Emancipation Day* celebrates the freeing of slaves in 1873.

April 16, Commemoration of the birthday of lawyer, writer and political leader, *José de Diego*, who was the first president of the Puerto Rico House of Representatives under US rule.

April. *Mavi Festival* is held in Juana Diaz with costumes, floats, artistic shows and crafts.

April. Anasco's *Anon Festival* includes a troubador competition and dancing.

April. *Puerto Rico Orchid Show* is held at Pedrin Zorrilla Coliseum, Hato Rey.

May. *Semana de la Danza* is a week-long celebration of the island's national dance, La Danza. It is held in the open-air court of the Dominican Convent, Old San Juan.

May. Annual 21km (13 ml.) *Marathon* which starts in front of the sanctuary of Virgin del Rosario, Sabana Grande.

May. *Puerto Rican Weaving Festival* at Isabela with weaving, mundillo lace making, food and music.

May. *Pineapple Festival* in Lajas to celebrate the harvest.

May. *Sugar Harvest Festival*s held in San German and Hormiqueros.

June. *Bomba y Plena Festival* celebrates the island's Afro-Caribbean heritage with music and dance at Ponce.

June. Two-week annual festival celebrating the work of the late cellist and composer *Pablo Casals*. Held in San Juan's Performing Arts Centre with performances in other cities.

June. *Aibonito Flower Festival* features acres of colourful flowers and annual competitions.

June 24. *San Juan Bautista Day*; the city celebrates its patron saint with a week of festivities and at midnight of the 23rd, *sanjuaneros* walk into the sea backwards three times to renew good luck for the coming year.

July 17. Commemoration of *Muñoz Rivera's* birthday. He was resident commissioner in Washington DC.

July. *Barranquitas Artisans Fair* is the island's oldest fair and has work by about 130 craftsmen on display.

July. Annual folk and religious ceremony honouring *St James the Apostle* with a carnival, parades and dancing, with particularly colourful processions from 26–28 July in the coastal town of Loiza.

July. *Vieques Folk Festival* with parade of floats, music and crafts.

September. *Annual International Billfish Tournament* is held at the Club Nautico, San Juan.

September. *Puerto Rico Symphony* starts its annual season of concerts.

October. Festival of typical *Puerto Rican dishes* held at Luquillo Beach.

October. *Annual Ceramic Festival* celebrates the island's crafts. Held in San Juan.

October. *National Plantain Festival* is held in Corozal.

November. *Kelly Club Regatta* is held at Club Nautico, Ponce.

November. *Jayuya Indian Festival* to celebrate the Taino Indian cultural heritage with craft shows, Indian ceremonies and dancing.

November. *Fiesta de la Musica* features the *cuatro* playing contest held at the Dominican Convent in Old San Juan on three successive weekends.

December. *Bacardi Arts Festival*; more than 200 craftsmen exhibit on the grounds of the world's largest rum manufacturing plant in Catano.

December 15–January 6. *Navidades* is celebrated island-wide with life-size nativity scenes, children's programmes and Christmas concerts and includes the lighting of the town of Bethlehem between San Christobel Fort and Plaza San Juan Bautista in Old San Juan.

December 25–28. *Hatillo Festival of the Masks* is celebrated with colourful masks and folk music at Hatillo.

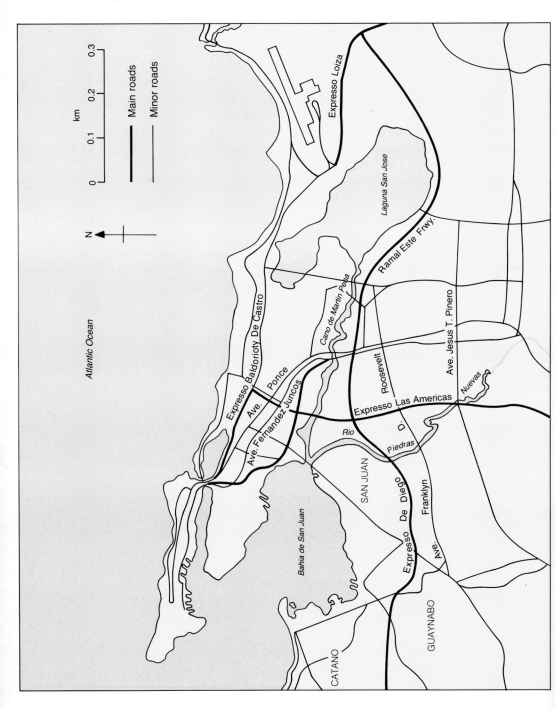

San Juan The island of Puerto Rico is dominated by its capital city, San Juan. About one million people live in the city on the north-eastern end of the island. The many high-rise buildings, fast-food outlets, and three-lane highways are more like America than the Caribbean, but the old centre is more like parts of Spain and seems a world apart. The majority of visitors are based around the Condado area and close to Old San Juan.

Old San Juan This is the oldest city under the American flag. There are over 400 buildings that have been restored to their original condition within the old city walls. The whole area was declared a National Historic Zone in 1949.

It is easier to walk around the Old City than to try to drive yourself. The alternative is the trolleys that run around the old city; you can hop on and off at any stage on its journey and there are no charges. The trolleys follow a circular route and run throughout the day.

This town was first developed in 1521 when the original Spanish settlers abandoned their town at Camparra because it was so unhealthy. The Spanish soon realized the potential of their new home as a gateway to the West Indies from Europe and started work on defences for the port.

El Morro Work on Castillo San Felipe del Morro, better known as El Morro, started in 1540 but took 243 years to complete. In the meantime, the fort saved the city from countless

Modern San Juan dominates the skyline

attacks and was only ever taken once – by the British, led by the Earl of Cumberland. He attacked the fort from inland and managed to defeat the soldiers inside but was himself defeated by an epidemic of dysentery which forced his men to retreat.

Today the fort strands 43m (140ft) above the sea on six levels, with a vast green field in front of it covering a network of tunnels. It is part of a World Heritage Site and a national historic site, administered by the National Park Service. The fort is open daily from 8 a.m. to 6 p.m., admission is free and there are orientation programmes in both Spanish and English. At the entrance gate, it is worth stopping to read the steel plaque embedded in the walls. It lists all those who attempted to capture the fort and is headed by Francis Drake.

The sea view from the top of the El Morro fortress in Old San Juan

Old San Juan was built in a seven-square block and was surrounded by an old city wall. The area has been a national historic site since the 1950s and has kept much of its old world charm. It is easier to walk around than to try to compete with the regular traffic jams in the narrow streets. The area is small enough to walk around comfortably in half a day but there is also enough to see to keep you occupied for much longer than that.

One of the first things to see on any tour around the city is El Morro. A quick walk around the fort not only gives you an idea of the power of the Spanish 400 years ago, but also gives you a good view of the old city, which is full of art galleries, museums and churches as well as historic houses, modern shops and excellent restaurants. If you only have a few hours in San Juan, a quick walk around will give you a feel of what the area is like. But people with longer to spend will soon find something to suit their tastes, whether it is for a lazy day watching life pass them by or a day packed with historic sites.

La Fortaleza Historians should start at El Morro and then move on to the Governor's palace, La Fortaleza. It was originally built as a fort to protect the new city against the Indians and was completed by 1540. But it soon proved ineffective as a fort and became the Governor's residence. Work on El Morro began in that year. La Fortaleza was twice occupied by invaders. The Earl of Cumberland moved in during his occupation of the city in 1598 and then, in 1625, the Dutch General Bowdoin Hendrick moved in. The building was modernized in 1846. It is open Monday to Friday from 9 a.m. to 4 p.m. but closed on holidays. There are guided tours every hour in English and every half-hour in Spanish. Do not miss out on the Treasure Room which can only be viewed by looking through a trap-door.

Casa Blanca As you walk from El Morro down to La Fortaleza you will pass the Casa Blanca. This white house was built to be the first residence of Juan Ponce de León, the pioneer of Puerto Rico. But, in 1521, he was wounded in his quest to find the Fountain of Youth in Florida, and died in Cuba on his way home. The house was destroyed by a hurricane but was rebuilt, and his descendants moved into the house in 1523. They stayed for the next 250 years until the Spanish Government decided it should be used as a residence for military commanders and, between 1898 and 1966, it was used as the residence of the US commander in Puerto Rico. It is now a museum of family life in the sixteenth and seventeenth centuries. Open daily between 9 a.m. and 12 p.m. and 1 p.m. and 4.30 p.m.; there are guided tours Monday to Friday by appointment, on 724-4102.

Next to Casa Blanca on Calle San Sebastián are Step Streets. These are the only two remaining streets that were built with steps for climbing the hill of Old San Juan. The steps run either side of the Caleta del Hospital and run alongside the El Convento Hotel. Down one of the streets, Callejon de las Monjas, you will find the *Casa del Callejon*. This building is owned by the Institute of Puerto Rican Culture and is home to the *Museum of Colonial Architecture* and the *Museum of the Puerto Rican Family*, and it was restored in 1990 (Tel: 725-5250).

La Rogativa once saved the city from capture by the British and is now immortalized in this statue in Old San Juan

Close to Casa Blanca, there is the *Plazuela de la Rogativa*. This statue of a clergyman followed by three women was given to the city in 1971 to mark the 450th anniversary of the night when the British were fooled into retreat by the sight of women carrying torches and following a bishop. The British thought they were facing reinforcements but, in fact, it was a *rogativa*, a religious service.

Museo de Felisa Rincon de Gautier Just off to the left at Caleta de San Juan, 51, this was once the home of forceful city major, Felisa Rincon de Gautier, who led the city from 1946 to 1968 and now contains furniture and memorabilia from his life. It is open from 9 a.m. to 3.45 p.m., Monday to Friday, and from 12.30 p.m. to 4 p.m. on Saturday and Sundays; groups by appointment, on 723-1897.

As you turn left down Caleta San Juan, look to your right at *San Juan Gate*. This was part of the sea defences and these large wooden gates opened on to a tiny cove where dignitaries landed. Officials would be met here and taken up Caleta San Juan to the city's Cathedral to give thanks for their safe arrival.

Turn left by La Fortaleza and take the next right off Calle La Fortaleza and find the *Parque de las Palomas*, Pigeon Park. Behind the park is the *Fine Arts Museum*. This has been restored recently and houses the Institute of Puerto Rican Culture's collection of paintings and sculpture (Tel: 724-5949).

Parque de las Palomas overlooks La Princesa jail and the coast-guard installations at La Puntilla. La Princesa has recently been restored and now houses the *Puerto Rica Tourism Company*. It is worth stopping there to pick up useful information about what to do and see, both in San Juan and out on the Island. Built in 1837, the building contains three of the original jail cells and two halls to display works of local Puerto Rican artists.

Arsenal de la Puntilla Opposite La Princesa on the waterfront, this Arsenal was built in 1800 as a naval station and was the last piece of Spanish ground in Puerto Rica after the Spanish-American war of 1898. The Americans allowed the Spanish troops to stay on the station until they could be evacuated. The station has regular exhibitions in its three galleries and is open from Wednesday to Sunday 9 a.m. to 12 p.m. and from 1 p.m. to 4.30 p.m.

Museum of the Seas A little further along the coast are the cruise-ship piers. On Pier one, you will find the museum of the Seas, housing a collection of antique maritime instruments, maps and pictures as well as models of ships. Information is in both English and Spanish and the museum is open whenever a cruise ship is in dock.

To the east of Las Palomas Park along the City Wall is the *Bastion de las Palmas*. A fortification built for gun emplacements, it has now been planted with trees and is a quiet place to sit and admire the view.

The *Cristobel Chapel* is next to Las Palomas Park. And on the north side of the Park is *La Casa del Libro*, which houses many pre-sixteenth-century books as well as exhibitions on printing. It is open Tuesday to Saturday (except holidays) from 11 a.m. to 4.30 p.m. This area is considered by many to be the prettiest in

Old San Juan and is worth a visit if you only have a short time in the area.

Adolfo de Hostos Museum On the corner of Calle Forteleza and Avenida Ponce de León is the Adolfo de Hostos Museum. Built in 1909 as a bath-house, it has been transformed into a museum in honour of one Puerto Rico's most famous historians. Adolfo de Hostos was the son of Puerto Rican writer and educator Eugenio Maria de Hostos. The exhibits have been collected by the Archaeologic, Anthropologic and Historic Foundation.

Alcaldia In the centre of Old San Juan on Calle San Francisco is the Alcaldia, or City Hall. This is the town's administrative centre and houses the mayor's office. Resembling Madrid City Hall, it was built in two stages, in 1604 and 1789 with two towers flanking its double arcade.

Provincial Deputation Building. This is just down the road, on the corner of Calle San Francisco and Calle San José. The Provincial Deputation was founded in the nineteenth century as Puerto Rico's first representative body. The building's site had originally been a cemetery and then later a market-place. The island was ruled from this building for eleven short days in between the time that Spain gave the island independence and the day that the United States took control. It is currently used by the US State Department but is open to the public Monday to Friday from 8 a.m. to 12 p.m. and from 1 p.m. to 4.30 p.m.

Intendencia This building stands on the opposite corner of Calle San Fransisco and Calle San José and was the Spanish Treasury from 1851 to 1898; it has been the Department of Education, Interior, Justice and Treasury this century. It is now Puerto Rico's State Department and has been recently restored to its original 1800s splendour. It is considered one of finest pieces of Puerto Rican architecture. Built on three floors, it has a large interior patio and neo-classical façade. The building is open Monday to Friday from 8 a.m. to 12 p.m. and from 1 p.m. to 4.30 p.m.

Plaza de Armes Opposite the Alcaldia, the Plaza de Armes which was named after the defence drills carried out by the city's residence. The square was carefully planned as the city's main square and is still used as a social gathering place. The four statues around the square represent the four seasons. The Colonial Guard marches from this square to Plaza de Colon and back along

Old San Juan is full of these narrow streets and old buildings

279

Calle San Francisco and Calle Forteleza. Dressed in sixteenth-century uniform, the band plays marches from that era. The marches happen daily from Tuesday to Saturday at 10.45 a.m., midday and 2 p.m. The march ends outside the City Hall where the band plays more music.

Museo Pablo Casals If you travel up Calle San José, heading north, opposite the junction with Calle San Sebastián you will find the Museo Pablo Casals, containing this famous cellist and composer's own instruments as well as manuscripts, photographs and video-tapes of successive Casals Festivals. It is open Tuesday to Saturday from 9.30 a.m. to 5 p.m., and on Saturday from 1 p.m. to 5.30 p.m. For tours or musical sessions, call 723-9185.

Museo Indio is on the corner of Calle San José and Calle Luna in the Casa de los Dos Zaguanes. Housing artefacts from the Taino Indian civilizations, some exhibits have been dated back 2,000 years to the time of Christ. The Institute of Puerto Rican Culture has added exhibits from the Smithsonian Institute in Washington DC. The Taino Indians were living on the island when Christopher Columbus first arrived and it was their tales of gold that lured Juan Ponce de León back to colonize the island.

Casa de los Contrafuertos is close by. It is believed to be the oldest private residence remaining in the city, dating from the early eighteenth century. Exhibitions are occasionally held in its Museum of Latin American Graphics on the first floor. On the ground floor, the recently restored Pharmacy Museum displays a nineteenth-century chemist shop. The Pharmacy Museum is open Wednesday to Sunday from 9 a.m. to 4.30 p.m.

Museo de Santos is another interesting museum. The *santos* are very much a part of Puerto Rican culture and religion. They are wooden carvings of saints and used to be kept in Puerto Rican homes and passed down from one generation to another. Originally brought from Spain, the craftsmen gradually took on their own designs for the santos and many have become works of art. A group called Rescate, meaning 'rescue', founded the museum in order to have a permanent collection of some of the more unusual santos. People often lend the Museum their private pieces and the exhibitions constantly change.

Continuing to the north until you reach the city wall, you will see the *Old San Juan Cemetery* on the other side between the wall and the sea. It is the burial place for many famous Puerto Ricans, including such names as José de Diego, José Celso Barbosa and José Gautier Benitez.

It is worth walking along the north wall to marvel at the strong fortifications laid down by the Spaniards. The wall surrounds the city from the US customs house in the south, round El Morro to Castillo de San Cristobal to the east of the old city. The wall is made of two 12m (40ft) high walls of sandstone blocks, with the gap in between filled with sand. The outer wall was sloped for added protection and the wall was patrolled day and night.

San Juan Museum of Art and History On the corner MacArthur, off the Norzagaray, this building started off life in 1850 as a bustling market-place and was restored in 1979 as a contemporary cultural centre. Two galleries exhibit Puerto Rican art while the largest interior patio on the island (40 x 30m/132 x 100ft), is used for concerts. An audiovisual show depicting the history of San Juan is screened at 11 a.m. every Friday. The suggested donation is US$1 for adults and 50 cents for children. The museum itself is open Monday to Friday 9 a.m. to 12 p.m. and 1 p.m. to 5 p.m., opening at 10 a.m. on Saturday and Sunday.

Castillo de San Cristobal The north wall ends to the east with the city's defences landward. Castillo de San Cristobal was built in 1772 to support El Morro and has five units connected by tunnels and dry moats. The idea was that any attackers would have to win all five units to capture the fort and not just breach one big building. It is open daily from 8 a.m. to 6 p.m. and admission is US$1 for adults, free for children.

Turning south at the Fort will take you to the *Casino de Puerto Rico*, which was built in 1917 in the style of a French Louis XIV mansion. It is now officially called the Manuel Pavia Fernandez Government Reception Centre and is used for official receptions. A little further south of the Casino is the *Teatro Tapia*. On the Plaza de Colon, this theatre is said to be one of the oldest in the western hemisphere. It was built in 1832 and named after the island's first playwright, Alejandro Tepia y Rivera. If you turn east from the theatre the road takes you through a narrow neck of land to Puerta de Tierra and the rest of modern San Juan.

Plaza de Colon was originally named in honour of St James but was dedicated to Christopher Columbus on the 400th anniversary of the discovery of Puerto Rico. The life of Christopher Columbus is described on bronze plaques which were put up in 1893 at the foot of a statue of the Spanish explorer. This area has been restored and cleaned up. There is a bus terminal on the plaza's north side.

Cathedral A city is not a city without a Cathedral, and San Juan's Cathedral is dedicated to our Lady of Providence, patron saint of Puerto Rico. Located on Calle Cristo, to the east of San Juan Gates, most of the building dates from the nineteenth century. The original building appeared in 1521 with a thatched roof. It was destroyed by a hurricane but was rebuilt in 1540 and the vaulted Gothic ceilings and circular belfry still survive. The remains of Juan Ponce de León were transferred here from San José Church in 1913 and are interred in a marble tomb near the transept. The remains of Roman martyr, San Pio, are also in the Cathedral. The Cathedral was restored in the 1970s and is open to the public daily from 6.30 a.m. to 5 p.m.; Monday to Friday, daily mass is at 7 a.m.; on Saturday mass is at 7.30 p.m., and on Sunday mass is at 9 a.m. to 11 a.m.

El Convento Continuing north along Calle Cristo takes you to El Convento. If you want to stay in Old San Juan, this is the only hotel. It started life as a Carmelite nunnery in 1651 after being granted a Royal decree. The present building dates from 1835 and has an interior courtyard with a restaurant and arched balconies. It is now the *Ramada Hotel El Convento* and costs around US$150 per night for a double room (Tel: 723-9020).

San José Church There are other churches in the area that are still in use. At the north of Calle Cristo is the San José Church. It was the original chapel for the Dominican monastery next door. It has a series of vaulted ceilings, probably introduced by friars who had come from Europe. Work began on the Church in 1532 and it was dedicated to St Thomas Aquinas. The church was abandoned for a time in 1838 before it was taken over by Jesuits in 1863. It was the family church of the descendants of Juan Ponce de León and his body lay in this church until 1913 when it was moved to the Cathedral. The only remaining family connection is the coat of arms belonging to his son-in-law Garcia

Trouche which is on the left wall of the chancel. Note the figure of Christ on the Cross, on the left of the church, which is said to date from the mid-sixteenth century. There are also some impressive processional flats stored at the back of the nave. The church is open from 8.30 a.m to 4 p.m., Monday to Saturday and a mass is held on Sunday at midday.

The Plaza de San José is a favourite meeting place for local people. It contains a statue of Juan Ponce de León which was made from a cannon. The cannon was captured from the British during Sir Ralph Abercromby's unsuccessful attack on the city in 1797.

Dominican Convent Museum The neighbouring Dominican Convent Museum was built by Dominican friars in 1523. The Convent has been used by many different groups since then, including women and children sheltering from Indian attacks and the staff of the headquarters of the Antilles Command of the US army. Now it is the Institute of Puerto Rican Culture and the library and chapel have been restored. The library contains relics from the Dominican order, including an eighteenth-century ornate altar, paintings and manuscripts. The Chapel Museum opens from Wednesday to Sunday, 9 a.m. to 12 p.m. and 1 p.m. to 4 p.m. The *Popular Arts Museum* opens from Monday to Saturday, 9.15 a.m. to 4.15 p.m.

Cristo Chapel At the south end of Calle Cristo is the Cristo Chapel. Legend has it that the Chapel was built after a young horse-rider plunged to his death in the sea at this point during a horse-race. Tomas Mateo Prats was watching the race, which was part of the 1753 patron saint festivities, when Baltaser Montanez failed to turn his horse at the end of Cristo Street and plunged over the precipice. Sr Prats offered to build a chapel in thanksgiving if the young man was saved. Unfortunately he died but the chapel was then built to protect others against a similar tragedy. It contains a small silver altar dedicated to the Christ of Miracles, paid for by contributions from the faithful, and is open every Tuesday from 10 a.m. to 4 p.m. but you can always see in through the chapel gate.

Galleries Old San Juan has several public art galleries as well as a mass of private galleries displaying a wealth of local art and crafts.

Wandering down Calle Cristo will take you to galleries belonging to some of the best of the local craftsmen. Stop in to see *M. Rivera* and his collection of handmade reproductions of Old San Juan houses, or, for modern art, try *Botello Galleria* at 208 Cristo Street. *Galeria Caliban*, *Galeria Luigi Marrozzini/Colibri Graphics* and *Galeria Palomas* are also on Calle Cristo. Walk down Fortaleza Street for more galleries, such as *The Butterfly People*. Many years ago a young couple with their baby daughter used to sell their butterflies in plexiglass on San Juan beaches but have now moved into their own shop at Calle Fortaleza, 152. It is also a restaurant specializing in steaks.

On San Sebastián Street, visit the *Galleria San Juan* in a restored eighteenth-century home of a captain of the Spanish artillery 'La Cueva del Indio'. The courtyards are filled with ceramics, sculpture and paintings. Calle San José houses *Galeria Coabey* and the *Galeria Liga de Arte*.

Shopping in Old San Juan is a pleasure. It is easy to walk around, stopping in parks or restaurants to rest weary feet and absorb the history while browsing through the myriad of little shops. There are the usual tacky T-shirt and souvenir shops but also good shoe shops, boutiques, antique shops and even places like *Go Bananas* where you can buy clothes and sit eating a snack in a sixteenth-century courtyard complete with wishing well. Go Bananas is on Cristo Street. *Perplexity Fashions* is also on Cristo Street and sells native print clothing and crocheted items. Recognized European names like Benetton are also represented as well as Indian styles in shops like the *Indian Art Palace* on Fortaleza Street and *Java Wraps* on Cristo Street.

The Book Store is open seven days a week on San José Street from 9 a.m. to 7 p.m. and contains a good selection of books on Puerto Rico and by local authors. Jewellers and leather workshops abound. Fortaleza Street has a wide selection of jewellers, some offering duty-free prices. *Leather and Pearls* on Cristo Street combines both crafts, and *Leather Boutique & Imports* on Fortaleza street has a wide range of leather luggage and bags as well as leather clothes. Porcelain and glass are also on sale, both imported and local work. Again, Cristo and Fortaleza Streets are the places to go.

For craft shops, try *Aquadilla en San Juan* on San Francisco Street or *Mercado de Artesanias*, Plaza de Hostos on Recinto Sur. *Puerto Rican Art and Crafts* is on Fortaleza street. But the main area is *Plazoleta del Puerto*, across the street from Pier Three at the

Marina. Built around a San Juan street scene, craftsmen work in small stalls so you can watch them work as well as do your shopping. The centre is open Monday to Saturday from 9 a.m. to 6 p.m. and some do open on Sunday between 10 a.m. and 6 p.m. (Tel: 722-3053). There is a bus terminal at the west of the centre.

Restaurants Some of San Juan's best restaurants are in the Old City. For snacks, try the turn of the century coffee shop, *La Bombonera*, on San Francisco Street (Tel: 722-4251), *Go Bananas* on Fortaleza Street (Tel: 724-7376) or *Asti's Pizzeria* on Cristo Street (Tel: 721-2006). And for ice-creams, there are some wonderful parlours on the Plaza Colon with exotic mixes.

Puerto Rican restaurants include *La Mallorquina*, on San Justo Street (Tel: 722-3261), which opened in 1848. Service is slow but the food and atmosphere is excellent. Other local restaurants include *La Tasca del Callejon* on Fortaleza Street (Tel: 721-1689) where the waiters double as musicians and where the tapas are a speciality. For an intimate evening out, try *La Zaragozana* on San Francisco Street (Tel: 723-5103). For seafood, try *El Siglo* on Fortaleza Street.

For meals with a view, try the Mexican restaurant *Amanda's* on Sol and Norzagaray Streets (Tel: 722-1682). It overlooks the ocean and the Castillo de San Cristobal. Or have a meal in the secluded courtyard restaurant of the *Ramada El Convento* just off Calle Cristo (Tel: 723-9020).

The main Post Office is opposite Pier One and is close to the two main car parks.

If you are driving into Old San Juan but intend to park and walk around, you can leave your car in three car parks. The furthest from town is the Covadonga Garage which is open 24 hours a day; a free shuttle service links the city from there. Two blocks closer to town is the Recinto Sur, known as Dona Fela's, but it is not open 24 hours and is not serviced by the shuttle. The third park is an open car park on La Puntilla. You can easily walk around the city from here and it is serviced by the free trolleys but is only open during the day.

Ferries leave from the marina in Old San Juan every 30 minutes for Catano, from 6.15 a.m. to 10 p.m. and on Sundays and holidays there are trips at 2.30 p.m. and 4.30 p.m. lasting 90 minutes which take you around the Old City by water. Adults us$2.50; children

US$1.25. Several tour operators also offer guided trips around the Old City, such as *Loose-Penny Tours* (Tel: 795-6351).

There are bus terminals in the Plazoleta del Puerto and in Plaza de Colon.

Useful Telephone Numbers

The Puerto Rican Tourism Company, Paseo de la Princesa. Tel: 721-2400.

Casa Blanca. San Sebastian. Tel: 724-4102.

Dominican Convent Museum, Calle Norzagaray, 98, Plaza de San Jose. Tel: 724-0700.

El Arsenal, La Puntilla (Tel: 724-5998/5949).

El Morro Fortress, San Felipe del Morro. Tel: 724-1974.

Fine Arts Museum, Calle Cristo, 253. Tel: 724-5949.

Fort San Cristobal. Tel: 724-1974.

La Casa del Libro, Calle Cristo, 255. Tel: 723-0354

La Forteleza. Tel: 721-7000, ext. 2211.

Museum of the Seas, Pier One. Tel: 725-2532.

Pablo Casals Museum. San Sebastian, 101, Plaza de San Jose. Tel: 723-9185.

Plazoleta del Puerto, Marina. Tel: 722-3053.

San José Church, Cristo and San Sebastian Street. Tel: 725-7501.

San Juan Cathedral, Cristo Street, 151. Tel: 722-0861.

San Juan Museum of History of Art, Calle Norzagaray, corner MacArthur. Tel: 724-1875.

The Pharmacy Museum, Casa de los Contrafuertes, San Sebastian, 101, Plaza de San José. Tel: 724-5998/5949.

New San Juan Most visitors to San Juan stay in the modern areas of town called the Condado and the Isla Verde. The Condado is a narrow strip of land between the Condado Lagoon and the Atlantic Ocean. It is linked to Old San Juan along another narrow strip called Puerta de Tierra. This is the home for two large international hotels. *The Radisson Hotel of San Juan* used to be called the Normandie and was designed to resemble a ship, complete with portholes for windows. The Art Deco building has recently been refurbished and costs around US$175 for a double room per night (Tel: 729-2929). Next door is the popular *Caribe Hilton Hotel* which is set in 17 acres of gardens. The hotel costs around US$260 for a double room per night (Tel: 721-0303).

San Jeronimo The Caribe Hilton Hotel stands on its own spit of land in front of San Jeronimo. This is a tiny fortress built in the eighteenth century to add to the fortifications of Old San Juan. It was badly damaged in the 1797 attack by the British. It has been restored and now houses a collection of weapons, uniforms and documents from that period. It is open Wednesday to Sunday, 9.30 a.m. to 12 p.m. and from 1 p.m. to 4.30 p.m. (Tel: 724-5949).

Follow Muñoz Rivera Avenue towards Old San Juan and you will come to *Muñoz Rivera Park*. This park is only fifty years old and was designed as an oceanfront square. It contains a statue of statesman, journalist and poet Luis Muñoz Rivera. The statue is sited close to an old ammunition depot, *El Polvorin*, which has been restored as a museum. Craft fairs are held in the Park, along with the occasional concert. Close by is the sports complex built for the 1979 Pan-American Games.

The parallel road travelling towards Old San Juan is Ponce de León. Opposite Muñoz Rivera Park is the *Central Archives and Library Building*. It was one of the last buildings the Spanish completed before their defeat in 1898. It was designed as a hospital but was first used in 1877 as a prison instead; later it was converted to a cigar factory and then to a rum distillery, becoming the central library after restoration in the 1970s. It has occasional exhibitions and a permanent room, La Sala de Eugenio Maria de Hostos, displaying memorabilia from the times of this Puerto Rican writer. The building also houses a small chapel behind a giant staircase. The library is open from Monday to Friday, 8 a.m. to 4.30 p.m. (Tel: 724-2680).

Further down Ponce de León is *The Capitol*. Built in the 1920s, it is the seat of Puerto Rico's bicameral legislature. It is a large white marble building, not particularly attractive but is open to the public from 8.30 a.m. to 5 p.m., Monday to Friday. Call 721-7305 or 721-7310 to book a guided tour.

The Condado is linked to Puerta la Tierra by a long white bridge, *Puenta Los Dos Hermanos* (Two Brothers Bridge). Fishermen congregate on this bridge at weekends, ice-cream sellers roam up and down and many Puerto Ricans just wander along meeting friends and watching the windsurfers glide across the Condado lagoon. As you cross the bridge, look out to sea and you will notice a small spit ending in a strange-shaped rock. The

**Overleaf
The Capitol Building in San Juan**

287

legend is that the lump is actually a solidified dog. The dog used to sit on the end of the spit every day and wait for his master, a fisherman, to return home. One day the fisherman drowned at sea but the dog continued to wait for so long that he eventually turned to stone.

The bridge leads straight on to Ashford Avenue, with its glitzy hotels, boutiques and restaurants. Ashford Avenue is also home to the San Juan Convention Centre and so during conventions, many of the hotels are packed and hold special convention functions. There are often a few craft stalls around the convention centre.

Just after leaving Puerto la Tierra, you will pass the *Isla Grande Flying School* which offers visitors sightseeing trips of Old San Juan by air (Tel: 722-1160) or 725-5760).

Hotels Among the better places to stay is the *Condado Plaza Hotel and Casino* (Tel: 721-1000) which costs up to us$330 for a double room per night. The hotel is also the base for *San Juan Water Sports* which offers everything on the water from harbour cruises and day trips to deserted beaches to snorkelling and kayaks (Tel: 721-1000), ext. 2619/2699/2105.

The nearby *Condado Beach Hotel* (Tel: 721-6090/6888) is quieter and less glitzy than the Condado Plaza but is often full up with local people. It costs about US$120 for a double room per night.

If you prefer somewhere cheaper and with a more personal service, try one of the many guest houses in the area. Some of the best include *Canario* (Tel: 722-3861) and its next door neighbour *Canario by the Sea* (Tel: 722-8640); both cost between US$60–80. Cheaper still is *Jewel's by the Sea* (Tel: 725-5313), which is on Seaview, to the east of Ashford Avenue; it costs around US$60. Guest houses off the main strip tend to be much cheaper than those in the middle of this busy area.

Most of the major hotels have private areas of beach but these tend to be quite small. Plans to develop the coastline to the east of San Juan will apparently give each hotel more space instead of the old policy of allowing buildings right onto the beach which has merely resulted in less sand.

Shopping Again, the shopping can be divided between the tacky souvenir shops and the more glamorous boutiques. Unfortunately, the souvenir shops seem to be winning the battle for space but there are still some good boutiques. Try *Level 1* or

Colombian Leather on Ashford Avenue. *Nativa* has younger fashions or try *Jolie* for beachwear.

Ashford Avenue is also home to an Avis car rental outlet, an American Airlines office as well as travel agents, chemists and newsagents.

Restaurants Some of the best restaurants in Condado are in the major hotels. The Condado Plaza Hotel (Tel: 721-1000) houses Italian restaurant *Capriccio*, Chinese cuisine at *Lotus Flower*, seafood cooking at *LK Sweeney* and steaks at *Tony Roma's*. Others that are recommended are the *Chart House* on Ashford Avenue (Tel: 728-0110) for seafood, and *Mama's Little Italy* (Tel: 722-2021) for a pasta meal.

Mirimar On the south side of the Candado Lagoon is the Mirimar area. There are lots of hotels in this area but it is mostly used by businessmen and is not a good area to walk around at night. The hotels are generally cheaper than those on the Condado or in Isla Verde. The *Clarion Hotel and Casino* is in the city's highest building and the restaurant at the top, *Windows of the Caribbean* (Tel: 721-4100), has magnificent views of the city and the ocean beyond. The hotel itself costs about US$150 for a double room per night. For a cheap hotel in a quiet street but with good service, try *El Toro* (Tel: 725-5150), which costs about US$40 per double room per night.

To the west of the Mirimar hotel area is Isla Grande. This area used to house American army garrisons but is now used for government offices and the Isla Grande airport. Flights from this internal airport go to the smaller islands of Culebra and Vieques.

Isla Verde To the east of the Condado along the coast is Isla Verde. This area is close to the international airport and some of the new hotels seem to be right underneath the flight path. Large hotels line the beach while, opposite, fast-food outlets and cheap shops line the road. But once inside the hotels, the American influence outside disappears. The top hotel has to be *El San Juan Hotel and Casino* (Tel: 791-1000) which costs up to US$300 for a double room per night. This beachfront hotel offers guests a wide range of facilities and shops, surrounded by an opulent decor of heavy, dark wood and chandeliers. It is worth coming to the hotel to try out one of the excellent restaurants or for some gambling in the casino.

Other top hotels along this coast are the all-inclusive *Sands* (Tel: 791-6100), which has recently been refurbished, for about US$245 per night, *ESJ Towers* (Tel: 791-5151) for about US$180 per night and *Empress Oceanfront* (Tel: 791-3083) for about US$128 per night.

There is little to do in this area that is not attached to one of the hotels. All watersports locally are arranged through them and they have the best beach areas. Most will book tours either of Old San Juan or out into the country.

Metropolitan Area San Juan is not just a coastal strip. As the city expanded it has swallowed up the neighbouring towns of Carolina, Bayamon, Catano and Rio Piedras, and all these individual towns are worth a visit. One of the most popular things to do in San Juan is to visit the *Ron Bacardi Factory* at Catano. A trip to the world's largest rum plant is often tied in with tours around Old San Juan and is reached by ferry from Old San Juan marina. Ferries leave every half-hour from 6.15 a.m. to 10 p.m. This rum factory has free 45-minute tours (Tel: 788-1500), between 9.30 a.m. and 3.30 p.m., Monday to Saturday. Other attractions around Catano include Cabras Island at the end of San Juan Bay with its *El Canuelo Fort*. This fort was built in 1608 to support El Morro. Along the road connecting Catano with Bayamon (Route 5), you will pass the grounds of the *Barrilito Rum Plant*, the site of a 200-year-old house and a 150-year-old windmill.

Caparra Shortly before reaching Bayamon on Route 2 you will come to the island's earliest settlement, Caparra. Juan Ponce de León tried to establish a settlement here in 1508 after he was given permission by the King of Spain to colonize the island. But it was an unhealthy place and the Spanish soon abandoned the town and started to build San Juan. You can still see the ruins of the old fort, and artefacts from that period are on display at the *Museum of the Conquest and Colonization of Puerto Rico*. It is open Monday to Friday from 9 a.m. to 5 p.m. and on weekends from 10 a.m. to 6 p.m. (Tel: 781-4795).

Bayamon Bayamon itself is worth a visit, particularly if you have children to entertain. Its *Science Park* on the north-west of town contains the *Museum of Natural Sciences* with both mounted animals and a living zoo surrounding a manmade lake with paddleboats. Other museums in the park include a *Museum of Geology and Physical Sciences*, a *Museum of Archaeology* and a *Museum of Transportation*. The park is open from 8 a.m. to 4 p.m. Wednesday to Friday, 10 a.m. to 6 p.m. on weekends and holidays. Admission is US$3 for adults and US$1 for children.

Bayamon's Central Park contains a functioning 1934 sugar-cane train and is open daily from 8 a.m. to 8 p.m. The Tourism Office (Tel: 798-8191/5552) has a display of local crafts, and the neighbouring *Braulio Castillo Theatre* concentrates on local culture.

The town's plaza houses an eighteenth-century church and the *Francisco Oller Art and History Museum*, full of Taino Indian ceramics, portraits by Francisco Oller and sculptures by Tomas Batista. The Museum is open Tuesday to Saturday from 9 a.m. to 4 p.m. The Barbosa Pedestrian Mall, with its fountains and benches, lead to the *Barbosa Museum* which was the birthplace and home of José Celso Barbosa who founded the island's Republican Party. It is open Monday to Friday from 8 a.m. to 12 p.m. and from 1 p.m. to 5 p.m.

Hato Rey Closer to the city centre, Hato Rey is home to the Caribbean's largest shopping mall with over 200 outlets in the Plaza Las Americas. The Plaza's Post Office is also a philatelic centre. Hato Rey is also home to one of the island's three water parks. Carefully designed to be safe for children the *Plaza Acuatica* is split into three park areas. It has wave pools, slides and children's pools. It also has a play castle, mini-golf and a children's dry-play area. Plaza Acuatica opens at 10 a.m. daily through the summer, at 12 p.m. Monday to Thursday during the winter and at 10 a.m. Friday to Sunday during the winter (Tel: 754-9500).

Santurce and the Sacred Heart University lie to the north. The University houses the Museum of Contemporary Puerto Rican Art on the first floor of the Barat Building, which opens between 9 a.m. and 4 p.m., Tuesday to Saturday, and from 11 a.m to 5 p.m. on Sundays. Between Santurce and Mirimar is the *Fine Arts Centre* on the corner of De Diego and Ponce de León Avenues.

To the east in Carolina, is El Commandante Racetrack where races are held every Wednesday, Friday, Sunday and on holidays, starting at 2.30 p.m. The restaurant opens at 12.30 p.m. on racedays (Tel: 724-6060).

One of the many waterfalls in the Caribbean National rain forest of El Yungue on Puerto Rico

A short drive south of Carolina takes you to Rio Piedras and the *Botanical Gardens*, containing over 200 exotic species. The *Agricultural Experiment Station Gardens* are at the entrance to Barrio Venezuela by the intersection of Routes 1 and 847. They are open from 9 a.m. to 4.30 p.m., Tuesday to Sunday but open on holiday Mondays, closing instead on the Tuesday.

Rio Piedras also has the *Luis Muñoz Marin Archives, Museum and Gardens* and you can have a guided tour through the gardens and library of Luis Muñoz Marin, a former governor of the island. The Museum is open from Tuesday to Saturday, 9 a.m. to 3 p.m., make group reservations on 755-7979. The Muñoz Marin Park has gardens, lakes and a small train to take you around. A cable-car links the Park to the car park and it is open Tuesday to Friday from 9 a.m. to 6 p.m. and at weekends from 8.30 a.m. to 6 p.m.

The main campus of the University of Puerto Rico is in Rio Piedras between Ponce de León Avenue and Barbosa Avenue. The *University Museum* and *Jose M. Lazaro Library*, the largest on the island, are both open to the public at varying times. Call 764-0000 for details.

If you travel to the east out of San Juan you will come to the Torrecilla Lagoon, a mangrove swamp and bird sanctuary. Boat trips around the lagoon last about two hours. *La Paseadora* launch takes up to 30 passengers at 2.30 p.m. on Saturdays and from 1 p.m. to 6 p.m. on Sundays and holidays. Trips cost US$3 for adults and US$2 for children.

San Juan Trips Plenty of day trips are organized from San Juan. These vary from trips to the beaches of the north-eastern coast, into the mountains and to the El Yungue rain forest.

El Yungue This is the Caribbean's National Rain Forest and covers an area of 28,000 acres. It is the only tropical rain forest in the US Forest Service. The rain forest used to cover virtually all the island but has shrunk to this small area in the north-east. There are other pockets of forest across the country worth visiting, but El Yungue is the most famous. Some 100 billion gallons of rain falls annually on the forest so, be warned, take an umbrella. It can rain fourteen or fifteen times a day.

The forest surrounds the El Yungue mountain which peaks at 1,075m (3,523ft). It was originally named Yuquiyu by the Indians after a kind spirit, and the name was changed by the Spanish.

295

Temperatures vary from the top to the bottom of the park, with the lowest temperatures at the peak of about 18°C (65°F), rising to 23°C (73°F) at the bottom.

The forest is the centre for several different kinds of research and the staff are always happy to talk to visitors about their work. There are newsletters, marked trails and guides to help visitors see the most of the forest and to understand the problems the area faces. One of these was Hurricane Hugo, which swept on to Puerto Rico in the north-east, damaging many trees in El Yungue. The Parks Service closed the area and spent several months clearing trails and replanting where possible; the climate also helped in regeneration.

A new approach has been taken with the forest. Local farmers are encouraged to work with the forest rather than just destroy it and the Parks Service is buying land on the edge of the reserve, trying to build up a wooded layer to protect the rare and old trees in the park.

Over 240 species of trees and plants can be found in El Yungue. One of the more unusual is a tree which has a white bark and broad green leaves. Legend has it that the bark changes colour when a storm approaches and locals will tell you that they saw it happen as Hurricane Hugo approached. Visitors can get a guide to some of the plants and the areas where they will be found.

Another special tree to Puerto Rico is the Ausubo Tree, a hard wood that the Spanish originally used in ship-building. In fact, the King of Spain considered it so valuable that he banned its export in case a ship load fell into enemy hands. The wood was also used as supporting beams in many of Old San Juan's fortifications and old buildings. Its reddish-brown colour made it attractive for furniture and over-use almost destroyed the species by the 1930s.

But the sights are not restricted to plants. There is wildlife, too. The *Puerto Rican parrot* is an endangered species and is only found in the forest. Its numbers dwindled to 19 in 1971, but intensive research and a breeding programme has helped build numbers back up to 84. Only 40 of those are in the wild while the remainder are in an aviary at the *Sierra Palm Visitors Centre*. The breeding programme does mean that the birds have to be kept quiet and undisturbed so visitors are often kept well away from the aviary. If you fancy your chances of spotting one of these rare birds in the

**Much of Puerto Rico is both
forested and mountainous**

wild, they are about 30cm (12in) long, mostly green with a red blaze above the beak and bright blue under their wings.

Another extremely difficult creature to spot is the *Coqui frog*. This brown frog makes a huge noise for its tiny body and creates one of the most memorable sounds of Puerto Rico. The frog grows to about 2.5cm (1in) long and blends into its surroundings extremely well. Puerto Ricans consider it a sign of good luck actually to see one of these tiny creatures and legend has it that the Coqui was once a bird that lost its wings. Later, fate took pity on the wingless bird and turned it into a frog able to climb the trees the bird had once perched on. Another less popular legend is that a naughty boy was punished by being instantly transformed into a frog and the frog's call is actually the noise of a boy whistling. The noise it makes – ko-kee – gave the frog its name. There are 13 species of Coquis in the Forest. Searching for these rare creatures is made easy by the well-marked trails. You can get details from the Sierra Palm Visitors Centre but they vary from easy, short walks taking you past waterfalls and to spectacular viewpoints to difficult trails that are really only for experienced hikers.

While the Park Service is spending literally millions of US dollars in saving the parrot and hoping that the resulting research can be used elsewhere in the world, there are other experiments being conducted in the Forest. El Yungue is also known as the Luquillo Experimental Forest. It has become an important site for watershed research. The US congress granted funds in 1985 and now there are three watersheds that are being constantly monitored as part of long-term studies into timber management in tropical rain forests.

The forest is open to visitors 24 hours a day, every day of the year. There are two information centres, one at Sierra Palm and the other at Palo Colorado. These are open from 9 a.m. to 5 p.m. daily, as is the Yokahu Observation Tower. The Ranger District Office hours are Monday to Friday, 7.30 a.m. to 11.30 a.m. and 12 p.m. to 4 p.m. There is a restaurant at the Sierra Palm Centre. For more information call 887-2875. Companies that organize tours to the forest include *The Gray Line Tours* on 727-8080 or 727-2156 and *Loose-Penny Tours* on 795-6351.

Just outside the Park on the way to Rio Grande is the Restaurante Las Vegas which is recommended for local food. It is

**Butterflies abound in the
Puerto Rican forest reserves**

one of the Mesones Gastronomicos, a scheme set up by the
Puerto Rico Tourism Company to highlight restaurants outside of
San Juan that offer good food at reasonable prices. These
restaurants all have a knife and fork symbol outside and are
checked regularly to make sure they are maintaining standards
while keeping prices down.

Luquillo Some of the best views of this seaside town are
from the El Yungue viewpoints The beach is one of the nicest in
Puerto Rico, stretching for over a mile and lined with palms. A
trip to the beach is often combined with trips into the El Yungue
Park or with horse-trekking tours. Luquillo is also home to the
island's annual Food Festival; held in October, it highlights typical
Puerto Rican dishes. If you want to stay at Luquillo reasonably
cheaply, try the *Parador Martorell*. This is one of sixteen-selected
hotels around the island. They are chosen for their local flavour
and reasonable prices. Many are close to tourist attractions, and
this one is close to the beach and costs in the region of US$60 a
night (Tel: 889-2710). Luquillo is under development and four
hotels of 300–500 rooms each are to be built by the owners of the
Sands Hotel in San Juan. There are also new hotels being built at
the inland town of Rio Grande, close to the entrance of El
Yungue, and at Fajardo south of Luquillo.

Fajardo This sleepy fishing village has been transformed in recent years and the latest scheme is for a US$350 million marina and hotel at Puerto del Rey. The *El Conquistador Hotel* was also re-opened and converted from 381 to 800 rooms. The area was hard hit by Hurricane Hugo but has been restored. It is a mecca for watersports lovers, both for its Seven Seas Beach and for its many aquatic activities. Ferries leave Fajardo to the outer islands of Culebra and Vieques. The ferry terminal is next to the pink US customs house.

Other smaller islands, *Icacos*, *Palominos* and *Palominitos*, are a favourite for snorkellers and divers. They are just off-shore from Fajardo and are meant to provide some of the best diving around the island. The Hurricane apparently left much of the coral reefs unscathed and, although local beaches are not as good as they were, they are still excellent for first-time visitors, unaware of what had been there. Dive operators around Fajardo include the *Scuba Shop* at the Villa Marina Shopping Centre (Tel: 863-8465), which will organize night dives, and many operators in San Juan organize day trips to the Fajardo area. The 12m (40ft) catamaran *Spread Eagle* is moored up at Fajardo and clients will be picked up from San Juan for day trips (Tel: 863-1905, 383-0162 or 863-5875).

The island's newest Parador is in Fajardo. La Familia has a swimming-pool and a solarium as well as a restaurant. It costs around US$60 a night (Tel: 863-1193). Another hotel in Fajardo is *Delicias* which costs about US$50 (Tel: 863-1818). Most restaurants in the town specialize in locally caught seafood. Among the best are *Anchor's Inn* (Tel: 863-7200) or *Timon* (Tel: 860-2244).

Loiza This coastal town lies half-way between San Juan and Fajardo. It is relatively undeveloped although, again, that is set to change. This coastal stretch was hit by Hurricane Hugo and still shows some signs of it: ramshackle huts are left in decaying heaps and many of the palms are missing their fronds. The people appear poorer along this stretch and it still has one of the highest proportions of African descendants as this was an area colonized by slaves after their freedom in 1873. But in many ways this is an interesting coastline, still rugged and untouched. Loiza is in the middle of 10km (6ml.) of beach and the road just gives you glimpses of the sand. First inhabited in the sixteenth century, it has the oldest church still regularly used in Puerto Rico, *San Patricio Church*, which was built in 1645.

Loiza still preserves many folk and craft traditions, including the coconut masks. The annual *Festival de Loiza Aldea* is held in July to honour St James the Apostle. There is a carnival, processions, dancing and singing. The coconut masks are a real speciality of Loiza; although each town has its own different masks, the ones from Loiza are said to be among the most exotic on the island.

Dorado To the west of San Juan along the coast is the resort town of Dorado. There is little on offer in the town itself but the resort hotels of *Hyatt Cerromar Beach* and *Hyatt Dorado* are on 3km (2ml.) of beach. The Cerromar has a long river pool with a jacuzzi and swim-up bar, while the Dorado has recently been refurbished. On the 1,000-acre estate, there are four Robert Trent Jones championship 18-hole golf-courses, 21 tennis courts and a health club. Prices vary from US$235 for a room through to US$1300 for suites (Tel: 796-1600).

There is a Mesones Gastronomicos in Dorado. The *Restaurante El Ladrillo* meets the high standards of the Puerto Rico Tourism Company for its local menu to belong to this group of restaurants. Other restaurants in the area include the Chinese restaurant, *Jewel of China*, on Route 693 (Tel: 796-4644).

Humacao The south-eastern part of Puerto Rico is accessible from San Juan but many people stop at Fajardo or travel through the centre of the island to Ponce, missing out on what many people consider to be the best beaches and prettiest areas of Puerto Rico. The town of Humacao is a few miles inland but it has a beach named after it.

The main attraction in the town is the *Casa Roig* residence which is open as a museum and cultural centre. It was built in the 1920s by architect Antonio Nechodoma and his work is the main focus of the museum. It is open Wednesday to Friday, from 9 a.m. to 12 p.m. and from 1 p.m. to 4 p.m., and on Sundays from 10 a.m. to 4 p.m.

For a Puerto Rican meal, try the Mesones Guastronomicos restaurant in Humacao, *Restaurante Tulio's Sea Food*. Other restaurants to try in town include *Daniel Seafood* (Tel: 852-1784) or *Paradise Seafood* (Tel: 852-1180), just out of town.

Palmas del Mar To the south of Humacao is the resort area of Palmas del Mar in a former coconut plantation. There has been more new development in this resort, with a new 475-room *Ritz-Carlton Hotel*. Again, this is a watersports centre, with dive operators like *Coral Head Divers* (Tel: 850-7208, 635-4529), or for sailing try the *Palmas Sailing Centre* (Tel: 852/6000/8114). There are deep-sea fishing trips as well as cruises to the nearby US Virgin Island of St Thomas for shopping. The island's major sailing regatta is held annually in Palmas del Mar in March. The annual *Copa Velasco Regatta* forms the first part of the Caribbean Ocean Racing Triangle and usually attracts over 100 racing yachts.

For landlubbers there is an 18-hole Gary Player designed golf-course (Tel: 852-6000), horse-riding at the *Palmas del Mar Equestrian Centre* (Tel: 852-6000), including Puerto Rico's own indigenous breed of horse, the Paso Fino, or tennis on any of the 20 courts, some floodlit.

There are several options for staying in the resort. There is the *Candelero Hotel* or suites at the *Palmas Inn* or time-share options in the villas of *Club Cala de Palmas*. Hotel rooms cost around US$150 per night for a double room (Tel: 852-6000).

The resort covers 6km (3.5ml.) of beach, 4km (2.5ml) of cliffs, and inland there are 70 acres of tropical forest. This is a place where you can have a complete holiday without leaving the resort. There is a variety of restaurants, from snack bars to gourmet, and there are shops, too, both for the sports enthusiast and the souvenir hunter.

From Humacao it is worth taking a drive along the coast down to the beach at *Punte Guilarte*. You will pass Tuna Point with its lighthouse and quiet beach. You will also pass the start of the Panoramic Route which runs from east to west across the island. This route takes about three days to do properly as the roads are not that good; slow-moving lorries hold up the traffic and you will be stopping every few kilometres to take in the breath-taking scenery, at roadside stalls or just to stop and chat to the locals.

Back on the coast there are some nice beaches at the small towns of *Maunabo*, *Patillas* and *Arroyo*. The beach south of Arroyo at Punta Guilarte is a public beach with changing facilities and lockers to stow your belongings. (On any beach in Puerto Rico you are always advised to leave your car locked and belongings out of sight to stop petty thieving.)

The port of Arroyo used to be the centre of smuggling on the island but, during this century, the legal occupation of sugar-cane growing has taken over. A trolley bus will take you around the town and surrounding areas. It operates on weekends and holidays from 8.30 a.m. It leaves from the port and costs US$2.

Nearby Guayama was also famous for its smuggling exploits. Now the most interesting feature is the *Casa Cautino Museum*, a former home on the edge of the town's plaza in Creole-style architecture. Built in 1887, it contains artefacts belonging to the former owners, the Cautino family. It is open from Wednesday to Sunday, 10.30 a.m. to 12 p.m. and 1 p.m. to 4.30 p.m.

To reach the Humacao area from San Juan, you can either take the coastal route through Rio Grande, Fajardo and south to Humacao, or you can travel inland across the mountains to Caguas, Gurabo Juncoe and Las Piedras. The third route to Humacao is from the southern town of Ponce. This is Puerto Rico's second city and one that will become increasingly popular with tourists.

Ponce This delightful city was named after Juan Ponce de León, the man who persuaded the King of Spain to colonize the

The Town Hall of Puerto Rico's second city, Ponce

303

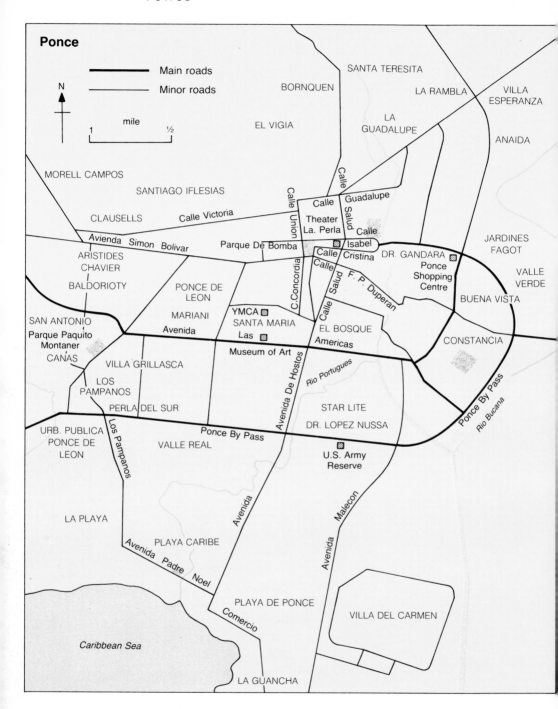

Ponce

—— Main roads

—— Minor roads

N

mile
1   ½

MORELL CAMPOS

SANTA TERESITA

BORNQUEN

LA RAMBLA

VILLA ESPERANZA

ANAIDA

EL VIGIA

LA GUADALUPE

SANTIAGO IFLESIAS

Calle Union

Calle Salud

Calle Guadalupe

CLAUSELLS

Calle Victoria

Calle Theater La. Perla

Avienda Simon Bolivar

Parque De Bomba

Calle Isabel

Calle Cristina

DR. GANDARA

Ponce Shopping Centre

JARDINES FAGOT

VALLE VERDE

ARISTIDES CHAVIER

BALDORIOTY

PONCE DE LEON

C.Concordia

Calle

Calle Salud

F. P. Duperan

BUENA VISTA

SAN ANTONIO

Parque Paquito Montaner

CAÑAS

MARIANI

Avenida

YMCA

SANTA MARIA

Las

Americas

EL BOSQUE

CONSTANCIA

Museum of Art

Ponce By Pass

Rio Bucana

VILLA GRILLASCA

LOS PAMPANOS

PERLA DEL SUR

Avenida De Hostos

Rio Portugues

STAR LITE

DR. LOPEZ NUSSA

URB. PUBLICA PONCE DE LEON

Los Pampanos

Ponce By Pass

VALLE REAL

U.S. Army Reserve

LA PLAYA

Avenida

Avenida Malecon

PLAYA CARIBE

Avenida Padre Noel

PLAYA DE PONCE

Comercio

VILLA DEL CARMEN

Caribbean Sea

LA GUANCHA

island. Ponce really made a name for itself between 1890 and 1930 when the area was at its most prosperous with sugar-cane plantations flourishing. Much of the architecture of the city was designed during this time and now it is being restored ready for the 1992 Columbus celebrations and for the 300th celebrations of the town itself.

A lot of the work has been done but it should all be finished in 1992 to create an atmosphere from a century ago. Visitors will be able to stroll down gaslit streets or take a horse and carriage around town. The US$440 million project has covered an area containing some 1,000 buildings. The restoration is not the only work going on in the city. A cruise-ship pier was built and opened in 1990, so for the first time cruise ships have been arriving. There are plans for an international airport so that tourists can fly direct from the USA to Ponce without changing to an internal flight at San Juan. Hotel accommodation has also been increased dramatically.

Until this renovation, people tended to stay in San Juan and limit themselves to day trips to Ponce. It was easy to see all the sights in just a day but now there is a move to encourage people actually to base their holidays in the town and travel out from Ponce to San Juan for a two-centre holiday. Ponce and San Juan are linked by an expressway that takes just over an hour but the alternative is to take your time and drive slowly through the mountains, stopping at the numerous towns and villages along the way.

The historic centre of Ponce is dominated by its Cathedral, the bright multicoloured fire station and the art museum. All the historic buildings are in a small area and easy to walk around in a day. In its heyday, Ponce was known as *La Perle del Sur* or the Pearl of the South. It was also known as the Aristocratic City because of its elegant houses and wide, tree-lined streets.

Most of the places of interest are within easy reach of the city's main square, *Plaza Las Delicias*. The square is surrounded by the Cathedral, the Town Hall, the Old Fire House and the Casa Armstrong-Poventud. The Square itself is split into two sections. The northerly part is known as Muñoz Rivera Plaza and the south side is Degetau Plaza. The whole square is planted out with fig trees and dotted with statues. It is an area for sitting in the sun, meeting friends or taking a rest before seeing the sights.

The courtyard inside Ponce's Town Hall where many criminals were said to have been executed in Puerto Rico

305

The Cathedral of Our Lady of Guadalupe in Ponce

The Cathedral is dedicated to Our Lady of Guadalupe and is worth a quick visit. Earthquakes and hurricanes have taken their toll over the years, but after each event the Cathedral has been carefully restored.

Old Fire House It is difficult to miss the Old Fire House or Parque de Bombas. Built in 1883 as an exhibition stall for the city's first agricultural fair, it should have been closed down at the end of the show. But it was adopted by the city's volunteer fire brigade as their headquarters and has been used to this day by the local firemen. It is a building of bright red and black stripes with small arched windows. Visitors are free to wander in, going around the fire engines and climbing up to the first floor where there is a small permanent display of memorabilia from the fire service over the past century. And every Sunday the town band gathers on the balcony overlooking the Plaza to entertain the crowds. There is also a modern fire station about one block away from the historic Fire House.

A bright red fire engine matches the décor at the Ponce Fire Station, Puerto Rico

Casa Armstrong-Poventud is on the opposite side of the Plaza from the Old Fire House. It has been restored by the Institute of Puerto Rican culture in its original neo-classical style with caryatid columns on its façade. It houses the *Tourism Information Centre* and a regional office for the Institute of Puerto Rican Culture. A team of architects is based in the building, who are responsible for the renovation work around the City.

About 60 per cent of the historic area had been lost by 1985 when the project was launched by Puerto Rican Governor, Rafael Hernandez Colon. The project organizers decided to restore as much of the façades of the buildings as possible and to open some as museums. They encouraged local people to restore the buildings with the help of Government grants and many of the buildings have been bought to ensure the whole street could be restored.

The Casa Armstrong-Poventud offices are open Monday to Friday from 8 a.m. to 12 p.m. and from 1 p.m. to 4.30 p.m., while the Museum hours are from Tuesday to Sunday, 9 a.m. to 12 p.m. and 1 p.m. to 4 p.m. The Museum houses a collection of antiques and also the furniture of Puerto Rican poet, José De Diego.

Another old building on the main plaza is the *City Hall* which is still the centre of local government. Inside the wrought-iron gates is a small courtyard where guides will tell you that prisoners used to be executed.

Walking down the side streets off the plaza takes you into the restored areas. Take a stroll down Calle Christina to find *Christina 70*, one of the city's latest Museums. It is just down the road from *La Perla Theatre*. This theatre, complete with Corinthian columns and capitals, is used around the year for plays, concerts and festivals. Next door is the city's *Public Library* which houses art and photographic exhibitions. Behind the Theatre is the *Morel Campos School of Music*. The whole block will eventually become the Ponce art and Cultural Centre.

Further down the street is Casa Serralles. The Serralles family were the first family to produce rum in Puerto Rico and are the makers of the Don Q brand. This is their former home, along with the Castillo Serralles perched on El Virgia Hill overlooking the city. Casa Serralles is to become an art centre.

The main Plaza in Puerto Rico's second city, Ponce

Another family home that has become a cultural centre is *Casa Villaronga* on Calle Isabel. The house was built by Ponce architect Alfredo Wiechers and is a fine example of the city's grace and style with its trellised roof-garden, stucco garlands, coloured glass and Spanish tiles.

Calle Isabel runs parallel to Calle Christina and alongside the Plaza las Delicias. It is one of the nicest streets in the central city and is the site of the *Fiestas de la Calle Isabel*, held on the third Sunday in every month. This street party is hosted by the Puerto Rican Tourist office and Department of Art and Culture as well as the residents of Calle Isabel. The festivities include Puerto Rican music, with bands playing on the balconies overlooking

309

the street, stalls selling local foods and stalls with craft work brought to the coast from inland artists. The Fiestas always start at 3 p.m. and restored homes are open to the public so that visitors can enjoy the neo-classical European architecture, touched by Creole influences. While looking up at the balconies, do not forget to look down at your feet. The pavement, too, has been restored, complete with its border of local pink marble.

The pink marble is a feature of many of the old buildings. Ponce Creole architecture is typified by the balconies and façades. The balconies often have columns and there are often inside balconies with a wall of small windows to let in light from the patio, and the houses often have a two- or four-sided roof. Many of the houses are twinned with the one next door and the balconies are built to look like one unit – no doubt to give the impression of having a house twice the size to impress visitors. The pavements are also unusual: as well as having pink marble edges, they have rounded corners, similar to those in Spain. Known as *chaflanes*, they are designed that way to make it easier to turn the corner faster.

Ponce Art Museum To the south of the Plaza las Delicias, is one of Ponce's main attractions, the Ponce Art Museum. This is a modern building and was purpose-built thanks to a foundation started by Luis A. Ferre, who was Puerto Rican Governor from 1968 to 1972. Designed by Edward Durrell Stone, who also designed the Kennedy Centre in Washington DC, it is the most extensive in the Caribbean, housing more than 1,000 paintings and 400 sculptures from five centuries of art from both America and Europe. Styles range from ancient classical to modern art. The actual building is made up of seven hexagons and also houses a library. The Museum, on Las Americas Avenue opposite the Catholic University, is open Monday to Friday (but closed on Tuesday) from 10 a.m. to 12 p.m. and from 1 p.m. to 4 p.m. On Saturday it is open from 10 a.m. to 4 p.m. and on Sunday from 10 a.m. to 5 p.m. It costs US$2.50 for adults and US$1.50 for children, with reductions for large groups (Tel: 840-1510 or 848-0505).

El Vigia Slightly further out of town to the north is El Vigia. The story is that, in days of old, people used to sit on this high ridge and watch for attacking ships. There is a small look-out post to mark where the watchman used to sit with his telescope. Now you can climb the 30m (100ft) high observation tower at La Cruz del Vigia to get the best views across the city and out to sea. From here, there are also good views of Coffin Island or Caja de Muertos Island, named because of its appearance from the El Vigia viewpoint.

Castillo Seralles Close to the viewpoint is Castillo Serralles, another former home of the Serralles family, the owners of the Don Q brand of rum. The castle has also been restored and houses a *Museum* on rum and sugar-cane production. It is a Spanish-style hacienda with a courtyard filled with fountains. The castle can be seen from just about anywhere in Ponce perched on El Vigia Hill.

Back in the downtown area, there is plenty for avid shoppers. The restoration work has not been limited to museum and historic buildings. The old market-place, *Plaza del Mercado*, has been transformed into a craft centre with artisan's stalls as well as stalls selling local food, fruit and flowers. The craft centre and new market-place are close together along Calle Estrella, which also houses the main Post Office.

Crafts are the focus of many of Puerto Rico's festivals. Ponce has an annual festival in February when *vejigantes*, local boys who dress up as devils, run around the city trying to scare people. Their masks are made of dried pig's bladders and coconut shells. This is also carnival time when the city's carnival queen is chosen and there is the traditional carnival parade and parties. Bomba dancers take to the streets along with *cabelleros*, dressed up as Spanish courtiers, *viejos* dressed up as old men in rags, and *locas*, men dressed like pantomime dames. Many of the costumes are in black, red and yellow to represent evil, and Ponce is famous for its horned masks. Live music includes the *plena* folk rhythms which originated in Africa.

Music is the focus of another of Ponce's celebrations, the *Bomba y Plena Festival*, held in June. It highlights the island's African heritage of music and dance.

In March, there is a *Regional Crafts Fair* for local arts and crafts. Another place to spot the craft stalls is along the by-pass, where boys sell hammocks among other crafts. These are expensive and not always as well made as those hammocks you can find in the mountains in areas such as San Sebastian.

For modern shopping centres, try the *Ponce Shopping Centre* on the by-pass or the *Santa Maria Shopping Centre*, just to the north of Avenida Las Americas. There are plenty of supermarkets and smaller shops in the city centre around the Plaza Las Delicias. You will see cars and vans travelling around the town centre with loudspeakers blasting out messages. They are not electioneering – just telling you what is on special offer at the supermarket.

In November, Ponce is the setting for the annual *Kelly Cup Regatta*, based at the Club Nautico Sailing Club on the waterfront.

Hotels If you want to stay right in the heart of the old city, try the *Hotel Melia*. With prices up to about US$70 per night, it offers good value in a friendly atmosphere and is also in easy walking distance of all the sights (Tel: 842-0260/1). The other older property is the *Ponce Holiday Inn*, to the west of the city, which costs around US$170 per night (Tel: 844-1200). The *Days Inn Ponce Resort*, opened in 1989 is on the road out to the airport and costs up to about US$130 (Tel: 841-1000), and *Hilton* is opening a hotel on La Guancha Beach, which is close to the harbour and new cruise-ship pier.

Restaurants Eating out in Ponce is easy, too, with plenty of choice, from the lines of fast-food outlets on the by-pass to the restaurants in the hotels. Or try seafood specialists *Ancla* on Calle Hostos (Tel: 840-2450). *Ambert Restaurant* on Calle Ferrocarril (Tel: 840-6434) specializes in Puerto Rican cooking as does *Lydia's Restaurant* at the Centro Commercial Los Caobos (Tel: 844-3933). There are some excellent seafood restaurants on the main road leaving the city heading west, close to the Holiday Inn. Perched on the top of a small cliff overhanging the sea, these are pleasant for lunch. Try *La Manserrate Sea Port* for its many local dishes in a peaceful setting.

Like San Juan, Ponce can be used as a base for trips around the island. It is only a 90-minute drive along the expressway to San Juan, and most other areas of the island are accessible. Within a short distance of the city you can visit an old coffee plantation, laze around on a secluded island or visit an old Indian ceremonial site.

Coffin Island is a short ferry ride away from the main port at Ponce. The journey takes about 45 minutes and costs US$5.50 for adults, US$3.50 for children. The ferry sails every weekend and on holidays at 7 a.m., returning at 4 p.m. You should take your own refreshments and just enjoy being on a tiny island with beautiful beaches, an old lighthouse and little else. Legend claims that the island was used as a pirate hideout. It is now owned by the Commonwealth Department of Natural Resources, which has built picnic sites and kiosks as well as started tours of the island caves and the still-functioning lighthouse, built in 1880. The island is a mecca for scuba divers. It is an underwater reserve with marked trails along the reef that is only 4.5m (15ft) from the shore. *The Marine Sports and Dive Shop* in Ponce will organize trips to the island, give you instructions or rent out equipment (Tel: 844-6175).

Tibes Indian Ceremonial Ball Park The old Indian site at Tibes was only discovered in the 1970s but archaeologists soon realized that it is the largest and oldest burial ground in the Antilles. They dug up the remains of about 190 Indians, which are believed to date from AD120–600. Alongside the graveyard are seven ceremonial plazas belonging to the Igneri culture, a tribe of Indians who pre-dated the Taino Indians on the island. The site could also have significance as an early astronomical observatory because the stone points on two dance grounds line up during equinoxes and solstices. It has been developed for tourism, and a documentary video is played to visitors on arrival, explaining what is on the site. A Taino village has been re-created alongside a museum and cafeteria. The Ceremonial Centre is open Tuesday to Sunday from 9 a.m. to 4.30 p.m. and costs US$2 for adults and US$1 for children. The centre is on Route 503 out of Ponce.

One unusual experience that your guide may introduce you to while at the Indian centre is that of a 'live earring'. Small lizards are crawling over every tree in the park and the guide will pick one off, open its mouth and then stick it on to your ear lobe. The lizards do stay there until flicked off or until the wearer can not stand it any more. It is not painful but is a weird sensation, particularly when their tails flick your neck.

Hacienda Buena Vista Slightly further up into the hills is Hacienda Buena Vista. This former coffee plantation has been restored and, in the right season, visitors can help grind some coffee before trying the brew for themselves. The Plantation was originally founded by Salvador de Vives. He emigrated to Puerto Rico from Venezuela in 1821 with his family and he worked for the Spanish Government for several years before deciding to invest in farming. He bought 482 cuerdas of land north of Ponce and named it Buena Vista because of its beautiful natural setting in the wooded mountains.

He grew a variety of crops including coffee, corn, plantains, yams, pineapples and cacao. Sugar-cane would not grow on the hilly farm, but, despite that, the farm prospered and eventually became one of the most important on the south of the island. De Vives relied heavily on his slave labour but also invested in the latest machinery, and a variety of engines and mills are still on the site. A water canal stretching the length of the farm fed a water mill which was used to power the corn mill. One of the prettiest parts of the farm is up among the trees above the farm buildings where there is a natural waterfall on the Canas River.

Over the years, the family changed crops to keep ahead of the market, surviving the disastrous hurricane of 1899 which destroyed 60 per cent of the country's coffee production. But politics eventually closed the farm when the Government expropriated most of the land and gave out small lots to local farmers. An earlier member of the De Vives family had helped to found the Credit and Saving Bank of Ponce and some of the family are still living in Ponce.

They gave many of their records to the Conservation Trust of Puerto Rico when the Trust bought the estate in 1984 and many are on show at the Hacienda. Bilingual guides will show you around the farm and explain what work the Trust has been doing, but admission is by reservation only (Tel: 722-5882, weekends 848-7020). It is open for visitors Friday to Sunday and two-hour tours start at 8.30 a.m., 10.30 a.m., 1.30 p.m., and 3.30 p.m. Admission costs US$4 for adults and US$1 for children. The Hacienda is on Route 10, leaving Ponce to the north.

Ponce Area Travelling a little further afield, there are phosphorescent bays, mineral springs and sandy beaches. There are also interesting inland towns and drives through the mountains. If you prefer to take the country route to San Juan rather than the expressway, your drive will take you through towns like Coamo, Barranquitas, Arbonito and Caguas.

Coamo lies to the north-east of Ponce on Route 14. The town was first developed by early Spanish settlers, but the Indians had recognized the power of the thermal springs centuries before.

Useful Telephone Numbers

Casa Armstrong-Proventud Museum. Tel: 844-8240, 840-7677.
Department of Natural Resources. Tel: 722-1726.
Hacienda Buena Vista, Barrio Magueyes. Tel: 722-5882.
La Guancha Pier ferry terminal. Tel: 848-4575.
Ponce Museum of Art, Las Americas Avenue. Tel: 840-1510, 848-0505.
Puerto Rican Tourism Office, Casa Armstrong-Proventud. Tel: 844-8240, 840-7677.
Tibes Indian Ceremonial Ball Park, Route 503. Tel: 844-5575, 840-2255.

Legend has it that the Indians had described the waters as the Fountain of Youth to the first Spanish settler Juan Ponce de León, which sent him off on his fateful quest to Florida. He was mortally wounded in battles in Florida while searching for the mythical Fountain of Youth and died in Cuba on his way home to Puerto Rico.

Coamo was the capital of southern Puerto Rico until the 1800s when the political power moved to Ponce, where the sugar-cane and coffee plantations brought great wealth to the region. Coamo is home to the annual *San Blas Marathon*. This race held in February has been known to attract over a quarter of a million spectators and is one of the island's main sporting events. It is run over a 21km (13.1ml.) course along Route 14.

The town contains an eighteenth-century Spanish-style church with vaulted naves and a masonry home converted to a museum. Next to the town's plaza, it is open Tuesday to Friday, 8 a.m. to 12 p.m. and 1 p.m. to 4 p.m., and on Sundays from 10 a.m. to 3 p.m. But most people come to Coamo for its thermal springs. The springs are now contained within the *Parador Banos de Coamo*, which has been a spa resort since 1947. The Parador has a Mesones Gastronomicos restaurant which is recommended for local food. It costs about us$55 per night to stay there (Tel: 825-2239/2186) and has a tennis court as well as the thermal pools and a swimming-pool.

San Cristobal Canyon Continue along Route 14 to Aibonito to get you to the San Cristobal Canyon between this tiny mountain town and Barranquitas. The canyon is just to the north of the Panoramic Route, which has been selected for its scenic views rather than the high standard of its roads. The speed limit is down to 16kph (10mph) on some corners – and that is fast – and remember to blow your car horn on every corner. But the views are worth it, and the canyon is probably the most spectacular area, with sheer drops of up to 214m (700ft). Lush, green vegetation fills the canyon and there are some roadside cafés with wonderful views.

Aibonito The only restaurants of note are the Mesones Gastronomios recommended *La Piedra*, or *Sierra Linda Steakhouse*. The *Aibonito Flower Festival* is held annually in June and features acres of brightly coloured flowers: lilies, carnations, roses and begonias.

In Barranquitas there is an annual *Artisans Fair* in July, attracting around 150 craftsmen and musicians.

Caguas has an added bonus for visitors with children – an aquatic theme park. Villa Coqui Wet N' Slide has a whole range of water slides, boats, swimming-pools and snack bars. It is open at weekends and on holidays from 9 a.m. to 5 p.m. (Tel: 747-4747).

Other restaurants that are recommended *en route* between Ponce and San Juan are *Restaurante Miramelinda* and *Restaurante Jalome Terrace* at Cayey, *Restaurante El Paraiso* at Caguas and *Restaurante Sirimar* at Aguas Buenas.

To the east of Cayey, there is the forest reserve of *Guavate Forest* with its picturesque lake. Another forest reserve within easy reach of Ponce is the *Toro Negro Forest*, which lines the Panoramic Route to the north of the city. This forest contains the island's highest peak, Cerro de Punta, at 1,339m (4,390ft) and the highest lake, Guineo Reservoir.

Travelling west of Ponce takes you to some of the best beaches in this area. *Bahia de Guanica* is another famous south-coast dive site and has a nice beach to sunbathe on in between dives. Divers drop about 30m (100ft) to the edge of the continental shelf where the wall drops about 365m (1,200ft). The drop-off is about 6km (4ml.) out from the shore and is a good place to spot some really big fish. This is the place where American troops first landed during their conquest of the island in 1898. Close to the coast along the main road heading west is a huge factory complex which rather spoils the scenery, but it is soon behind you and you can again feel like you are in the Caribbean of beautiful beaches and scenery rather than modern America.

Mayaguez This bustling city on the west coast is well worth a visit. It is not easy to reach the city from San Juan but is a day trip to Ponce. It is easier to explore Mayaguez and its surrounding sights by car, taking your own time, rather than trying to rush through in an organized tour. There are two distinct areas to see: the coastal strip and the mountains inland. Mayaguez is a mix of new and old, with botanical gardens, a large zoo and a large university nestling in the hills to the east of the coastal city centre.

Downtown, the city centres around its plaza with pedestrian areas and benches to sit on. Lap up the sun and admire the statue of Christopher Columbus. Driving through the town, it seems a warren of narrow streets filled with traffic, but if you stick to the main roads, you should not get too held up. Route 102 takes you past the modern docks and tuna processing plants. Sights to stop off for in the city include *Our Lady of Candelaria Cathedral* and the *Yaguez Theatre*. For shopping, try the modern Mayaguez Shopping Mall on the edge of town.

For a slower way of life, travel east into the hills to find the University of Puerto Rico, Mayaguez Campus. Next to the main campus and opposite Patriot's Park is the *Tropical Agricultural Research Station* with its many hundred species of trees and flowers. Admission is free and the gardens are open between 7.30 a.m. and 4.30 p.m., Monday to Friday (Tel: 831-3435). The gardens are worth a visit on a sunny day when the bright colours will cheer anybody up.

Mayaguez Zoo is at the top of a long road winding uphill through the University. Mid-week, the Zoo has a forgotten air with just a few visitors meandering around the small, concrete cages but at weekends it is a popular spot for Puerto Ricans to bring their families for a day out. There are picnic facilities and cafés, so many people with young children are there all day. There is also a small children's zoo. The animals did not look particularly happy in their small areas but there are some unusual South American birds and animals that do not find their way to European zoos. The Zoo is open from Tuesday to Sunday, 9 a.m. to 4.30 p.m. Admission is US$1 for adults and US$0.50 for children (Tel: 834-8110)

November is the month to find the city's main *Arts and Crafts Fair*. There are similar fairs at many of the smaller towns in the area, like Cabo Rojo.

Hotels There are not many places to stay in the city. There is one parador, *El Sol*, on Palmer Street which costs about US$55 per night (Tel: 834-0303), or try the *Mayaguez Hilton* on Route 2 which costs about US$182 (Tel: 831-7575, 724-0161) and has recently been refurbished. Holiday Inn is building a new hotel in the city.

Mayaguez Surroundings Between Mayaguez and Ponce is the quaint old town of San German, a phosphorescent bay at La Paraguera and a lighthouse and beach at Cabo Rojo.

San German was the second town to be developed by the Spanish settlers and still has much of the Spanish flavour. The

Useful Telephone Numbers
Department of Natural Resources.
  Tel: 722-1726.
Mayaguez Zoo, Route 108, Barrio
  Miradero. Tel: 834-8110.
Tropical Agricultural Research Station,
  Route 65 and Route 108.
  Tel: 831-3435.
Tourism Office, open Monday to Friday
  8 a.m. to 12 p.m. and 1 p.m. to
  4.30 p.m. Tel: 831-5220.

The Porte Coeli church in San German

town dates back to the fifteenth century and still has one of its original churches, *Porta Coeli*, which was built in 1606. The chapel has been restored by the Institute of Puerto Rican Culture and still retains its original dark wooden pews and pillars. It does not hold religious services but is open as an art museum, with Mexican religious paintings from the eighteenth and nineteenth century. It is open Wednesday to Sunday from 8.30 a.m. to 12 p.m. and from 1 p.m. to 4.30 p.m. Admission is free (Tel: 892-5845).

The Porta Coeli church is on one of the towns two plazas. The other is home to the *San German de Auxerre* church which is far more elaborate. The church, which is still used, faces the old town hall. The town also contains the *Inter-American University Campus* and the oldest pharmacy in Puerto Rico, *Dominguez Drugstore*. The annual town carnival is held in February, and the residents celebrate the sugar-cane harvest in May with crafts, foods, music and dancing.

Hotels If you want to stay in San German, try the *Parador Oasis* (Tel: 892-1175) which costs around US$55 and is close to the Porta Coeli church. This house is 200 years old, and old coins belonging to King Alfonso XII of Spain have been found there. It also has underground tunnels leading from the house which are believed to have been used for smuggling.

318

La Parguera is a small fishing village in the Lajas Valley to the south of San German. This village is a popular destination, both with day trippers from Ponce and with those who stay overnight to view the phosphorescent bay. If you are travelling in this area, it is worth an overnight stop at one of the village's two paradors to catch a glimpse of this rare phenomenon. It is best seen on a moonless night when the millions of tiny marine creatures, *miniscent dinoflagellates*, give off a chemical reaction when disturbed. The microscopic life form only develops in areas of sheltered tropical waters. If you are unfortunate enough to be in town on a bright moonlit night, it is still worth cruising around the bay. Take a bucket with you and, when in the bay, fill it with water and you should get an idea of what the whole bay would look like. Another phosphorescent bay is found on the eastern island of Vieques. Hour-long boat trips leave La Parguera between 7.30 a.m. and 12.30 a.m.

The town has not just been developed for sightseers on the water, scuba divers have also helped turn this town into a resort. The divers can combine the phosphorescent creatures with diving when they immerse themselves in the tiny creatures at a depth of about 15m (50ft) at Enrique Reef. Divers often see large fish in this area, where there is another wall, like the one off Coffin Island. The water around the bay is protected by a series of mangrove swamps, and it is interesting to hire a small boat and meander through them during the day. People often go to the *Mata la Gata Island* for swimming or to *Rosada Beach* for lazing in the sun.

Other things to see in the village are a *Sea-Shell Museum* which is open Friday to Sunday. And, in May, the nearby town of Lajas celebrates the pineapple harvest with music, crafts and foods.

Hotels To see the phosphorescent bay, you need to stay in town. There are guest houses as well as two paradors. These are *Parador Posada Porlamar* (Tel: 899-4015), costing around us$50, and the *Parador Villa Parguera* (Tel: 899-3975), which is slightly more expensive at around US$60. The Posada Porlamar does not have its own restaurant but has kitchen facilities for guests and there are restaurants nearby. As with many of the Puerto Rican resort areas, it will get much busier at weekends and it is worth booking accommodation in advance.

319

**The restaurant in the Oasis
Parador, San German**

Boqueron Around the coast on the western side of the island is Boqueron, known for its beautiful beach. The bay is sheltered, protecting the mile-long beach of white sand. So far this area has remained relatively undeveloped but that could all change within the next few years. The place is dotted with beaches so there should always be somewhere secluded. This area wakes up at weekends, with many local people flocking down to the beach to lie in the sun, buy snacks from the seafood stalls or to visit the bird sanctuary at *Boqueron Lagoon*, which has become a refuge for ducks and seabirds. The main beach at Boqueron is the *El Combate Beach*, slightly to the south of town.

Between Boqueron, which is in the Cabo Rojo district, and La Parguera is the *Cabo Rojo lighthouse* marking the south-western tip of the island. The lighthouse was built in 1882 by the Spanish and has spectacular views of the ocean. This is a strange area of limestone boulders and salt flats, completely different to the more typical tropical coastline further north.

Slightly further north toward Boqueron is the *US Fish and Wildlife's Caribbean refuge headquarters* with marked trails for bird-watching. Open on weekdays from 7.30 a.m. to 4 p.m., there is a small visitors' centre at the refuge.

Hotels Boqueron has one parador to stay at. *Parador Boquemar* is a small hotel with a swimming-pool and costs around US$60 per night (Tel: 851-2158). When eating out, try the local speciality, oysters.

Joyuda Beach This beach is on the northern half of Cabo Rojo and should soon be in the middle of a major development. There are plans for a US$45 million resort with 275 villas, a golf-course and a marina. At the moment there is one parador, *Parador Perichi's*, which costs about us$60 per night (Tel: 851-3131). The rooms have a sea view and it has a recommended restaurant.

Maricao Further into the mountains from San German is the *Maricao Forest Reserve*. Trails are marked for bird-watching walks. The *Maricao Fish Hatcheries* are open daily from 8 a.m. to midday and from 1 p.m. to 4 p.m. Thousands of fish are reared here to re-stock island lakes. The tanks are laid out in gardens.

Each February the area celebrates its coffee harvest with music, dancing, a parade and demonstrations of coffee drying and grinding.

Hotels You can go on walking trails from the area's parador, *Parador Hacienda Juanita*. This peaceful hotel costs about US$40 per night. Hammocks swing on the terrace for guests to snooze in, and the whole atmosphere is of a place where you should catch up on some reading, do some walking or sample some of the coffee grown on the plantation surrounding the hotel. The hotel was built in 1830 and has antique tools used in coffee production adorning the walls.

Sabana Grande To the south of Maricao and east of San German is the small town of Sabana Grande which, like Maricao, has a fishy flavour to it. It is home to the United States' largest freshwater *prawn farm*. The fish farm is open to the public daily from 8 a.m. to 5 p.m. (Tel: 873-1026).

Mona Island This is one of Puerto Rico's bigger offshore islands. It used to be inhabited by Taino Indians but was deserted centuries ago and is now owned and run by the Government's Department of Natural Resources. There are no hotels on the island but there is camping. Most people visit the island for day trips to spot some off the island's wildlife, which includes iguanas, seals and a wide range of seabirds. There are cliffs, caves and sandy beaches. Most people prefer to catch a plane across to the island rather than go by boat as the Mona Passage can get rough. You need to take everything with you, including water, and camping costs US$1 per night. Permission is needed from the Department on 722-1726.

Rincon Back on the coast, this sleepy town was once a mecca for surfing. Surfers still come to this north-western town in winter but most head just out of town to guest houses along the beaches,

321

A typical Puerto Rican church

rather than stay in the main town. The town itself has the feel of a British Victorian seaside town on a rainy day. There are surfing shops and a few craft shops but not much else. The World Surfing Championships were held in the town in 1968. As an added bonus for those on the water, humpbacked whales visit this particular stretch of coast during their winter stay in the Caribbean.

To find the best beaches and most spectacular views, drive out of Rincon to the north. The coastal road ducks and weaves around the mountains, which drop straight down to the beach. Small guest houses are dotted amongst the lush, green vegetation and every so often you will get a glimpse of the sandy beach and crashing waves. There is a lighthouse on the coastline, along with a strange white dome next door. This turned out to be a relic of the island's foray into thermonuclear energy in the 1960s.

Hotels The town's parador is *Parador Villa Antonio* which costs around US$80 per night. It has a swimming-pool, two tennis courts and is set in a secluded area close to the beach (Tel: 823-2645).

Aguadilla This is the spot where Christopher Columbus first stepped on to Puerto Rican soil, and in the town centre is a natural spring where Spanish sailors used to collect their water. The spring is now part of *El Parterre Park*. Water is the theme of a great attraction for children. The *Cascadas Aquatic Park* has nine different water play areas. It is open on Fridays from 2.00 p.m. to 9.00 p.m. and on weekends and holidays from 9.00 a.m. to 6.00 p.m. The Park is on Route 2 (Tel: 882-3310).

Aguadilla is another mecca for surfers but it also attracts divers. The Crash Boat site is only just off the shore and there are many underwater caves and reefs to explore all along this coastline. The Crash Boat area was named after the rescue boats kept in the area in the days when the US Air Force occupied the nearby base at *Borinquen Point*. This disused base is now a sports centre with a golf-course, tennis courts, a bowling alley and a baseball field. A new event that looks set to become an annual fixture is the *Budweiser/Puerto Rico Surf Challenge*. It attracts hundreds of surfers to the 11-day competition at the end of January, five days of which are held along the north-western coast.

Hotels There are several small hotels as well as one parador in the town. Try the *Parador Montemar*, which has two swimming-pools and two restaurants (Tel: 891-5959/4383).

Restaurants For eating out, try the Mesones Gastronomicos recommendation, *Restaurante Dario's Gourmet* (Tel: 890-6143).

San Sebastian This mountain town lies inland from Rincon and is worth a visit for the friendliness and warmth of its people. Speaking Spanish does help, although you can get by with sign language. San Sebastian is famous for its crafts, particularly hammock-making. Finding the craftsmen is not as easy as finding the town. Most of them live in the tiny villages and you just have to drive around, asking people and try to follow their directions. Once at a craftsman's house, the trip will be worth it. They all have great pride in their work and are usually happy to show you how to make a hammock, will let you try a few for size and then will haggle furiously over the price. The Spanish word for hammock is *hamacas* – very useful when trying to find these remote craftsmen.

At Pedro Hernandez's place, you might get a shock. His brother-in-law spent over 20 years in New York and it is a surprise to hear this thick Brooklyn accent emerging from an old man sitting in the sun high in the Puerto Rican mountains. Most of the craftsmen have other jobs as well and just have a little hut or garage for their crafts. Most will have a sign outside the house but do not be disappointed if no one is home as you are bound to find someone else round the corner.

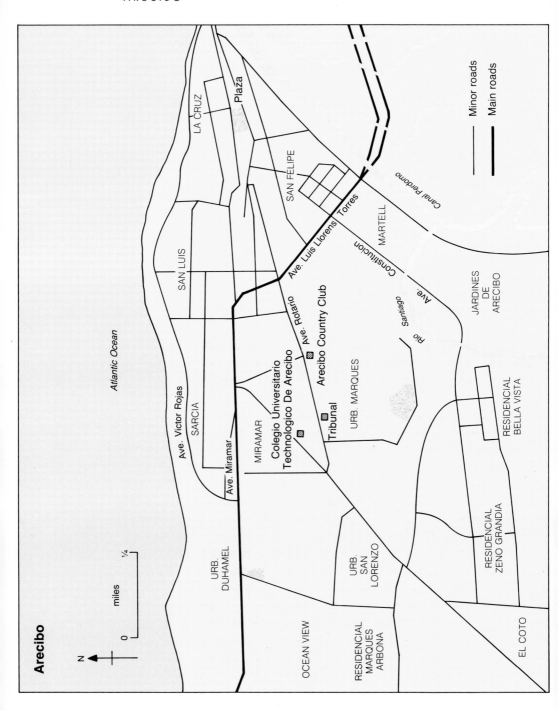

Arecibo

Arecibo This is a quiet town on the northern coast, first settled by the Spanish in 1556. There is not much to see or do in the town itself but it is a central point for some of Puerto Rico's major attractions. The town's annual festival is in February when it holds the *Captain Correa Carnival*. There are parades of floats, music and dancing. Most of the activity is based around the town's main plaza, the Luis Munoz Rivera Plaza.

Arecibo Observatory The name Arecibo is well known but not because of the town. The Arecibo Observatory is well known world-wide by astronomers and many other scientists. The Observatory lies to the south of the town, high in the mountains. Once near it you cannot miss it. The Puerto Rico Tourism Company describes it as a 'space station suspended above the world's largest wok', and that sums it up pretty neatly. Run by Cornell University and the National Science Foundation, the station was set up to probe radio emissions from far-off galaxies.

It has the world's largest telescope and its dimensions are enormous. The dish itself is 305m (1000ft) in diameter and 51m (167ft) deep and covers an area of 20 acres. Covering such a large area, the dish has created its own little world under the dish, with flourishing vegetation including many ferns and orchids, while wildlife includes mongeese, lizards and frogs. Even more amazing is the station lifted above the dish. It weighs a staggering 600 tons. Held in position by twelve cables, it is supported by three concrete towers.

The space station is one of the world's most serious attempts to discover any extra-terrestrial life. Working on the theory that any other civilization might communicate by radio waves, the station is used to monitor radio waves and to try to interpret them – so far, without success.

Scientists at Arecibo are not just looking for ET and his mates, they are also involved in research work into the mysterious quasars, pulsars and galaxies. Although the scientists are hard at work, the experts will take time out to give visitors tours and try to explain their work. Visiting hours to the station are very restricted but, even if you are not scientifically minded, it is an impressive place. The tours are also restricted to an observation platform in front of the dish to avoid disturbing any of the research work. Tours are given daily from Tuesday to Friday at

The Arecibo Observatory dominates the surrounding countryside in Puerto Rico

2.00 p.m. and the observatory is open to the public on Sundays from 1.00 p.m. to 4.30 p.m. The facility is totally closed to the public on Mondays, Saturdays and Sundays (Tel: 878-2612).

The observatory is in a strange area of karst limestone and forest. This area has really only been opened up to tourism in the past few years but for centuries has been used by Indians and then the Spanish colonists.

Rio Camuy Caves One area that was missed until the 1950s is a huge area of sink-holes, leading down to vast underground caves and rivers. It is staggering that such an area could remain undiscovered for such a long time on a relatively small island that has been colonized for so long. The Rio Camuy Caves were used by the Taino Indians for the shelter from hurricanes and to hide from the invading Spanish forces. Local people have always known about the caves but it was not until 1958, when Russell Gurnee took a plane journey in the area, that the extent of the caves was realized. Professional explorers went into the system and discovered what experts say is one of the most spectacular cave systems on earth.

Russell Gurnee persuaded the Government to purchase surrounding land to protect the caves, and so the 300 acre park was created. It was not until 1976 that the caves were opened to the public, but now visitors can explore the cave system without even climbing down the massive sink-hole that leads into the system. A trolley takes visitors down the 107m (350ft) deep sink-hole to the cave entrance.

The Rio Camuy is the longest underground river in the world and can be seen from the Empalme Cave, which has concrete walkways for the public to use. This protects the rest of the cave from human interference and allows the stalagmites and stalactites to continue to grow and develop. There is still quite a lot of movement in the caves, there are landslides and collapses – but do not worry, the caves are monitored constantly and are closed if there is any danger to the public.

There are actually three sink-holes in the park, called *Tres Pueblos*, and they measure 198m (650ft) in diameter and are 107m (350ft) deep. There is an observation point from which you can marvel at their size. The caves are equally impressive. Only the *Empalme Cave* is open to the public but from there you can get

327

glimpses of the massive system. It is up to 60m (200ft) deep in places and very little light penetrates. Bats have made their home in some of the caves and you can actually feel the warmth that they have generated. At dusk they swarm out of the caves in their thousands but during the day you will not see any of them. The Rio Camuy has carved the caves and canals. In the dry winter season the river is about 21m (70ft) below the cave but in the rainy season it can rise dramatically through the caves.

Visitors are welcome from Wednesday to Sunday, 8.00 a.m. to 5.00 p.m. The Park can only take 1,500 visitors at any time and will close if it reaches that capacity. It is run very much like an American attraction. Visitors are given a video demonstration and talk about the caves and how to behave while in them, before being taken to the trolley and down into the caves. There are bilingual guides ready to answer any question. Back on the high ground, there is a small café and shop. Car parking and entry costs about US$5 (Tel: 898-3100). Another of the strange things about the caves is that at one stage you are actually standing underneath the road that you have driven along to get to the Park on Route 129. The whole area is dotted with caves and tunnels.

Cueva de Camuy. This is another Park close by, a good place to take children as it has attractions for them as well. It has privately owned caves, Cueva de Camuy, which has also been developed with walkways so that you can admire the spectacular caves in relative comfort. Guided tours are also available. To keep the children amused there are pony rides, go-karts and a swimming-pool. There is a small café and shop. On Route 486, the cave is open Monday to Saturday from 9.00 a.m. to 5.00 p.m. and on Sundays from 9.00 a.m. to 8.00 p.m. The admission price of US$1 for adults and US$0.50 for children includes the cost of a guided tour (Tel: 898-2723).

Getting to this area is not easy. Day trips from San Juan tend to go east, not west, and you really need to hire a car to explore this region. Free trollies will take guests of the local paradors to see the sights but it is easier to travel on your own. Having your own transport gives you the freedom to explore this inland region which is relatively free of tourists and contains some spectacular scenery. One of the most peaceful and pretty spots is at the *Taino Indian Park* near Utuado.

The Indian Ceremonial Centre at Caguana is one of the largest of the former Indian sites in the area. The Caguana site is believed to have been used by the Taino Indians for ball games and for ceremonies. The village always had a permanent population but archaeologists believe that Indians from the whole surrounding area used to converge on the site for religious events.

The Taino Indian culture reached its peak in Puerto Rico in about AD 1200. It was an agriculture-based culture, with the main crops being yucca, corn and sweet potatoes. The Indians were also keen fishermen. The ball game united the local villages. The indications are that it was a strongly competitive game with religious overtones. They believed in a supreme god but also in lesser gods who supported him. These gods were represented in carvings of gold, wood and stone.

It was their use of gold that proved the downfall of the Taino Indians. When Christopher Columbus first arrived, the Indians wanted to show they were peaceful and gave the Spanish gifts of gold. They told a young Spaniard, Juan Ponce de León, that the gold was just lying there ready to be picked out of the rivers. The Indians did find gold in rivers but, unfortunately, while it seemed a lot to them, it did not seem much to the Spanish. But their stories had fuelled the questioning fire in Ponce de León and he returned to Spain to persuade the King of Spain to allow him to colonize the island. This happened and then the gold ran out. Within a century of the Spanish arrival, the Indians were wiped out and their culture disappeared. At the time of the Spaniards arriving, the Taino Indians were led by Chief Caguana and were still holding rituals at the Caguana site.

The Caguana site has now been restored and there is a small museum of artefacts. There are ten *bateyes* (courts), each named after a Taino Indian chief, with some monoliths scattered around. The park was restored by the Institute of Puerto Rican culture and is in a pleasant spot with dramatic mountains behind it, a river running through the park and pretty flowering trees scattered across the area. Guides will explain the significance of the site and there are picnic spots throughout the park. Admission is free and the park, on Route 111, is open daily from 8.30 a.m. to 4.30 p.m. (Tel: 894-7325).

Lake Dos Bocas and Rio Abojo Forest Reserve If you go to the Caguana Indian Site, you should continue a little further along Route 111 to Lake Dos Bocas. This is a lake with two fingers high in the mountains and close to the forest reserve of Rio Abajo. It is a very picturesque area and boat trips will take you around the lake. The launches are actually set up to take residents around the lake but they are happy to take tourists, too. Run by the Public Works Department, the trips are free and last about two hours. The Rio Abajo Forest is under strict forest management to preserve mahogany and teak and now there are large plantations of these trees. The forest is open from 6.00 a.m. to 6.00 p.m. and has numerous picnic spots and walks.

Hotels Lake Dos Bocas is to the north of Utuado. For exploring this area you can stay locally in Utado at *Parador Casa Grande*. Costing about US$45 a night, all the rooms have balconies with breath-taking mountain views. The restored hacienda has 100 acres with mountain hiking trails and its own swimming-pool (Tel: 721-2884).

Jayuya There is a lake as pretty as Lago Dos Bocas to the east of Utuado: *Lake Caonillas*, just north of Route 111. The lake is excellent for fishing and the nearby Parador at Jayuya will organize trips, but guests need to bring their own equipment. This Parador, *Parador Hacienda Gripinas*, is one of the cheaper hotels in the scheme, costing around US$40 per night. It was the old house belonging to the owners of the surrounding coffee plantation. Its restaurant is also listed under the Mesones Gastronomicos system and it has a swimming-pool (Tel: 721-2400). Another recommended restaurant in this high mountain town is *Restaurante El Dujo* which specializes in Puerto Rican dishes.

This mountain area is home to many wood carvers. One of Puerto Rico's most famous carvings is that of the rooster which is usually brightly painted. The story is that a well-known carver, Emilio Rosado, tripped over while chasing a rooster and began a life-long fascination with the bird. He started carving chickens and the practice spread among the mountain craftsmen who started depicting other birds and animals. Jayuya is just to the north of the Forest Reserve of Toro Negro and is not far off the Panoramic Route, making it a useful place to stop if you are doing the three-day trip across the mountains. It is also within easy reach of Ponce to the south. Each year, usually in November, Jayuya hosts the *Indian Festival* which celebrates Puerto Rico's

Indian heritage. There are visits to the local Indian sites, Indian ceremonies, craft shows and dancing.

Another lake to attract freshwater fishermen is Lake Guajataca, to the south-west of Arecibo. Anglers report good fishing in the lake but visitors need to take their own fishing tackle. Guajataca is another pretty area to drive around and is mostly easily accessible from Quebradillas where there are two Paradors to stay in.

Parador Vistamar is perched in the hills overlooking the ocean, while *Parador El Guajataca* is below on the edge of the small beach. The Parador Vistamar is owned by Iris and Carlos Fernandez, who have plans to build another hotel at Isabela where a big hotel project is planned also. The two hotels at Quebradilla both offer guests their own swimming-pools, good restaurants and a friendly atmosphere. Both are popular with Puerto Ricans so it is worth booking ahead, particularly for weekends. The Vistamar costs around US$80 for a double room with a sea view (Tel: 895-2065) and the El Guajataca costs around US$70 per night (Tel: 895-3070). The municipal authorities run free trolley services every weekend from both Paradors to the local sights, such as the Arecibo Observatory and to the Rio Camuy Caves. The Quebradilla beach is popular with the locals because of its long arc of sand, protected by high cliffs behind it.

Isabela Further along the north coast from Arecibo to the west is Isabela. This quiet town is set to be transformed by 1992 as a massive US$1 billion project comes to fruition. By the end of 1992, the IDG Development Corporation intends to have opened two hotels and two golf-courses on the site. It has plans for a further three hotels and three golf-courses.

At the moment, the town is best known for its diving. This whole section along to Aguadilla is a mass of underwater caves, and divers choose Isabela because the first are (40ft) off the beach. Lobsters and crabs live in the caves while divers can also spot schools of fish and stingrays. Contact *La Cueva Submarina* (Tel: 872-3903) for details of the diving in the area and also to hire equipment.

Camuy Hatillo lies to the east of Quebradilla and is another north-coast town which most people just drive straight past. The town has a colourful annual festival at Christmastime. Masks and costumes are the order of the day as the townsfolk celebrate

Christmas with music and parties. There is not much to see in Hatillo, but if you want to stop for lunch, try the *Restaurant El Buen Café* on Route 2 (Tel: 898-3495) which is recommended under the Mesones Gastronomicos scheme.

Route 2 has recently been upgraded and much of it converted into an expressway, cutting the journey time along the north coast from San Juan. This will probably lead to far more tourism along this coast which, for the moment, is tranquil and full of secluded bays lined by white sandy beaches. A word of warning: if you use the expressways, remember to take plenty of change with you as there are tolls at regular intervals. If you prefer to avoid the expressway, drive back to San Juan along the coast road which takes you past some of the nicest beaches on the island.

The Offshore Islands Many visitors to Puerto Rico miss out on the offshore islands of Cuelebra and Vieques. Each island is accessible by both plane and ferry. Planes leave from the Isla Grande airport in San Juan and ferries leave from Fajardo on the east coast. These are undeveloped and there is little to do except soak up the sun and go diving, snorkelling or fishing.

Unfortunately, both islands were in the path of Hurricane Hugo and were hit hard. They remained closed for some time and many of the hotels were only able to open half the number of rooms. Local people say it is not quite the same as it once was, but as a first-time visitor the islands are still beautiful places. The hotels and facilities are coming back on line and there is no sense of having to rough it because of the hurricane. The big hurricanes only seem to hit each area of the Caribbean every fifty or sixty years, so local people will tell you that you are quite safe for many years to come. The new hotels are also being built with hurricanes in mind and it is really only the small wooden shacks or glass windows that get smashed up.

The islands are very much a weekend get-away spot for Puerto Ricans so if you want to visit at a weekend book ahead. But during the week it is usually easy to book a flight the day before or even on the day you want to fly. Try to book accommodation before you go , particularly at weekends or at holiday times.

Vieques This island is the closest to mainland Puerto Rico, about 10km (6 ml.) east of Fajardo. Much of the island is closed off to the public and is occupied by the US Navy. The Navy gained title to the land during World War II and will allow the public access to the beaches unless it is practising any manoeuvres. The main town is Isabel Segunda, or Isabel II, and only about 8000 people live on the island. Most visitors head for Esperanza where there is a beautiful beach and somewhere to stay and eat.

The island's natural beauty has attracted film-makers and the best-known films to have been made on Vieques are *Lord of the Flies* and *Heartbreak Ridge*. Wildlife, including the native Paso Fino horses, roam around the island, along with mongeese, lizards and crabs.

To get to the island you have a choice of flying from the Isla Grande airport in San Juan with Vieques Air-Link (Tel: 722-3736) or catching a ferry from Fajardo on the east coast of Puerto Rico. There are also ferry connections between Vieques and Culebra. Call the ferry port at Fajardo before making plans as the weather does affect the timetable (Tel: 863-0705). The ferry ticket costs US$2 for adults; US$1 for children one-way. During the week there are usually two sailings a day but at weekends and on holidays there are four scheduled sailings in each direction. There are also daily connections to Culebra.

Once on the island it is easy to get around. There are jeeps or bikes available for hire from the airport. The *publicos* will pick you up wherever you hail them and drop you off anywhere along the route. If you want to go off the usual route they simply become a taxi, but negotiate the fare first. In the towns you can easily walk around to all the sights.

Isabel Segunda is a pleasant little port with an attractive main square. The fort was the last to be built by the Spanish anywhere in the Americas and was built when the English and French were vying for control of the island with the Spanish. Built in 1843, when the town was founded, *El Fortin* is partially restored and is worth the trip for its views across the north coast. An old lighthouse also stands guard over the port. It was built in 1896 but is now deserted.

Esperanza, on the south coast, used to be the island's centre for sugarcane industry. In the heyday of the industry there were over 25,000 people on the island and there were four sugar mills. Today, all of that has gone but Esperanza remains as a centre for visitors because of its beautiful beaches.

The beach that makes the town lies just to the east. *Sun Bay*, or Sombe as it is also known, is over 1.5km (1 ml.) of white sand fringed by coconut palms. The beach is run by the Government, which charges US$1 for car parking. That money is used to provide changing huts, keep the beach clean and provide picnic tables. But do not worry, this organization does not ruin the beach. It rarely gets crowded, except occasionally on holidays, but even then it is always easy to find a quiet spot.

All along the south coast, there are beautiful secluded beaches to visit including the quiet waters of *Half Moon Beach* or *Blue Beach*, while to watch the waves crashing on to the rocks guarding the beach try *Third Beach*. These three are all to the east of Sun Bay. Between Blue Beach and Half Moon Beach, there is a phosphorescent bay at *Mosquito Bay*. The lights, only seen clearly on moonless nights, are actually hundreds of thousands of tiny dinoflagellates which show their luminescence when disturbed. Like the bay at La Parguera on the mainland, it is still worth a visit even on a moonlit night. The local advice is to take a bucket with you and then scoop up some water and you will see what the bay is like on a dark night.

The snorkelling is excellent on the beaches, with quiet water, but for scuba diving, most divers head to the south-west corner and sites such as *Green Beach*, *Dog's Paw* and *Caballo Blanco*. You need a day pass to get through the restricted naval area to reach Green Beach but these are easily obtained while on the island.

Hotels There are plenty of cheap and cheerful places to stay on the island, but if you are going across to Vieques at a weekend or on a public holiday it is a good idea to book in advance. There are snack bars and local restaurants but those recommended tend to be attached to the hotels or guest houses. Vieques has one Parador, *Parador Esperanza*, which is within walking distance of Sun Bay. It is geared up for watersports and has its own marina with a small fleet of sailing dinghies. Guests can take daily or weekly sailing trips or hire scuba diving, snorkelling or windsurfing equipment. Water-skiing is also available. There is a freshwater swimming-pool and a tennis court. The restaurant serving fresh fish and lobster is recommended under the Government's Mesones Gastronomicos scheme for offering cheap, good local dishes. The Parador costs up to US$90 for a double room in high season.

Another highly recommended place to stay is *Casa del Frances* which sits high on a hill above Esperanza. Costing around US$55 per night, the guest house is in a restored sugar plantation and is full of character; its restaurant serves excellent Puerto Rican food (Tel: 741-3751). The *Tradewinds* guest house is down on the beach at Esperanza and costs around US$45 a night and it also has one of the best locations for its seafood restaurant (Tel: 741-8588).

There is virtually no nightlife on Vieques but the young tend to meet at *Bananas*, facing the beach at Esperanza. The outdoor bar serves up American snack food such as burgers, pizza and chilli.

Culebra There are actually 24 islands clustered around Culebra, which is the largest at just 18sq.km (11sq.m). It is quieter still than Vieques and is the ideal spot for those really wanting to get away from it all. The islands are teeming with wildlife, particularly turtles, lizards and a wide range of sea-birds. Underwater there is an amazing selection of fish. Divers say they are often overwhelmed by all the fish around them, from tiny bright-coloured fish to large angel fish, rays and grunts.

About 200 people live on Culebra and most of them live in the main town of Dewey, known locally as Pueblo. The town is on Ensenada Honda on the south coast. Like Vieques, there are plenty of beautiful, clean beaches and inland there are rolling hills.

To get to the island you can fly from Isla Grande airport in San Juan with *Flamenco Airlines* (Tel: 724-7110 or 725-7707). There are flights twice daily. From Fajardo the ferry takes one hour and operates once a day, Tuesday to Sunday. The tickets cost about US$2.25 for adults or US$1 for children. Check with the ferry terminal for sailing times (Tel: 863-0705). There are ferries between Vieques and Culebra on Mondays, weekends and holidays. The ride costs about US$1 and takes about half an hour.

All the tourist development is on the main island of Culebra. The other 23 islands in the archipelago, along with four tracts of land on Culebra, are all part of the *Culebra National Wildlife Refuge* which was established in 1909 to protect the large sea-bird breeding colonies. Two of the islands, *Culebrita* and *Luis Pena*, are open daily from sunrise to sunset. Culebrita is home to the endangered hawksbill turtle and is also a good scuba-diving area with a 1.5km (1ml.) long coral formation just off the coast. The island has a small lighthouse on it .

To find out more about the Refuge there is an *Information Centre* at the city hall in Dewey. This centre will also give you information about where to stay, visit or eat on the island (Tel: 742-3291). There is not much to see in Dewey, which was named after US Admiral George Dewey, but it is an attractive laid-back town with a very friendly population, who live in pretty pastel-coloured houses. The town is in a picturesque spot between two lagoons, Ensenada Honda Bay and Sardinas Bay.

On the main island, the best beaches are on the north coast. *Playa Flamenco* is one of the whitest and best known. Watch out for the surf which can be a bit rough. Divers prefer the north-western coast at *Impact Area* where there are spectacular coral formations in still waters. Another good spot is the trio of tiny islands off the west coast, *Cayo Yerba*, *Cayo Raton* and *Cayo del Agua*, where the schools of fish are reported to be so large that you cannot see through them. Diving equipment can be hired from the *Flamenco Resort and Fishing Club* (Tel: 742-3144), *Fiesta* (Tel: 742-3555) or the *Culebra Underwater Diving Association* (Tel: 742-3839).

Bikes or jeeps can be rented to get you around the island, or you can hire horses from Flamenco Beach for treks along the north coast (Tel: 742-3811). Back on the water, the local fishing around Culebra is said to be excellent. For fishing charters, contact *Cielo y Mar* (Tel: 742-3167) or *Taso Pena* (Tel: 742-3567). Boats can also be hired to cruise around the islands or for picnicking on nearby cays.

Hotels There are several places to stay at Dewey and around the island. In Dewey, try the *Posada la Hamaca*, which costs about US$40 a night (Tel: 742-3516). It does not have a restaurant but there is *Milca's Bakery* close by where you can buy delicious fresh bread for breakfast. And at most island guesthouses there are barbecue areas, where guests can cook their own fish. If you have not caught it yourself, you can buy some from the *Associacion de Pescadores* on Sardinas Beach.

Also close to Dewey is *Casa Bohéme* which costs US$325 per week (Tel: 742-3508). The cost includes the use of vehicles and boats if you stay for the full week.

On the other side of the island is the *Flamenco Resort and Fishing Club*. On the beach at Flamenco the hotel has a selection of villas and the only camp site on Culebra (Tel: 742-3144).

Further Information

Sports As with most of the large Caribbean islands, there is a wide range of sports available. Most of the large hotels offer their guests everything from tennis to watersports. Puerto Ricans are keep sportsmen and the most popular sports are horse-racing, cock fighting and baseball.

Baseball There are six professional baseball clubs in Puerto Rico and their season starts in October. North American teams visit the island for matches in February and most of the large towns have a stadium.

Boxing So far, Puerto Rico has produced 18 world champions and it is very proud of its achievements. Matches are held monthly at the International Ballroom of the *El San Juan Hotel and Casino* and at the *Caribe Hilton*. Fights are also held at the *Roberto Clemente Coliseum*, where there are also basketball courts, a swimming-pool and a sports museum.

Central Park This sports stadium was built in reclaimed mangrove swamp for the 1979 Pan Am Games and is close to the Condado area of San Juan. There are plenty of tennis courts available from US$2 an hour, soccer and baseball fields, a running track, free fitness classes and a café.

Cock Fighting The main cock-fighting arena is in *Isla Verde* just outside San Juan. The season runs from November through to April. The fighting is a weekly event at *Club Gallistico* on Saturday from 1 p.m. to 7 p.m. (Tel: 792-1557/6005). There are a total of 40 cock-fighting arenas across the island.

Diving Divers are well catered for with a choice of dive sites all around the island and with some of the best diving on the off-shore islands of Culebra and Vieques. There are wrecks, coral reefs and caves to explore. Many of the dive shops will arrange boat trips out to the less accessible areas but many sites are within a short distance of the shore. Companies that offer diving trips include *Aquatica Underwater Adventures*, Aquadilla (Tel: 890-6071); *Caribbean School of Aquatics*, Condado (Tel: 723-4740); *Caribe Aquatic Adventure*, Old San Juan (Tel: 765-7444); *Coral Head Divers*, Palmas del Mar (Tel: 635-4529); *La Cueva Submarina Training Centre*, Isabela (Tel: 872-3903); *Marina de Salinas*, Salinas (Tel: 752-8484); or *Mundo Submarino*, Isla Verde (Tel: 791-5764).

Hell on earth in Grand Cayman

Fishing Both deep-sea and freshwater fishing are available around Puerto Rico. The freshwater fishing tends to be in the mountains on lakes such as Lago Dos Bogas, Lake Caonillas or Lake Guajataca. At these lakes you will need your own fishing tackle. Boats can be organized locally, often through the Paradors in the area. Call the *Department of Natural Resources* for more details on Tel: 722-5938. Deep-sea fishing charters are available all around the coast from most resort towns.

The world's oldest *Billfish Tournament* is a well-established annual event in Puerto Rico. Based at the *Club Nautico*, San Juan, fishermen from across the world compete for blue marlin of up to 408kg (900lb). Other fish caught regularly in these waters are sailfish, wahoo, tuna, tarpon, jack and bonefish. Companies offering charter include *Aquatica Underwater Adventures*, based in Aquadilla (Tel: 890- 6071); *Benitez Deep Sea Fishing*, Club Nautico de San Juan (Tel: 723-2292 or 724-6265); or *Castillo Watersports*, Isla Verde (Tel: 791-6195 or 726-5752).

Golf There are fourteen courses across Puerto Rico, which is home to some major tournaments. Golf really started on the island with the construction of two Robert Trent Jones courses at the Dorado Beach resort in 1958. Now there are nine championship courses. There are now four Robert Trent Jones courses at the *Hyatt resort* in Dorado, all 18 holes and with a golf pro (Tel: 796-1234 ext 3238). *Berwind Golf Course*, Rio Grande is 18-hole, with a golf pro (Tel: 876-3056) and is open Tuesday, Thursday and Friday, except holidays. *Club Riomar*, Rio Grande, is a 18 holes with a golf pro (Tel: 887-3964). *Dorado del Mar Country Club* has a 9-hole course and a golf pro (Tel: 796-2030); *Luis Ortiz*, San Juan (Tel: 786-3859); *Palmas del Mar Resort*, 18-hole course with a golf pro (Tel: 852-6000, ext. 54); and *Punta Borinquen*. Aguadilla has an 18-hole course with a golf pro (Tel: 890-2987).

Hiking Untarmacked roads and forest tracks are the haunt of hikers who can find nearly 500km (300ml.) of trails through the mountains. Most forest reserves have well-marked trails which are kept clean. Walks vary from the high mountain paths to trails through mangrove forests on the coast. For details, call the *Department of Natural Resource Forest Service* on Tel: 724-3724.

Horse-Racing The island's only race-track is at *El Commandante* on Route 3 at Canovanas. Race meetings are held every Wednesday, Friday, Sunday and on holidays at 2.30 p.m. the dining-room opens at 12.30 p.m. on race days (Tel: 724-6060).

Horse Trekking There are horse-riding facilities in the mountains and on the coast as well as on the offshore islands of Vieques and Culebra, where you can hire native Paso Fino horses. *Hacienda Carabali* will organize treks along the north-coast beaches and around the El Yungue rain forest (Tel: 795-6351 or 887-4954). *Loose-Penny Tours* will also organize north-coast rides (Tel: 795-6351). At Palmas del Mar, south of Humacao, you can get tuition or go on beach rides (Tel: 852-6000 ext. 12721).

Every January there is a *Horse Show* exhibiting the Paso Fino horse. This breed of horse is unique to Puerto Rico and is named after its gait: only one hoof is raised in the air at any one time. The show is held at *Loubriel Stadium*, Bayamon. Another exhibition of this breed is held annually during March at *Guayama*.

Running If you are not actually taking part, the Puerto Ricans are equally keen spectators. Thousands turn up to watch the *San Blas Half-Marathon* every year in Coamo. Each February international and local runners compete along Route 14. And in May there is a 21km *Marathon* which starts in front of the sanctuary of Virgin del Rosario, Sabana Grande. Local roads are also the setting for the many cycling races held every year.

Sailing Like fishing charters, there are boats for hire at most of the resort towns. Some companies also organize day trips and will lend snorkelling equipment, organize barbecues on some of the small offshore islands and provide transfers to and from your hotel. Companies that do day trips include *Captain Jayne* (Tel: 791-5174), *Caribe Aquatic Adventures* (Tel: 765-7444); *Island Safari* (Tel: 723-4740 or 721-6090; *Captain Jack's Catamaran*, based at Fajardo (Tel: 863-1905); or *Palmas Sailing Centre* at Humacao (Tel: 852-6000 ext. 10310).

There are several annual sailing regattas, including the *Annual Copa Velasco Regatta* at Palmas del Mar. About 100 racing yachts compete in this first leg of the Caribbean Ocean Racing Triangle. The race is usually held in March. In November, the *Kelly Cup Regatta* is held at the Club Nautico in Ponce.

Tennis Most of the large hotels have tennis courts and several of the Paradors also have courts, many of them floodlit. Other tennis courts can be found at *Central Park* in San Juan, where a court costs about US$2 for one hour. There are 17 courts, all floodlit (Tel: 722-1646).

Watersports Water-skiing, wind-surfing, snorkels and small boats are available at most resorts and large hotels. Surfing is concentrated on the north-western corner of Puerto Rico between Rincon and Aquadilla and each January there is the *Budweiser/Puerto Rico Surf Challenge* which is the first tournament in the Budweiser US Pro Surfing Tour.

Children There is plenty to keep children entertained. Most of the island's major attractions welcome children, and places like the Camuy Caves will probably fascinate them. Many of the beaches are quite safe for children, with shallow, calm waters, and in many of the hotels and paradors there are children's pools as well as other play areas.

The island's many festivals also include children who are encouraged to dress up in costumes and masks. The singing, dancing and parades usually involve children. There are plenty of sports for children, from tennis to watersports. There are some mini-golf courses, the riding tours are open to children and there are three water parks.

Theme Parks The closest park to San Juan is in the metropolitan area at Hato Rey. *Plaza Acuatica* has water parks, play areas and a miniature golf-course as well as a restaurant. The Park, at Federico Ciosta and Chardon, Hato Rey, is split into passive areas and water areas. The passive areas open at 11 a.m. Monday to Friday and at 10 a.m. on weekends. The water areas open at 12 p.m. on Friday and at 10 a.m. on weekends (Tel: 754-9500). *The Villa Coqui Wet N'Slide*, at Route 763, Caguas, has water slides, canoes and boats as well as swimming-pools and cafés. It is open on weekends and holidays from 9 a.m. to 5 p.m. (Tel: 747-4747). There are nine water areas at *Cascades Aquatic Park*, on Route 2, Aquadilla, which is open on Fridays from 2 p.m. to 9 p.m. and on weekends and holidays from 9 a.m. to 6 p.m. (Tel: 882-3310).

Old San Juan and Ponce Museums and art galleries may not appeal to many children but the historic areas of Old San Juan and Ponce are lively places to walk around, with street parties every third Sunday in the month in Ponce or with the craft stalls and ice-cream parlours in the old squares in Old San Juan.

Boat Trips There are plenty of boat trips around the island: the boat tour of Old San Juan, the trips around the phosphorescent bays of La Parguera and Vieques, the lake trips in the mountains or the ferry rides to the offshore islands of Vieques and Culebra.

Kites Every Sunday the area in front of *El Morro Fortress* in Old San Juan comes alive with children playing with kites. Many Puerto Rican families bring picnics to the green field in front of the castle for the children to play footballor fly kites.

Zoos Puerto Rico's only large zoo is at Mayaguez. It has a large variety of South American animals with a few imported from other continents, such as elephants, lions and tigers. The animals do not look particularly happy, though. There is a small children's area with a playground and café. On Route 108 at Barrio Miradero, it is open Tuesday to Sunday from 9 a.m. to 4.30 p.m. and admission is US$1 for adults, half-price for children.

There is also a small zoo at the Science Park in Bayamon as part of the Museum of Natural Sciences. The caged animals surround a small lake with boats. The *Luis A. Ferre Science Park* is on Route 167 and is open Wednesday to Friday from 8 a.m. to 4 p.m. and on weekends and holidays from 10 a.m. to 6 p.m. Admission is US$3 for adults and US$1 for children and OAPs.

Flora and Fauna Puerto Ricans are very proud of their natural heritage. There are several major parks and reserves which have been established for over fifty years. The most famous of these is the El Yungue Forest, or the Caribbean National Forest as it is also known. There are about ten other forest reserves across the island. The small offshore islands have also been protected as reserves. The National Wildlife Refuge on Culebra and the island of Mona are both havens for sea-birds and small animals. There are only a few phosphorescent bays across the world but there are two in Puerto Rico, both of which are carefully looked after.

Forests El Yungue covers 28,000 acres in the Luquillo Mountain range in the north-east. Open to the public 24 hours a day, the reserve is home to many native plants and animals. The only surviving Puerto Rican parrots are found in the forest and are the subject of a major breeding project to try to save the species. The visitors' centres have plenty of information about walking trails and the flora and fauna.

Other forest reserves include the nearby *Pinones Forest* which

342

has large mangrove swamps and lagoons. Another coastal forest is *Guanica Forest* to the west of Ponce which has the largest number of bird species anywhere on the island. Inland forests include *Maricao Forest, Guajataca Forest, Abajo Forest, Cambalache Forest, Monta Guilarte Forest, Toro Negor Forest* and *Carite Forest*.

Phosphorescent Bays These are at La Parguera and on Vieques. The bays are actually filled with millions of luminescent dinoflagellates which light up when disturbed. Best seen on moonless nights there are regular boat trips through the bays.

Fauna Puerto Rico is home to a variety of lizards, iguanas and mongeese. Snakes are found on the island but none of them is poisonous. The largest is the Puerto Rican Boa which can grow to nearly 2.5m (100in) long. The island caves are filled with a variety of bats and the forests filled with frogs. The most commonly heard frog in Puerto Rico is the coqui. This tiny frog grows to a maximum of 2.5cm (1in) long, is a brown-green colour and is named after its loud, distinctive call. There are fourteen varieties of coqui. They are extremely difficult to spot but it is considered good luck to see one. Legend claims that the coqui was originally a bird but fate struck its wings off. Later, a kinder fate gave the frog the ability to climb trees. Another creature unique to Puerto Rico is the Paso Fino horse. Herds still run wild on the offshore island of Vieques while the breed is still used for exhibitions and for trekking through the mountains and along the coast.

Birds Puerto Rico's most famous bird is its parrot. This bird is about 30cm (12in) long and is green with a red blaze above its beak and bright blue under its wings. There are only about forty left in the wild and they are very difficult to spot. Another common Caribbean bird is the Bannaquit which has distinctive yellow and black colouring. The Puerto Rican tody has a distinctive beep or bee-beep and is related to kingfishers. This tiny bird has green, red, white and yellow colourings.

Colonies of sea-birds inhabit the westerly offshore island of Mona, while there is another sea-bird refuge on the mainland nearby at boqueron with bird-watching trails. The twenty-four islands of Culebra, off the east coast, are all part of another bird refuge. Four areas of the largest island, along with the twenty-three smaller ones make up the refuge where terns and boobies are the most common birds.

There are over fifty species of birds living in El Yungue and many others across the whole island.

Sea Marine life around Puerto Rico is abundant. Humpback whales pass the north coast during their winter migration into the Caribbean. Turtles nest on the quiet beaches of Culebra, which is one of the few nesting sites left for turtles; now local people are educated about the risk of destroying turtles by killing too many or by destroying the breeding grounds. There are coral reefs around the island, teeming with colourful tropical fish. Game and competition fishing is good all around the coastline, while there are well-stocked lakes in the mountains. Trout and freshwater prawns are farmed and then used to restock lakes.

Flora With such a kind climate, flowers and trees thrive on the island. Trees include the Sierra Palm; Caimitillo Blanco which grown to 18m (60ft) with a straight trunk 60cm (24in) in diameter; Palo Colorado, a large tree, can live for up to 300 years and is one of the favourite nesting trees for Puerto Rican parrots, the Achitillo tree is commonly known as the parrot tree: the Yagrumo tree has silvery leaves and is known as the trumpet tree; Roble Blanco is a delicate pink cedar tree; the orange-red Mountain Immorelle blooms in the spring; while the scarlet African Tulip trees bloom all year round; Motillo trees are very hard with a dense canopy of dark green leaves and its wood is used for furniture; the Ausubo tree is such a hard wood that it was declared a protected tree by the King of Spain who did not want a ship load to leave the island to be captured by the enemy. Instead, the wood has been used in many of the historic buildings across the island. It can be identified by its wide flat leaves and white flowers. There are 240 tree species on the island and twenty-six are endemic. Orchids, ferns and mosses are found everywhere throughout the forests.

Health There are state hospitals but, like America, there are plenty of private hospitals, too. These are expensive, so make sure your insurance will cover you. For details of local hospitals, check the Blue Pages (English language) of the telephone book.

For *ambulance and emergencies*, call 343-2550 or 754-2550.

For the *Fire Department*, call 343-2330.

For Police Emergencies, call 343-2020

Tourist Zone Police, on Vieques Street, Condado. Tel: 722-0738, 724-5210. Open 24 hours a day, seven days a week.

If you have a road accident, there is an accident compensation system called *Automobile Accident Compensation Administration*. Report the accident to the police and then contact the AACA within 15 days on Tel: 759-8989.

Essential Addresses

Tourism Offices: from England you can call the Puerto Rico Tourism Company offices in Madrid on a freephone number: 0800-898920 or write to Officina de Turismo del Estado Libre Asociado de Puerto Rico, Calle Pedro Teixeira, 8 – 4ta Planta, 28020 Madrid, Spain.

Miami: 200 SE First Street, Suite 903. Miami FL 33131. Tel: 305-381 8915.

New York: 575 Fifth Avenue, 23rd Floor, New York, NY 10017. Tel: 800-223 6530.

San Juan: Luis Muñoz Marin International Airport, Isla Verde. Tel: 791-1014, 791-2551. El Centro Convention Centre, Condado. Tel: 723-3135, 722-1513. Paseo de la Princesa, Old San Juan, PO Box 4435, Old San Juan Station, San Juan. Tel: 721-2400.

Ponce: Casa Armstrong-Poventud, Plaza Las Delicias. Tel: 840-5695.

Rafael Hernandez Airport, Aguadilla. Tel: 890-3315.

Other offices can be found in many town plazas and are usually open from 8 a.m. to 12 p.m. and from 1 p.m. to 4.30 p.m., Monday to Friday.

Language *Driving*:

Alquiler de Autos – car rental offices

Calle sin salida – dead end

Carretera cerrada – road closed to traffic

Carretera dividida – divided road

Carretera estrecha – narrow road

Cruce – crossroad

Cruce de peatones – pedestrian crossing

Cuesta – hill

Desvio – detour

Estacion de peaje – toll station

Lanchas y barcos – ferry terminals

Mantengase a la derecha – keep right

No estacione – no parking

Parada/Parada de guaguas – bus stop

Peligreo – danger

Publicos – a taxi that runs a scheduled service

Puente estrecho – narrow bridge

Velocidad maxima – speed limit

Zona escolar – school zone.

Jamaica Index

Note

Page references in *italics* indicate illustrations. Page references followed by m indicate maps.